JOHNSON THE ESSAYIST

JOHNSON THE ESSAYIST

HIS OPINIONS ON MEN, MORALS AND MANNERS

A STUDY

BY

O. F. *Octavius Francis* CHRISTIE, M.A.

HASKELL HOUSE
Publishers of Scholarly Books
NEW YORK
1966

First Published 1924

HASKELL HOUSE PUBLISHERS Ltd.
Publishers of Scarce Scholarly Books
280 LAFAYETTE STREET
NEW YORK, N. Y. 10012

Library of Congress Catalog Card Number: 68-688

Standard Book Number 8383-0527-X

Printed in the United States of America

PREFACE

In Johnson's lifetime a selection of " the most condensed and brilliant sentences " from *The Rambler* was published under the name of *Beauties*. In 1888 Dr Birkbeck Hill made a collection of extracts from his sayings and writings entitled *The Wit and Wisdom of Dr Johnson*, and in 1889 edited some *Select Essays*. In 1907 Mr W. Hale White edited, with an interesting Preface, for the Clarendon Press, *Selections from Dr Johnson's Rambler*. But I am not aware that his Essays have yet been examined with a view to grouping his opinions on various subjects, religious, moral and social. This has been my endeavour, and to show that these opinions, though they may not form a system of philosophy, do form a consistent and coherent whole.

Whenever the occasion offered, I have compared Johnson's opinions with those of previous essayists, and especially with Addison's. This comparison is sometimes instructive as illustrating not only the difference between Johnson's mind and character and Addison's, but also between English manners and ideas in 1710 and in 1750.

I have also here and there contrasted Johnson's point of view with that of Lord Chesterfield. Chesterfield's *Letters* are in substance essays, albeit written mostly on one principal favourite topic. Not seldom were these two notable men in agreement, and it is to be regretted that their relations were not more friendly ; for no man of his time rated wit and genius higher than did Lord Chesterfield.

It is of obvious interest to compare Johnson the Essayist with Johnson the Talker. The two are not always in harmony; sometimes the divergence is striking. But this, of course, is not surprising. Many a conversationalist indulges in brilliant paradoxes, which he never expects will be printed. It was fated that Johnson's conversation should be published; and it is now read by everybody, while his Essays are neglected. And yet, as his friend the learned Mrs Elizabeth Carter declared, " his real opinions are to be found in his books."

Whether the reader will be interested in the following pages will depend upon whether he is attracted by Johnson's wit and wisdom and the style which adorns them, for my book consists largely of quotations. In his *Plan of an English Dictionary* Johnson said: " I have determined to consult the best writers for explanations real as well as verbal; and perhaps I may at last have reason to say, after one of the augmenters of *Furetier*, that my book is more learned than its author." On the same principle, I may at least claim that these many quotations have made my own book wiser and wittier than its author.

" We used to say to one another familiarly in Streatham Park," wrote Mrs Thrale, " ' Come, let us go into the library, and make Johnson speak *Ramblers*.' " Let us, as a second best, sometimes still go into the library and *read* Johnson's *Ramblers*—and *Idlers* and *Adventurers*; wherein, as Boswell says, we shall find " a true representation of human existence." " In no writings whatever," he adds with equal truth, " can be found *more bark and steel for the mind*, if I may use the expression; more that can brace and invigorate every manly and noble sentiment."

CONTENTS

SAMUEL JOHNSON

Born	18th Sept. 1709
Married Mrs Porter . . .	1735
Left Lichfield for London . . .	1737
First *Rambler*	20th March 1750
Last *Rambler*	14th March 1752
Death of Mrs Johnson . .	17th March 1752
First *Adventurer* . . .	3rd March 1753
Last *Adventurer* . . .	2nd March 1754
Publication of *Dictionary* . .	15th April 1755
First *Idler*	15th April 1758
Last *Idler*	5th April 1760
Introduction to Boswell . .	16th May 1763
Introduction to the Thrales . . .	1764
Journey to the Hebrides . . .	1773
Died	13th Dec. 1784

I

INTRODUCTION

" Johnson has a large following of enthusiastic admirers who would indignantly repudiate any slur cast upon their devotion. Yet some of them perhaps are worshippers rather than lovers, and lovers rather than friends. At any rate, they do not read his books." SIR WALTER RALEIGH: *Six Essays on Johnson.*

AT the Johnson bicentenary of 1909 Lord Rosebery, speaking of Johnson's writings, asked: " But who reads the rest ? I speak only for myself. The *Ramblers* and the *Idlers* are dead for me. I hope there are others more fortunate. *Rasselas* I read not voluntarily, but assiduously, at school ; and, probably for that reason, never wish to read again." [1]

Thus Lord Rosebery bore witness to our modern neglect of Johnson's writings. Johnson the Conversationalist has long ago eclipsed Johnson the Essayist. Of the crowds of enthusiasts from both hemispheres who attend the Johnson celebrations, or reverently peep at his chair in the " Cheshire Cheese," how many have read through a single *Rambler* ? To these he is a strange " character," a wit, a sage, a philosopher of life, a great Londoner. The title " Lexicographer " has survived, and, since the days of Miss Pinkerton's Academy, has carried a jocular flavour. By many, indeed, Johnson is regarded as an odd, worthy fellow ; a sort of glorified Mr Pickwick, with Boswell, a concentration of Tupman Snodgrass and Winkle, ever in attendance.

Johnson is scarcely visualized without Boswell. But where was Boswell when Johnson began writing his *Ramblers* ? He was a boy of ten, running wild in his

[1] *Miscellanies Literary and Historical*, i. **32.**

9

native Auchinleck ; thirteen years were to pass before
he even became acquainted with his master. It might
almost be asked :

> " What do they know of Johnson,
>   Who only Boswell know ? "

The Rambler was written when Johnson's fortunes were
still low, and long before his life was cheered by the
advent of Boswell. The first number appeared in March
1750, and the last in March 1752. *The Rambler* soon
had admirers, men whose admiration was worth having ;
but the circulation scarcely reached five hundred copies,
only one-sixth of the sale *The Spectator* had enjoyed
forty years before.[1] Success came later, and Johnson
lived to see ten English editions, besides others published
in Scotland and Ireland.[2]

But Johnson would have been the last man to measure
a book by its sale. How has the reputation of *The Rambler*,
and of Johnson's other essays, flourished from his age to
our own ?

Let us begin with the author's own judgment. " My
other works," said he to an acquaintance, " were wine
and water, but my *Rambler* is pure wine." [3]

Next to the author comes, as is fit, the author's wife.
" Mrs Johnson, in whose judgment and taste he had great
confidence, said to him, after a few numbers of *The
Rambler* had come out, ' I thought very well of you before,
but I did not imagine you could have written anything
equal to this.' " [4]

Let us now pass from the wife to the disciple. " In 1750
he came forth in the character for which he was eminently
qualified, a majestick teacher of moral and religious
wisdom." [5] " I profess myself to have ever entertained a

---

[1] *Spectator*, No. 10.
[2] Boswell's *Life of Johnson* (Birkbeck Hill), i. 213.
[3] *Ibid.*, i. 210n.   [4] *Ibid.*, i. 210.   [5] *Ibid.*, i. 201.

profound veneration for the astonishing force and vivacity of mind which *The Rambler* exhibits." [1] ". . . But I may shortly observe, that *The Rambler* furnishes such an assembly of discourses on practical religion and moral duty, of critical investigation, and allegorical and oriental tales, that no mind can be thought very deficient that has, by constant study and meditation, assimilated to itself all that may be found there." [2] "Every page of *The Rambler* shows a mind teeming with classical allusion and poetical imagery ; illustrations from other writers are, upon all occasions, so ready, and mingle so easily in his periods, that the whole appears of one uniform vivid texture." [3]

But, it may be said, what is the worth of Boswell's admiration ? Is it not usual for the worshipper to fall prostrate before his idol ? I admit the point of the question ; it may be prudent to discount Boswell's praise. And, if Macaulay was right, to be praised by Boswell would be disastrous ; it would be *laudari a vituperato*. For of Boswell Macaulay has written : " There is not in all his books a single remark of his own on literature, politics, religion, or society, which is not either commonplace or absurd. . . . Logic, eloquence, wit, taste, all these things which are generally considered as making a book valuable, were utterly wanting to him." [4] But Macaulay was wrong, and his vilification of Boswell has hurt his own reputation more than Boswell's. Read Boswell's estimate of Goldsmith,[5] his comparison of Johnson's style with Addison's,[6] of Fielding with Richardson,[7] or the character of Johnson which concludes his biography [8] : are all these either " commonplace or absurd " ? I think they are sound

---

[1] Boswell's *Life of Johnson* (Birkbeck Hill), i. 213.
[2] *Ibid.*, i. 214.   [3] *Ibid.*, i. 217.
[4] Essay on *Croker's Boswell*.
[5] Boswell's *Life of Johnson* (Birkbeck Hill), i. 412.
[6] *Ibid.*, i. 224.   [7] *Ibid.*, ii. 49.   [8] *Ibid.*, iv. 46.

criticism and good literature. Or could the above-quoted sentences in praise of *The Rambler* have been written by " a man of the feeblest and meanest intellect " ?

Johnson was not blind to his follower's failings, and neither gave nor endured excessive praise ; but he said of Boswell : " He has better faculties than I had imagined ; more justice of discernment, and more fecundity of images." [1] Would Johnson have endured for more than twenty years the constant and close companionship of " a dunce, a parasite, and a coxcomb " ? The point is no longer worth arguing, for Boswell's genius has now been recognized ; it entitles him to rank with the great ones of the eighteenth century. But a man cannot have earned the name of the greatest biographer in English literature, without possessing considerable literary and critical powers. I have formed the impression that, from the day he made himself known to Johnson, Boswell grew steadily in wisdom and in literary art.

Arthur Murphy, who had himself published a weekly periodical, says of *The Rambler* : " In this collection Johnson is the great moral teacher of his countrymen ; his Essays form a body of ethics ; the observations on life and manners are acute and instructive, and the papers professedly critical serve to promote the cause of litera- ture." [2] " Johnson is always lofty ; he seems, to use Dryden's phrase, to be o'er-informed with meaning, and his words do not appear to himself to be adequate to his conception. He moves in state, and his periods are always harmonious." " In matters of criticism, Johnson is never the echo of preceding writers. He thinks and decides for himself." And, comparing Johnson with Addison : " Addison makes virtue amiable ; Johnson represents it as an awful duty. Addison insinuates himself with an air

---

[1] Boswell's *Life of Johnson*, ii. 267.

[2] *An Essay on the Life and Genius of Dr Johnson* (published 1792).

of modesty; Johnson commands like a dictator; but a dictator in his splendid robes, not labouring at the plough. Addison is the Jupiter of Vergil, with placid serenity talking to Venus :

" 'Vultu, quo coelum tempestatesque serenat';

Johnson is JUPITER TONANS : he darts his lightning and rolls his thunder, in the cause of virtue and piety." " *The Idler* is written with abated vigour, in a style of ease and unlaboured elegance. It is the Odyssey after the Iliad. . . . Johnson forgets his austere manner, and plays us into sense. He still continues his lectures on human life, but he adverts to common occurrences, and is often content with the topic of the day."

I have quoted Murphy at some length, because he has not only well contrasted Johnson with Addison, and Johnson's *Rambler* with Johnson's *Idler*, but also because he probably represented the opinion which most educated men held about Johnson's Essays at the end of the eighteenth century and the beginning of the nineteenth. Murphy belonged to Johnson's circle (though not to the inner circle), and held him in awe.[1] Those who had a great personal respect for the Doctor extended that respect to his writings, and set the tone to other readers. After his death a more critical spirit began to prevail.

But, even while Johnson was at his zenith, " with the flatterers were busy mockers." Horace Walpole was an accomplished mocker, and, for some reason, had an intense personal dislike for Johnson. He wrote to Mason of " the fustian of his style, and the meanness of his spirit "[2]; to the Countess of Ossory : "I have no patience with an unfortunate monster trusting to his helpless deformity for indemnity for any impertinence that his arrogance suggests."[3] He ridicules his triple tautology,[4] and his long words.[5]

[1] Boswell's *Life of Johnson* (Birkbeck Hill), ii. 338*n*.
[2] 18th August 1774.   [3] 27th December 1775.
[4] 1st February 1779.   [5] 14th November 1779.

He is " a saucy Caliban." [1] " Yet he has other motives than lucre,—prejudice, and bigotry, and pride, and presumption, and arrogance, and pedantry are the hags that brew his ink, though wages alone supply him with paper." [2] Of Boswell's *Journal* of his tour : " It is the story of a mountebank and his zany." [3] " Johnson had all the bigotry of a monk, and all the folly and ignorance too." [4] " That well-bred usher to the graces, Dr Johnson." [5] Of Johnson's *Life of Pope* : " a most trumpery performance, and stuffed with all his crabbed phrases and vulgarisms, and much trash as anecdotes." [6]

I could give other instances, but these are enough to show that Boswell was justified in his remark that Walpole " never was one of the true admirers of that great man." [7]

Boswell sought to explain Walpole's dislike by the theory that he resented the bad arguments which Johnson, when reporting Parliamentary debates, put into the mouth of Sir Robert Walpole. But Walpole ridiculed this idea. There is no need to account for the antipathy otherwise than by the difference in the dispositions and habits of the two men. Not long before Walpole's death Joseph Farington records him as saying : " I have a doubt of Johnson's reputation continuing so high as it is at present. I do not like his *Ramblers*." [8] Farington adds : " Lord Orford never was acquainted with Johnson ; Sir Joshua Reynolds offered to bring them together, but Lord Orford had so strong a prejudice against Johnson's reported manners, that he would not agree to it." [9]

Certainly the good-will of Walpole would not have been

---

[1] 9th February 1781.   [2] 7th February 1782.
[3] 6th October 1785.   [4] 29th August 1785.
[5] 7th May 1782.   [6] 14th April 1781.
[7] Boswell's *Life of Johnson* (Birkbeck Hill), iv. 314.
[8] *The Farington Diary*, i. 154.
[9] " Nor did I ever exchange a syllable with him ; nay I do not think I ever was in a room with him six times in my days " (Horace Walpole to Miss Berry, 26th May 1791).

conciliated by the 56th *Idler*, in which Johnson censures
" the love of curiosities or that desire of accumulating
trifles, which distinguishes many by whom no other distinction could ever have been obtained." This " fills the
mind with trifling ambition ; fixes the attention upon
things which seldom have any tendency towards virtue or
wisdom, employs in idle inquiries the time that is given
for better purposes." [1] The virtuoso is generally a sensitive
creature.

But for perhaps a generation after his death the reputation of Johnson was maintained ; his *Ramblers* and other
works were reprinted again and again. Then, as a writer
in *The Times Literary Supplement* [2] has put it : " The
Romantics had their way. About the year 1825, the
publishers and their public concluded that the works of
Johnson were no longer necessary to salvation." The time
had arrived of readers and of critics who would have been
described by Boswell as " not strongly impregnated with
the Johnsonian æther."

In 1831 Macaulay, in his essay on Croker's edition of
Boswell, wrote : " The reputation of those writings, which
he [Johnson] expected to be immortal, is every day
fading." Carlyle, writing in the same year, said : " already
indeed they are becoming obscure for this generation, and
for some future generation may be valuable stuff as
Prolegomena and explanatory scholia to the Johnsoniad
of Boswell." But Macaulay himself was too much a lover
of eighteenth-century literature not to appreciate *The
Rambler*. In his *Biographies* he says that the best critics
" did justice to the acuteness of his observations on morals

[1] " To procure rare engravings and antique chimney-pieces,
to match odd gauntlets, to lay out a maze of walks with five
acres of ground, these were the grave employments of his long
life " (Macaulay's essay on *Horace Walpole*).

[2] In a fine essay called " Johnson's Reputation " (1st September
1921).

and manners, to the constant precision and frequent
brilliancy of his language, to the weighty and magnificent
eloquence of many serious passages, and to the solemn yet
pleasing humour of some of the lighter papers."

M. Taine praised Johnson's style: " Classical prose
attains its perfection in him, as classical poetry in Pope." [1]
But as to his matter: " His truths are too true ; we already
know his precepts by heart. We learn from him that life
is short, and we ought to improve the few moments
granted to us ; that a mother ought not to bring up her
son as a fop ; that a man ought to repent of his faults
and yet avoid superstition ; that in everything we ought
to be active, and not hurried. . . . We should like to know
who could have been the lovers of *ennui* who bought up
13,000 copies of his works." Other shafts follow, winged
with Gallic wit.

That Johnson perpetrated some platitudes cannot be
denied. He was a journalist, often writing in a hurry. " I
was awakened from this dream of study by a summons
from the press : the time was come for which I had
been thus negligently purposing to provide, and, however
dubious or sluggish, I was now necessitated to write." [2]
And even when the author has leisure, " the mind finds
sometimes an unexpected barrenness and vacuity." [3]
But Johnson was not fond of platitudes ; he could be
as amusing as M. Taine about them. In his criticism
of Pope's *Essay on Man* we find him censuring Pope's
matter and praising his style, in a passage curiously
similar to M. Taine's criticism of *The Rambler*: " To
these profound principles of natural knowledge are added
some moral instructions equally new ; that self-interest,
well understood, will produce social concord ; that men
are mutual gainers by mutual benefits ; that evil is some-

[1] *History of English Literature* (translation by Van Laun),
iii. 322.
[2] *Rambler*, No. 134.   [3] *Adventurer*, No. 138.

times balanced by good ; that human advantages are unstable and fallacious, of uncertain duration and doubtful effect. . . . Surely a man of no very comprehensive search may venture to say that he has heard all this before ; but it was never till now recommended by such a blaze of embellishments, or such sweetness of melody." I shall have more to say of Johnson's alleged tendency to platitude, but I fancy that half M. Taine's quarrel with Johnson is not so much that he is a " platitudinarian," as that he is a moralist. " We then remember that sermons are liked in England, and that these Essays are sermons." But sermons need not be platitudes.

To pass to more modern critics, Sir Leslie Stephen gave *The Rambler* poor commendation. Johnson's allegory is " unendurably frigid and clumsy." [1] He consigns these Essays " to the dustiest shelves of libraries." [2] " The pompous and involved language seems indeed to be a fit clothing for the melancholy reflections which are its chief staple, and in spite of its unmistakable power, it is as heavy reading as the heavy class of lay-sermonising to which it belongs." [3] " Of these Essays there is a fair proportion which will deserve, but will hardly obtain, respectful attention." [4]

Even Austin Dobson, who was an eighteenth-century man heart and soul (much more so, I think, than Johnson), committed himself to a questionable statement : " To select positively humorous examples from his papers would be a difficult task." [5]

An ultra-modern critic has gone further, and maintained that it " seems absurd to call Johnson an Essayist." [6]

---

[1] English Men of Letters Series : *Johnson*, p. 40.
[2] *Ibid.*, p. 56.   [3] *Ibid.*   [4] *Ibid.*, p. 167.
[5] Preface to *Selected Eighteenth-Century Essays.*
[6] Mr G. K. Chesterton, " Lecture on Cobbett," *Morning Post*, 27th April 1922.

B

Thus the process of depreciation has been continuous. Perhaps the unfavourable judgment of the encyclopædist need not weigh too heavily. Mark Pattison said that twenty years were not too many to spend in editing the works of Pope. By a sum in proportion, to write a History of English Literature with a just appraisement of every author would require much more than the longevity of Jahred or Mahalaleel. For a writer, whose limit is three-score or fourscore years, is it possible to do much more than sketch " tendencies," adumbrate " movements," and delimit " periods," linking each with apt quotations and appropriate names ? And then, how strange is the classification ! M. Taine places Johnson with the Novelists ! Is this on the strength of *Rasselas* ? To Johnson as a Novelist he devotes thirteen pages ; to Miss Burney as a Novelist he gives a line and a half ! And what exceptions to every rule of classification ! And how prone are really great authors to slide backward from their own proper " period," or trespass forward into the succeeding one ! " Canst thou draw out Leviathan with a hook ? or his tongue with a cord which thou lettest down ? "

With " movements " and " tendencies " Johnson had little to do. He was static rather than dynamic. In morals and religion, politics and literature, he stood for principles which were unfashionable even in his own day, and are now considered obsolete. Yes, in religion and politics Johnson may have been behind his time ; but we shall see that as a hater of injustice and cruelty he was in front of it. At least he knew his world well ; his pictures of social life are rich in interest and humour. Even here his reputaton is eclipsed by Addison's, not so much because Addison is more humorous, and certainly not because he knew life better than Johnson, but because Addison invented a sort of story to keep some of the characters in *The Spectator* together, and thereby nearly became a novelist. If Johnson had developed the histories of some of his own

entertaining personages—Mr Frolick, Lady Bustle, Squire
Bluster, Mr Squeeze—and contrived to interconnect the
fortûnes of some of them, the *Ramblers* and *Idlers* might
boast more readers in the present day.[1] But I do not
contend that he could have drawn a Sir Roger.

Whatever be the reason, the general opinion of Johnson's
Essays, as compared with Addison's, was expressed by
Lady Mary Wortley-Montagu : " *The Rambler* followed
The Spectator as a pack-horse would do a hunter." And
yet Johnson the Essayist still has, and ever will have, his
select and fervent admirers. Mr Birrell, after reading Lord
Rosebery's confession, says he returned for refreshment
to the 55th *Rambler*, the story of " the Maypole." [2] Perhaps the tide is turning. Sir Walter Raleigh appraised
The Rambler in language Boswell might have used, as
" that splendid repository of wisdom and truth " [3] ; and
the writer in *The Times Literary Supplement*, to whom
I have already referred, concludes his essay with this
passage : " We are no longer prepared without misgiving
to discard *The Rambler* as merely pompous, and the *Life
of Milton* as merely malignant ; to dismiss the criticism
of Gray as ineptitude, and the *Preface* to Shakespeare as
impertinence. Johnson's best books have only to be read,
and read without prejudice, for their truth and beauty
to become plain to us, as they were plain to Burke and
Scott." [4]

[1] Madam Bombasin, in *Rambler* No. 12, is not unworthy of
Fielding.
[2] The story of a daughter who " begins to bloom before the
mother can be content to fade "—to use an expression of the
Princess in *Rasselas*.
[3] *Six Essays on Johnson*, p. 12. " Raleigh was perhaps the
first to point out " (wrote Mr R. W. Chapman in *The London
Mercury* of July 1922) " that the smooth generalizations of *The
Rambler* are the mask of passionate conviction."
[4] " Johnson's Reputation " (*The Times Literary Supplement*,
1st September 1921).

My aim is to lure the Boswellian-Johnsonians (if I may coin such a term; or may I call them Roseberians?) into new paths of enjoyment, and to convince them that they may find in the Essays wit and wisdom equal to the wit and wisdom they have tasted in Johnson's familiar conversation. Remember that Johnson spoke exactly as he wrote. He told Sir Joshua Reynolds " that he had early laid it down as a fixed rule to do his best on every occasion, and in every company; to impart whatever he knew in the most forcible language he could put it in; and that, by constant practice, and never suffering any careless expressions to escape him, or attempting to deliver his thoughts without arranging them in the clearest manner, it became habitual to him." [1] The consequence of this was, " that his common conversation in all companies was such as to secure him universal attention, as something above the usual style was expected." [2] " I could not help remarking," wrote Miss Burney, " how very like Dr Johnson is to his writing, and how much the same thing it was to hear or to read him." [3] " Very true," said Mrs Thrale, " he writes and talks with the same ease, and in the same manner." " Every sentence which dropped from his lips," wrote Macaulay, " was as correct in structure as the most nicely balanced period of *The Rambler*." [4] " How he does talk!" exclaimed Miss Beresford, an American lady, " every sentence is an Essay." [5] Such testimonies might be multiplied, but I will conclude with one from Lord Rosebery: " Another signal feature of his conversation is this, that his little discourses spring forth unpremeditated but full-fledged; he gives the number of his reasons before he utters them, as if what he

[1] Boswell's *Life of Johnson* (Birkbeck Hill), i. 204.
[2] *Ibid.*, iv. 183.
[3] *Diary and Letters of Madame d'Arblay*, September 1778.
[4] *Biographies* (Johnson).
[5] Boswell's *Life of Johnson* (Birkbeck Hill), iv. 284.

were going to say were already complete in his own mind, though the subject has only just been put before him." [1] But if Johnson spoke as he wrote, the converse is true ; he wrote as he spoke. In the *Ramblers, Idlers* and *Adventurers* will be found things as good as in Boswell, and the same " union of perspicuity and splendour." But here will not be found the talking " for victory," the quick retorts, the verbal blows as from a pistol's butt-end —those outbreaks of brutal rudeness which, however amusing now to read, shocked Johnson's best friends at the time, and distressed himself in the retrospect.[2] In wordy warfare Johnson outrivalled the sophist Thrasymachus, he fell on his opponents like a savage beast, to " toss and gore " them.[3] They feared and trembled—

[1] *Miscellanies Literary and Historical*, i. 51.

[2] These are the " methods of argument " that Johnson himself has condemned in the 85th *Adventurer* : " A man heated in talk, and eager of victory, takes advantage of the mistakes or ignorance of his adversary, lays hold of concessions to which he knows he has no right, and urges proofs likely to prevail in his opponent, though he knows himself that they have no force ; thus the severity of reason is relaxed, many topicks are accumulated, but without just arrangement or distinction ; we learn to satisfy ourselves with such ratiocination as silences others ; and seldom recall to a close examination that discourse which has gratified our vanity with victory and applause." Certainly the " severity of reason was relaxed " when Johnson, declaiming against " action " in oratory, replied to Mrs Thrale (who had objected Demosthenes' saying, " Action Action, Action "): " Demosthenes, Madam, spoke to an assembly of brutes, to a barbarous people "—*Autobiography of Mrs Piozzi* (Abraham Hayward), i. 51. In October 1782 Madame d'Arblay wrote in her Diary of Johnson's " satirical and exulting wit," " how greatly he made himself dreaded by all, and by many abhorred." She also observes that he was omitted from invitations.

[3] συστρέψας ἑαυτὸν ὥσπερ θηρίον ἧκεν ἐφ᾽ ἡμᾶς ὡς διαρπασύμενος (*Plat. Rep.*). Johnson could be " the greatest sophist that ever contended in the lists of declamation " (Boswell's *Life of Johnson* (Birkbeck Hill), iv. 429).

and hated. It is said that Thomas Sheridan was the only victim who *never* forgave, but I should imagine there must have been others. I have often wished he could have met an opponent who had the spirit and wit to pay him in his own coin, often wondered how he escaped personal violence from someone "who" (in Cowper's words) "could thresh his old jacket" till he "made his pension jingle in his pocket." But in his Essays we have wit and wisdom without petulance ; language sometimes bri'liant, more often sombre, but unmarred by wilful paradox ; a strong sense of humour indulgently exercised.

Here too is a mine, which has lain for long too little worked, a treasure-house too long neglected ; for here are the fruits of Johnson's observations on the social system of his day—on town and country, City and West End, Tyburn and debtors' prisons, women and virtuosos, awkward scholars and younger sons. They are the observations of one who knew his world as few knew it, and had suffered much therein ; who sternly and consistently condemned the vices of his fellow-men, but could laugh at their foibles, and make allowance for their follies.

There is yet one more good reason for studying these Essays. Johnson was a great man ; greater even as a man than as a writer. Long before his death the fame of him had spread over England, and far into Scotland. The landlady of the inn at the little town of Ellon asked Boswell: "Is not this the great Doctor that is going about through the country ? . . . There's something great in his appearance." And the landlord said: "They say he is the greatest man in England, except Lord Mansfield." [1] To simple folk as to wiser, Johnson stood for something very large ; something national and typical. Sir Leslie Stephen bore witness to this prestige when he sarcastically wrote : "George the Third, as the last representative of some

[1] Boswell's *Life of Johnson* (Birkbeck Hill), v. 96. A Scot may be forgiven for having made this exception.

shadow of divine right, found his Abdiel in the last of the
Tories, Johnson." [1] It was a humorous stroke to liken
the stout Doctor to a celestial seraph ; but of Johnson, as
of Abdiel, it might be said :

> " Nor number nor example with him wrought
> To swerve from truth, or change his constant mind,
> Though single."

To the truth, as he saw truth, he was faithful. He
yielded neither to the old Whig doctrine that resistance
may be justifiable,[2] nor to later popular cries which (as
he thought) intimidated even the judges in Westminster
Hall. He stood firm for subordination. Though never a
politician, he was—in a sense—the first man in England.

Carlyle described the eighteenth century as " so steeped
in falsity, and impregnated with it to the bone, that—in
fact the measure of the thing was full, and a French
Revolution had to end it." [3] But in England there has
been no such revolution, and Carlyle himself gives one
reason for our salvation : " If England has escaped the
blood-bath of a French Revolution, and may yet, in virtue
of this delay and the experience it has given, work out
her deliverance calmly into a new Era, let Samuel Johnson,
beyond all contemporary or succeeding men, have the
praise for it." [4]

The thoughts, then, of such a man on religion, on
morals, on literature, and on the manners of his age are
surely worth our examination. We read them with delight
when given out in his familiar conversation. Why should
we neglect to study them as closely in his Essays ?

[1] *English Thought in the Eighteenth Century*, ii. 205, 206.

[2] He denounced Russell and Sidney as " rascals." Boswell's
Life of Johnson (Birkbeck Hill), ii. 210.

[3] *History of Frederick the Great*, i. 11.

[4] Carlyle's essay on *Johnson*.

II

JOHNSON'S STYLE AND MANNERISMS

" I have laboured to refine our language to grammatical purity, and to clear it from colloquial barbarisms, licentious idioms, and irregular combinations. Something, perhaps, I have added to the elegance of its construction, and something to the harmony of its cadence. When common words were less pleasing to the ear, or less distinct in their signification, I have familiarized the terms of philosophy, but have rarely admitted any word not authorized by former writers." *Rambler*, No. 208.

IN order to understand why Johnson was so fond of using long Latinized words, we must turn to certain passages in his *Plan of an English Dictionary* and his *Preface to the English Dictionary*, which explain his theory of our language, and of the duty he had undertaken towards it :

" Of antiquated or obsolete words, none will be inserted but such as are to be found in authors who wrote since the accession of *Elizabeth*, from which we date the golden age of our language." [1]

" When I survey the Plan which I have laid before you, I cannot, My Lord, but confess, that I am frighted at its extent, and like the soldiers of *Cæsar*, look on *Britain* as a new world, which it is almost madness to invade. But I hope, that though I should not complete the conquest, I shall at least discover the coast, civilize part of the inhabitants, and make it easy for some other adventurer to proceed farther, to reduce them wholly to subjection, and settle them under laws." [2]

" So far have I been from any care to grace my pages with modern decorations, that I have studiously

[1] *The Plan of an English Dictionary.*   [2] *Ibid.*

endeavoured to collect examples and authorities from the writers before the restoration, whose works I regard as *the wells of English undefiled*, as the pure sources of genuine diction. Our language, for almost a century, has, by the concurrence of many causes, been gradually departing from its original *Teutonick* character, and deviating toward a *Gallick* structure and phraseology, from which it ought to be our endeavour to recal it." [1]

" But as every language has a time of rudeness antecedent to perfection, as well as of false refinement and declension, I have been cautious lest my zeal for antiquity might drive me into times too remote, and crowd my book with words now no longer understood. I have fixed Sidney's work for the boundary, beyond which I make few excursions. From the authors which rose in the time of *Elizabeth*, a speech might be formed adequate to all the purposes of use and elegance." [2] He then mentions Hooker, Bacon, Raleigh, Spenser, Sidney and Shakespeare, as authors who between them supply a vocabulary sufficient for every need.

" Those who have been persuaded to think well of my design, will require that it should fix our language, and put a stop to those alterations which time and chance have hitherto been suffered to make in it without opposition." [3]

With these passages should be read one from his *Preface* to Shakespeare : " The English nation in the time of *Shakespeare* was yet struggling to emerge from barbarity. The philology of *Italy* had been translated hither in the regin of *Henry the Eighth* ; and the learned languages had been successfully cultivated by *Lilly, Linacre*, and *More* ; by *Pole, Cheke*, and *Gardiner* ; and afterwards by *Smith, Clerk, Haddon*, and *Ascham*. *Greek* was now taught to boys in the principal schools ; and those who united elegance with learning, read, with great diligence, the *Italian* and

---

[1] *Preface to the English Dictionary.*
[2] *Ibid.*   [3] *Ibid.*

Spanish poets. But literature was yet confined to professed scholars, or to men and women of high rank. The public was gross and dark ; and to be able to read and write, was an accomplishment still valued for its rarity."

From these quotations we may educe Johnson's opinion (1) that our English language had, by the end of the sixteenth century, developed from its original barbarism into a state approaching perfection, but (2) that in his own day there was danger of a decline. His aim was to stay this decline ; to check (amongst other abuses) the growth of " Gallick structure and phrase " ; and, in " fixing " the language, to exclude alike "antiquated and obsolete " words, words used by illiterate writers, and words used by translators who would " reduce us to babble a dialect of France."

True it is that, at the conclusion of his task, he became despondent of its success, and feared a lexicographer might be derided who should " imagine that his dictionary can embalm his language," and that he dwelt on the futility of academies that pursued such an object. But, none the less, to " fix " our language, and to preserve its ancient perfection, was the aim that Johnson had set before him.

Now what, in Johnson's view, had been the principal instrument of rescuing the English language and the English people from " barbarity " ? Clearly, the cultivation of the learned languages, Greek and Latin.[1] And it was Greek and Latin that permeated and interpenetrated his own words, phrases, and sentences. He would have nothing to do with the old words, even when found in authors whom he approved and praised. There are, for instance, words common in Spenser, such as " surquedry,"

---

[1] " Some part of their superiority [*i.e.* of the ancients] may be justly ascribed to the graces of their language, from which the most polished of the present *European* tongues are nothing more than barbarous degenerations " (*Rambler*, No. 169).

" hardiment," " belgard," " whileare," " yold," " harrow
and wealaway," that are admitted to the *Dictionary*, but
described there as " now out of use," " not in use," " an
old word, now wholly disused," " obsolete." Doubtless
they had become obsolete, but Johnson never made any
effort to revive them. Some of them are quaint, pretty
words, and I can imagine many an author of our own time
re-discovering and re-introducing them, with no apology
for using words from Spenser. But Johnson, with the
pedantry of a classical scholar, preferred a Greek-English
and Latin-English vocabulary.[1]

There are a great many long words in the Essays,
and especially in *The Rambler*; in *The Adventurer* and *The
Idler* they are by no means so frequent. Of these I have
noted only one, *speculatist*, which is not to be found in
the *Dictionary*; of this word Johnson is decidedly fond.
But there are others in Boswell's pages that have not
obtained entrance—*e.g. formular, conglobulate, anfractu-
osities, labefactation*. Johnson claimed [2] " that he had not
taken upon him to add more than four or five words to
the English language, of his own formation," but I think
he put his additions at too low a figure. In this manu-
facture he displayed a striking ingenuity. " He said to
me, as we travelled, ' these people, sir, that Gerrard talks
of, may have somewhat of a *peregrinity* in their dialect,
which relation has augmented to a different language.' I
asked him if *peregrinity* was an English word : he laughed,
and said ' No.' I told them this was the second time that

[1] It is true that Johnson writes of Spenser as our first poet :
"we consider the whole succession from Spenser to Pope, as
superior to any names which the continent can boast " (*Idler*,
No. 91), but he condemns his " studied barbarity " (*Rambler*,
No. 37). " His style was in his own time allowed to be vitious,
so darkened with old words and peculiarities of phrase, and so
remote from common-sense, that *Jonson* boldly pronounces him
to have written no language " (*Rambler*, No. 121).

[2] Boswell's *Life of Johnson* (Birkbeck Hill), i. 221,

I had heard him coin a word. When Foote broke his leg,
I observed that it would make him fitter for taking off
George Faulkner as Peter Paragraph, poor George having
a wooden leg. Dr Johnson at that time said, ' George
will rejoice at the *depeditation* of Foote,' and when I
challenged that word, laughed, and owned he had made
it, and added that he had not made above three or four
in his *Dictionary*." [1]

There are other words used in the Essays, which are
found indeed in the *Dictionary*, but without any authority being given for them; amongst these are *adscititious*,
abscinded, *officinal*; in *Rasselas* we have *indiscerptible*.

For long words of yet another class the authorities given
are technical or scientific treatises; one might well think
they should have been confined to such uses. Johnson
thought otherwise: " When common words were less
pleasing to the ear, or less distinct in their signification,
I have familiarized the terms of philosophy." So we
have *papilionaceous*,[2] *colorifick*, *frigorifick*, *fugacity*, *alexi-
pharmick*, and (in Boswell) *circumduction* (a term of Civil
Law).

Other long words in the Essays, supported in the
Dictionary by quotations from general literature, are
*equiponderant, reposited, orbity, cathartics, argumental, equili-
brations, concatenations* (much a favourite of Johnson's),
oraculous, subducted. From other works, or his letters,
we get *intenerate, oppugner, divaricate, irremeable*.

Tainted by this same Latinization are the names Johnson
gives to his characters. Fungosa is a stockbroker; Fulgentia,
Tetrica, Turpicula, Charybdis are names of ladies !

---

[1] Boswell's *Life of Johnson* (Birkbeck Hill), v. 130. Boswell,
the next day, invented " equitation " (*ibid.*, 131). " It is
remarkable that my noble, and to me most constant friend, the
Earl of Pembroke, . . . has since hit upon the very same word."

[2] Carlyle, adopting this word, described Mrs Thrale as " a bright
papilionaceous creature " (Essay on *Johnson*).

Boswell speaks of " those uncommon but apt and ener-
getick words, which, in some of his writings have been
censured, with more petulance than justice," [1] and Johnson's own attitude towards those who criticized them
was characteristically sturdy and contemptuous. " But
words are hard only to those who do not understand them ;
and the critick ought always to inquire, whether he is in-
commoded by the fault of the writer, or his own." [2] But
they incurred ridicule. " Before I left Norfolk in the year
1760," said Dr Burney, " the *Ramblers* were in high favour
among persons of learning and good taste. Others there
were, devoid of both, who said that the *hard words* in *The
Rambler* were used by the author to render his *Dictionary*
indispensably necessary." [3] " Sir R. Payne and Dr Johnson are answering General Burgoyne, and they say the
words are to be so long that the reply must be printed
in a pamphlet as large as an atlas, but in an Elzevir type,
or the first sentence would fill twenty pages in octavo." [4]
" He seems to have read the ancients with no view but
of pilfering polysyllables." [5] After Thrale's death, some
ingenious verses, suggesting that Johnson was inclined to
marry the widow, were written in the Latinate language :

> " Cervisial coctor's viduate dame,
> Opin'st thou this gigantick frame,
> Procumbing at thy shrine,
> Shall, catinated by thy charms,
> A captive in thy ambient arms
> Perennially be thine ? " [6]

[1] Boswell's *Life of Johnson* (Birkbeck Hill), i. 184.
[2] *Idler*, No. 70.
[3] Boswell's *Life of Johnson* (Birkbeck Hill), i. 208n.
[4] Horace Walpole to the Countess of Ossory, 14th November 1779.
[5] To Mason, 14th April 1781.
[6] Mrs Piozzi's *Autobiography* (Hayward), i. 251. She herself
wrote opposite these verses : " Whose silly fun was this ? Soame
Jenyns ? "

But Johnson, with his genial sense of humour, excelled all the other wits in parodying himself. " Mrs Carter, having said of the same person, ' I doubt he was an Atheist.' JOHNSON. ' I don't know that. He might perhaps have become one, if he had had time to ripen (smiling). He might have *exuberated* into an Atheist.' " [1] " Talking of the Comedy of *The Rehearsal*, he said, ' It has not wit enough to keep it sweet.' This was easy ; he therefore caught himself, and pronounced a more round sentence ; ' It has not vitality enough to preserve it from putrefaction.' " [2] Of this remark Macaulay observed : " Sometimes Johnson translated aloud." It is, in fact, a translation from English to Latin.

We need not concern ourselves to defend these " hard " words. Those that Johnson invented have not survived to afflict posterity ; we may say of them as Johnson said of Dryden's Gallicisms : " They continue only where they stood first, perpetual warnings to future innovators." But it must be said for Johnson that his motive was a good one—to dignify the English language ; he aimed at " perspicuity and splendour." His contemporaries found the long words " disgusting," in the eighteenth-century sense of the word—*i.e.* wearying and distasteful. His style, like the haughty manner of Chatham, may sometimes repel ; at any rate, it is never mean.

Let us pass to another fault that has been alleged against Johnson's style—his use of triple phrases, which may be conveniently called " triplets." " Triple tautology " is Horace Walpole's name for this mannerism, " or the fault of repeating the same sense in three different phrases, that I believe it would be possible, taking the ground-work for all three, to make one of his *Ramblers* into three different papers, that should all have exactly the same purport

[1] Boswell's *Life of Johnson* (Birkbeck Hill), iv. 97, 98.
[2] *Ibid.*, iv. 320.

and meaning, but in different phrases." [1] I do not think
Walpole was justified in this definition of the " triple
tautology " ; there is always a separate and distinct description or idea in each member of the triplet, as appears
in Johnson's *quadruple* condemnation of bad mutton—
" it is ill-fed, ill-killed, ill-kept, and ill-dressed." Macaulay's
name for the triplets is " pompous triads," [2] and he is
glad they are not found in Johnson's conversation. But
this is not surprising ; for, pompous though they may be,
they are by no means easy to compose ; and even Johnson
could scarcely have achieved them as *impromptus*.

But this affectation (if we may so term it) is really not
very frequent. In my edition of Johnson's *Works*,[3] *The
Rambler* occupies 1285 pages, *The Adventurer*, 191, and *The
Idler*, 415. Of " triplets " I have counted in *The Rambler*
27 instances, in *The Adventurer* 2, and in *The Idler* 4.
But it has to be admitted that, in addition to " triplets,"
Johnson must plead guilty to " quartettes " ; of these
The Rambler has 7 and *The Idler* 2.

Let me offer the reader a few samples of " triplets."
The simplest " triplets " consist of three sets of double
nouns :

On the Infatuation for Writing.—" A disease for which,
when it has attained its height, perhaps no remedy will
be found in the gardens of philosophy, however she may
boast her physick of the mind, her catharticks of vice, or
lenitives of passion." [4]

The Use of Retirement and Abstraction.—" By this
practice he may obtain the solitude of adversity without

[1] Letter to the Countess of Ossory, 1st February 1779.

[2] Mrs Gaskell invented another name : " Indeed, she never could
think of the Browns without talking Johnson ; and, as they were
seldom absent from her thoughts just then, I heard many a rolling,
three-piled sentence " (*Cranford*, ch. ii.).

[3] 1810. Twelve volumes, " with an Essay on his Life and Genius,
by Arthur Murphy, Esq."

[4] *Rambler*, No. 2.

its melancholy, its instructions without its censures, and its sensibility without its perturbations." [1]

The Mind afflicted by Disease.—"Knowledge may be easily lost in the starts of melancholy, the flights of impatience, and the peevishness of decrepitude." [2]

Factions in the Republic of Letters.—"Each has called in foreign aid, and endeavoured to strengthen his own cause by the frown of power, the hiss of ignorance, and the clamour of popularity." [3]

The Function of Criticism.—"Criticism reduces those regions of literature under the dominion of science, which have hitherto known only the anarchy of ignorance, the caprices of fancy, and the tyranny of prescription." [4]

The Youth of Tranquilla.—"I was not condemned in my youth to solitude, either by indigence or deformity, nor passed the earlier part of life without the flattery of court-ship, and the joys of triumph. I have danced the round of gaiety amidst the murmurs of envy, and gratulations of applause ; been attended from pleasure to pleasure by the great, the sprightly, and the vain ; and seen my regard solicited by the obsequiousness of gallantry, the gayety of wit, and the timidity of love." [5] Tranquilla, it may be noted, goes from " strength to strength," from " twins " to " triplets " — if this expression be not indecorous concerning a lady who ends her letter by informing *The Rambler* that she intends to remain single.

Poor Debtors.—"The rest are imprisoned by the wanton-ness of pride, the malignity of revenge, or the acrimony of disappointed expectations." [6]

The Corruptions of Gaols.—"They are filled . . . with all the shameless and profligate enormities that can be produced by the impudence of ignominy, the rage of want, and the malignity of despair." [7]

[1] *Rambler*, No. 28.   [2] *Ibid.*, No. 48.
[3] *Ibid.*, No. 83.   [4] *Ibid.*, No. 92.
[5] *Ibid.*, No. 119.   [6] *Idler*, No. 22.   [7] *Ibid.*, No. 38.

Sometimes each part of the " triplet " is a substantive coupled with an adjective :

Good Humour.—" It recommends those who are destitute of all other excellencies, and procures regard to the trifling, friendship to the worthless, and affection to the dull." [1]

On the Advantages of Living in a Garret.—" As an elaborate performance is commonly said to smell of the lamp, my commendation of a noble thought, a sprightly sally, or a bold figure, is to pronounce it fresh from the garret." [2]

Or a verb is united with an adjective or substantive :

" *Know Thyself.*"—" A precept dictated by philosophers, inculcated by poets, and ratified by saints." [3]

The Gloom of a Sick Chamber.—" Where all human glory is obliterated, the wit is clouded, the reasoner perplexed, and the hero subdued." [4]

The Spendthrift.—" A very short time will give him up to the gripe of poverty, which will be harder to be borne, as he has given way to more excesses, wantoned in greater abundance, and indulged his appetite with more profuseness." [5]

The Peevish Man.—" A little opposition offends, a little restraint enrages, and a little difficulty perplexes him." [6]

Why People retreat to the Country.—" The general, ruffled with dangers, wearied with labours, and stunned with acclamations, gladly snatched an interval of silence and relaxation." [7]

The Courtier Uncle.—" By some occult method of captivation, he animated the timorous, softened the supercilious, and opened the reserved." [8]

---

[1] *Rambler*, No. 72. [2] *Ibid.*, No. 117.
[3] *Ibid.*, No. 28. In this *Rambler* Johnson gives an epitaph on Pontanus which must have pleased him : " Quem amaverunt bonæ musæ, suspexerunt viri probi, honestaverunt reges domini."
[4] *Ibid.*, No. 48. [5] *Ibid.*, No. 53.
[6] *Ibid.*, No. 74. [7] *Ibid.*, No. 135. [8] *Ibid.*, No. 147.

The Idler's Dearth of Correspondents.—" I have therefore no opportunity of showing how skilfully I can pacify
resentment, extenuate negligence, or palliate rejection." [1]

Here is a more complicated and ingenious " triplet,"
consisting of three collocations of a verb with two substantives :

The Encouragement of New Actors.—" I saw the ranks
of the theatre emulating each other in candour and
humanity, and contending who should most effectually
assist the struggles of endeavour, dissipate the blush of
diffidence, and still the flutter of timidity." [2]

Perhaps the reader is now sufficiently fortified by a
diet of " triplets " to digest a pair of " quartettes " :

An Uniformity in the State of Man.—" We are all
prompted by the same motives, all deceived by the same
fallacies, all animated by hope, obstructed by danger,
entangled by desire, and seduced by pleasure." [3]

Effect of Age on Conduct.—" We grow negligent of time
in proportion as we have less remaining, and suffer the
last part of life to steal from us in languid preparations
for future undertakings, or slow approaches to remote
advantages, in weak hope of some fortuitous occurrence,
or drowsy equilibrations of undetermined counsel." [4]
Here we have four sets of linked pairs of adjectives and
substantives.

A " quintette " (and I think the only one of which
Johnson is guilty) may fitly conclude this selection :

" Difficulties embarrass, uncertainty perplexes, opposition retards, censure exasperates, or neglect depresses." [5]

A taste for " triplets," it may be admitted, is an acquired taste ; they are a mannerism tempting to imitators,
who might not be so skilful as Johnson.[6]   They are, at any

---

[1] *Idler*, No. 2.   [2] *Ibid.*, No. 96.
[3] *Rambler*, No. 60.   [4] *Ibid.*, No. 111.   [5] *Ibid.*, No. 207.
[6] Mrs Elizabeth Carter, the blue-stocking, who wrote the
44th *Rambler*, was fairly successful with her " triplets " : " Where

rate, easier to ridicule than to construct ; and for Johnson's triplets it may be claimed that each part of the trio always bears a separate sense, and contributes something to the whole. Every substantive is exactly appropriate to its adjective, and every verb to its substantive ; they are, in fact, an exercise in neatness and precision of composition, and show, if rather aggressively, Johnson's mastery of his language.

If we pass from words and phrases to a general estimate of Johnson's prose, what can be said but that he has a good style and a bad style ? The bad has been called " Johnsonese " ; it is characterized by the copious use of the long Latin words, but the essence of its badness is that the words are not only too long, but too many. Sometimes, but rarely, this results in obscurity of meaning ; as, for instance : " When the radical idea branches out into parallel ramifications, how can a constructive series be formed of senses in their nature collateral ? " [1] Boswell praises this effort as an instance of " the perspicuity with which he has expressed abstract scientifick notions," [2] but I cannot help recalling Johnson's own pleasant remark on one of Donne's metaphysical poems : " If the lines are not easily understood, they may be read again." [3]

are the painful toils of virtue, the mortifications of penitents, the self-denying exercises of saints and heroes ? " " The true enjoyments of a reasonable being . . . do not consist in unbounded indulgence, or a luxurious ease, in the tumult of passions, the languor of indolence, or the flutter of amusements."

In *The Times* of 10th August 1922 I read a very creditable " triplet " : " But it is ours to acknowledge and to share, and over vast spaces of the earth to distribute a priceless inheritance, which has helped to discipline the understandings, to smooth the intercourse, and to increase the comforts of mankind " (" Lord Shaw's Address to the American Bar Association at San Francisco," 9th August 1922).

[1] *Preface to the English Dictionary.*
[2] *Life of Johnson* (Birkbeck Hill), i. 291.
[3] *The Lives of the English Poets* (Cowley).

Horace Walpole ridiculed this lack of compression in a letter to Mason [1] : " The machinery in *The Rape of the Lock* he calls ' combinations of skilful genius with happy casuality,' in English I guess ' a lucky thought.' " And Cowper has a sly dig : " My brother and I meet every week, by an alternate reciprocation of intercourse, as Sam. Johnson would express it." [2] Macaulay says of *The Rambler* that, while some pronounced it perfect, " Another party, not less numerous, vehemently accused him of having corrupted the purity of the English tongue." [3] Let it be granted that Johnson's style often fell short of his description of Addison's : " His sentences have neither studied amplitude, nor affected brevity ; his periods, though not diligently rounded, are voluble and easy." [4]

And yet, even when the " amplitude " of his sentence is over-studied, Johnson is always Johnson. The parodists have never quite succeeded. Boswell, who makes some excellent comments on the imitators,[5] in another passage [6] mentions Campbell's effort, of which Dr Birkbeck Hill gives a sample : " Without dubiety you misrepresent this dazzling scintillation in totality, and had you had that constant recurrence to my oraculous dictionary, which was incumbent upon you from the vehemence of my monitory injunctions." Is this the style of Johnson ?

" No, but a most burlesque, barbarous experiment."

As Johnson said of another attempt : " Sir, these are not the words I should have used. No, Sir ; the imitators of my style have not hit it. Miss Aikin has done it the best ; for she has imitated the sentiment as well as the diction." [7] But Burke explained the failure of another imitator in

---

[1] 14th April 1781.
[2] Letter to Major Cowper, 18th October 1765.
[3] *Biographies* (Samuel Johnson).
[4] *The Lives of the English Poets* (Addison).
[5] *Life of Johnson* (Birkbeck Hill), iv. 385.
[6] *Ibid.*, ii. 44.   [7] *Ibid.*, iii. 172.

words which are worthy of Johnson himself : " No, no, it
is *not* a good imitation of Johnson ; it has all his pomp
without his force ; it has all the nodosities of the oak
without its strength. . . . It has all the contortions of
the Sybil, without the inspiration." [1]

Was Disraeli consciously essaying an enterprise, in
which others had failed, when he made a famous onslaught
on his rival ?—" A sophisticated rhetorician, inebriated
with the exuberance of his own verbosity, and gifted with
an egotistical imagination, that can at all times command
an interminable and inconsistent series of arguments to
malign his opponents and glorify himself." For Disraeli,
too, was speaking in the Latin tongue—and perhaps with
his own tongue in his cheek.

Here we are concerned with the Essays, and, though
these contain many " hard " words and " triplets," I have
found in them very little, if any, " Johnsonese." They
are not quite devoid of platitudes,[2] but a good style
may make even platitudes attractive. The true style of
Johnson, his better style—how are we to describe it ?
Style is something indefinable,

> " But what it is, hard is to say,
>   Harder to hit,
> Which way soever men refer it."

But some things we can say of Johnson's style. First
there is dignity, that which Mr Birrell calls his " unrivalled
stateliness." [3] Then there is order, " movement from

---

[1] *Life of Johnson* (Birkbeck Hill), iv. 59.

[2] I fear the following sentences are obnoxious to this charge :—
" As it is presumption and arrogance to anticipate triumphs, it
is weakness and cowardice to prognosticate miscarriages." "That
all are equally happy, or miserable, I suppose none is sufficiently
enthusiastical to maintain." " Hope is indeed very fallacious, and
promises what it seldom gives." " Whatever is left in the hands
of chance must be subject to vicissitude."

[3] *Obiter Dicta : First and Second Series complete*, p. 200.

point to point, which can only be compared to the
measured tread of a well-drilled company of soldiers." [1]
Then there is imagery; often and often he presents vivid
pictures to the mind's eye. Again, though he can be
diffuse, he can also be terse and epigrammatic. And he
is always scrupulously grammatical, which cannot be said
of Addison. But the style is the man; and what was this
man? He was fundamentally sad; his finest passages are
those that are pervaded by his profound melancholy. So
let us not forget his "cadences"; for if Johnson was
(as he owned) "very insensible to the power of music,"
he knew how to introduce harmonies into his prose, into
many a sentence that, after swelling with majestic sound,
fades away with simple words and phrases, and ends with
a "dying fall." But wit and humour were also his; a
native wit polished and embellished by learning, the
genuine playful humour of a strong, wise, kind, tolerant
nature. Wit and humour, dignity and order, picturesque
phrase and epigram—of all these Johnson was master;
but, as it is my plan that the Essayist should speak for
himself, I will try no more at definition, but place before
the reader some examples of Johnson's prose style:

Theory and Practice.—"The speculatist is only in danger
of erroneous reasoning; but the man involved in life, has
his own passions, and those of others, to encounter, and is
embarrassed with a thousand inconveniences, which confound him with variety of impulse, and either perplex or
obstruct his way." [2] . . . "He that is most deficient in
the duties of life, makes some atonement for his faults,
if he warns others against his own failings, and hinders,
by the salubrity of {his admonitions, the contagion of his
example." [3]

A Theoretical Soldier.—"He therefore studied all the
military writers, both ancient and modern, and, in a short

---

[1] *Obiter Dicta: First and Second Series complete*, p. 217.
[2] *Rambler*, No. 14.   [3] *Ibid.*

time, could tell how to have gained every remarkable battle that has been lost from the beginning of the world. He often showed at table how Alexander should have been checked in his conquests, what was the fatal error at Pharsalia, how Charles of Sweden might have escaped his ruin at Pultowa, and Marlborough might have been made to repent his temerity at Blenheim. He entrenched armies on paper so that no superiority of numbers could force them, and modelled in claim many impregnable fortresses, on which all the present arts of attack would be exhausted without effect." [1]

Hedonism of the Ancient Poets is no Excuse for Modern.— " It is no wonder that such as had no promise of another state should eagerly turn their thoughts upon the improvement of that which was before them ; but surely those who are acquainted with the hopes and fears of eternity, might think it necessary to put some restraint upon their imagination, and reflect that by echoing the songs of the ancient bacchanals, and transmitting the maxims of past debauchery, they not only prove that they want invention, but virtue." [2]

An Apprehensive Temper.—" A temper which keeps the man always in alarms ; disposes him to judge of everything in a manner that least favours his own quiet, fills him with perpetual stratagems of counteraction, wears him out in schemes to obviate evils which never threatened him, and at length, perhaps, contributes to the production of those mischiefs of which it had raised such dreadful apprehensions." [3]

A Fortune-Hunter.—" Chance threw in her way Philotryphus, a man vain, glittering, and thoughtless as herself, who had spent a small fortune in equipage and dress, and was shining in the last suit for which his tailor would give him credit. He had been long endeavouring to retrieve his extravagance by marriage, and therefore soon paid

[1] *Rambler*, No. 19. [2] *Ibid.*, No. 29. [3] *Ibid.*

his court to Melanthia, who after some weeks of insensibility saw him at a ball, and was wholly overcome by his performance in a minuet. They married; but a man cannot always dance, and Philotryphus had no other method of pleasing." [1]

An Antidote against Sorrow.—" The safe and general antidote against sorrow is employment. It is commonly observed, that among soldiers and seamen, though there is much kindness, there is little grief; they see their friend fall without any of that lamentation which is indulged in security and idleness, because they have no leisure to spare from the care of themselves." [2]

" *Crabbed Age and Youth.*"—" If dotards will contend with boys in those performances in which boys must always excel them; if they will dress crippled limbs in embroidery, endeavour at gayety with faltering voices, and darken assemblies of pleasure with the ghastliness of disease, they may well expect those who find their pleasures obstructed will hoot them away; and that if they descend to competition with youth, they must bear the insolence of successful rivals.

" ' Lusisti satis, edisti satis, atque bibisti :
Tempus abire tibi est.' " [3]

Foolish Envy of the Great.—" As themselves have known little other misery than the consequences of want, they are with difficulty persuaded that where there is wealth there can be sorrow, or that those who glitter in dignity, and glide along in affluence, can be acquainted with pains and cares like those which lie heavy upon the rest of mankind." [4]

Nemesis of the Spendthrift.—" But the time is always hastening forward when this triumph, poor as it is, shall vanish, and when those who now surround him with

---

[1] *Rambler*, No. 39.   [2] *Ibid.*, No. 47.
[3] *Ibid.*, No. 50.   [4] *Ibid.*, No. 58.

obsequiousness and compliments, fawn among his equipage, and animate his riots, shall turn upon him with insolence, and reproach him with the vices prompted by themselves." [1]

The Death of One we have injured.—"Our crime seems now irretrievable, it is indelibly recorded, and the stamp of fate is fixed upon it. We consider, with the most afflictive anguish, the pain which we have given, and now cannot alleviate, and the losses which we have caused, and now cannot repair." [2]

Existence without Thought.—"He that lives in torpid insensibility, wants nothing of a carcass but putrefaction." [3]

Manners and Fashions.—"Of all these, the savage that hunts his prey upon the mountains, and the sage that speculates in his closet, must necessarily live in equal ignorance." [4]

The Great Corrupters of the World.—"There have been men splendidly wicked, whose endowments threw a brightness on their crimes, and whom scarce any villainy made perfectly detestable, because they never could be wholly divested of their excellencies ; but such have been in all ages the great corrupters of the world, and their remembrance ought no more to be preserved, than the art of murdering without pain." [5]

A Good Conscience makes Patience easier.—"And surely, if we are conscious that we have not contributed to our own sufferings, if punishment falls upon innocence, or disappointment happens to industry and prudence, patience, whether more necessary or not, is much easier, since our pain is then without aggravation, and we have not the bitterness of remorse to add to the asperity of misfortune." [6]

A Soul well principled.—"Yet, lest we should think

[1] *Rambler*, No. 53. [2] *Ibid.*, No. 54.
[3] *Idler*, No. 24. [4] *Adventurer*, No. 131.
[5] *Rambler*, No. 4. [6] *Ibid.*, No. 32.

ourselves too soon entitled to the mournful privileges of irresistible misery, it is proper to reflect, that the utmost anguish which human wit can contrive, or human malice can inflict, has been borne with constancy ; and that if the pains of disease be, as I believe they are, sometimes greater than those of artificial torture, they are therefore in their own nature shorter ; the vital frame is quickly broken, or the union between soul and body is for a time suspended by insensibility, and we soon cease to feel our maladies when they once become too violent to be borne. I think there is some reason for questioning whether the body and mind are not so proportioned, that the one can bear all that can be inflicted on the other, whether virtue cannot stand its ground as long as life, and whether a soul well principled will not be separated sooner than subdued." [1]

The Happiness of Youth.—" It is not easy to surround life with any circumstances in which youth will not be delightful, and I am afraid that whether married or unmarried, we shall find the vesture of terrestrial existence more heavy and cumbrous, the longer it is worn." [2]

The Motives for Matrimony.—" When I see the avaricious and crafty, taking companions to their tables and beds without any inquiry, but after farms and money ; or the giddy and thoughtless uniting themselves for life to those whom they have only seen by the light of tapers at a ball ; when parents make articles for their children, without enquiring after their consent ; when some marry for heirs to disappoint their brothers, and others throw themselves into the arms of those whom they do not love, because they have found themselves rejected where they were most solicitous to please ; when some marry because

---

[1] *Rambler*, No. 32. Boswell said he never read this sentence " without feeling his frame thrill " (Boswell's *Life of Johnson*, Birkbeck Hill, i. 215). [2] *Ibid.*, No. 45.

their servants cheat them, some because they squander their own money, some because their houses are pestered with company, some because they will live like other people, and some only because they are sick of themselves, I am not so much inclined to wonder that marriage is sometimes unhappy, as that it appears so little loaded with calamity." [1]

Nature provides no Remedy for Sorrow.—"But for sorrow there is no remedy provided by nature; it is often occasioned by accidents irreparable, and dwells upon objects that have lost or have changed their existence; it requires what it cannot hope, that the laws of the universe should be repealed; that the dead should return, or the past should be recalled." [2]

Complaints of the Rising Generation.—"Every old man complains of the growing depravity of the world, of the petulance and insolence of the rising generation. He recounts the decency and regularity of former times, and celebrates the discipline and sobriety of the age in which his youth was passed; a happy age, which is now no more to be expected, since confusion has broken in upon the world and thrown down all the boundaries of civility and reverence." [3]

Age not always to be revered.—"If men imagine that excess of debauchery can be made reverend by time, that knowledge is the consequence of long life, however idly or thoughtlessly employed, that priority of birth will supply the want of steadiness or honesty, can it raise much wonder that their hopes are disappointed, and that they see their posterity rather willing to trust their own eyes in their progress into life, than enlist themselves under guides who have lost their way?" [4]

The Universal Friend.—"Nor can the candour and frankness of that man be much esteemed, who spreads

[1] *Rambler*, No. 45.   [2] *Ibid.*, No. 47.
[3] *Ibid.*, No. 50.   [4] *Ibid.*, No. 50.

his arms to humankind, and makes every man, without distinction, a denizen of his bosom." [1]

Domestic Happiness.—" To be happy at home is the ultimate result of all ambition, the end to which every enterprise and labour tends, and of which every desire prompts the prosecution." [2]

The Highest Panegyrick.—" The highest panegyrick, therefore, that private virtue can receive, is the praise of servants." [3]

The Miseries of Learned Men.—" The miseries of the learned have been related by themselves, and since they have not been found exempt from that partiality with which men look upon their own actions and sufferings, we may conclude that they have not forgotten to deck their own cause with the brightest ornaments and strongest colours." [4]

The Wickedness of Loose or Profane Authors.—" By the instantaneous violence of desire, a good man may sometimes be surprised before reflection can come to his rescue ; when the appetites have strengthened their influence by habit, they are not easily resisted or suppressed ; but for the frigid villainy of studious lewdness, for the calm malignity of laboured impiety, what apology can be invented ?   What punishment can be adequate to the crime of him who retires to solitudes for the refinement of debauchery ; who tortures his fancy, and ransacks his memory, only that he may leave the world less virtuous than he found it ; that he may intercept the hopes of the rising generation ; and spread snares for the soul with more dexterity ? " [5]

Our Familiarity with Death.—" Yet we to whom the shortness of life has given frequent occasion of contemplating mortality, can, without emotion, see generations of men pass away, and are at leisure to establish modes of sorrow,

[1] *Rambler*, No. 64.   [2] *Ibid.*, No. 68.   [3] *Ibid.*
[4] *Ibid.*, No. 77.   [5] *Ibid.*

and adjust the ceremonial of death. We can look upon funeral pomp as a common spectacle in which we have no concern, and turn away from it to trifles and amusements, without dejection of look, or inquietude of heart." [1]

Gaming.—" A man may shuffle cards, or rattle dice, from noon to midnight, without tracing any new idea in his mind, or being able to recollect the day by any other token than his gain or loss, and a confused remembrance of agitated passions and clamorous altercations." [2]

Dead Counsellors are safest.—" It was the maxim, I think, of Alphonsus of Arragon, that *dead counsellors are safest.* The grave puts an end to flattery and artifice, and the information that we receive from books is pure from interest, fear, or ambition. Dead counsellors are likewise most instructive, because they are heard with patience and with reverence." [3]

Lessons learnt from a Public Library.—" No place affords a more striking conviction of the vanity of human hopes, than a public library ; for who can see the wall crowded on every side by mighty volumes, the works of laborious meditation, and accurate enquiry, now scarcely known but by the catalogue, and preserved only to increase the pomp of learning, without considering how many hours have been wasted in vain endeavours, how often imagination has anticipated the praises of futurity, how many statues have risen to the eye of vanity, how many ideal converts have elevated zeal, how often wit has exulted in the eternal infamy of his antagonists, and dogmatism has delighted in the gradual advances of his authority, the immutability of his decrees, and the perpetuity of his power ? " [4]

The Fear of being rejected by God.—" That to please the Lord and Father of the Universe, is the supreme interest of created and dependent beings, as it is easily proved, has

[1] *Rambler*, No. 78.   [2] *Ibid.*, No. 80
[3] *Ibid.*, No. 87.   [4] *Ibid.*, No. 106.

been universally confessed; and, since all rational agents are conscious of having neglected or violated the duties prescribed to them, the fear of being rejected, or punished by God, has always burdened the human mind." [1]

Beauty desired, in spite of its Danger.—" Beauty is well known to draw after it the persecutions of impertinence, to incite the artifices of envy, and to raise the flames of unlawful love ; yet, among the ladies whom prudence or modesty have made most eminent, who has ever complained of the inconveniences of an amiable form? or would have purchased safety by the loss of charms ? " [2]

A Mistake made by some Great Poets.—" They seem to have thought that as the meanness of personages constituted comedy, their greatness was sufficient to form a tragedy ; and that nothing was necessary but that they should crowd the scene with monarchs, and generals, and guards ; and make them talk, at certain intervals, of the downfall of kingdoms, and the rout of armies." [3]

The Difficulty of raising Reputation.—" Yet such is the state of the world, that no sooner can any man emerge from the crowd, and fix the eyes of the publick upon him, than he stands as a mark to the arrows of lurking calumny, and receives in the tumult of hostility, from distant and from nameless hands, wounds not always easy to be cured."[4]

Avarice.—" Avarice is generally the last passion of those lives of which the first part has been squandered in pleasures, and the second devoted to ambition. He that sinks under the fatigue of getting wealth, lulls his age with the milder business of saving it." [5]

Every Man intends to reform himself. — " As we all know our own faults, and know them commonly with many aggravations which human perspicuity cannot discover, there is, perhaps, no man, however hardened by impudence or dissipated by levity, sheltered by hypocrisy

[1] *Rambler*, No. 110.   [2] *Ibid.*, No. 111.   [3] *Ibid.*, No. 125.
[4] *Ibid.*, No. 144.   [5] *Ibid.*, No. 151.

or blasted by disgrace, who does not intend some time to review his conduct, and to regulate the remainder of his life by the laws of virtue." [1]

The Conquering of Bad Habits.—" The influence of custom is indeed such, that to conquer it will require the utmost efforts of fortitude and virtue ; nor can I think any man more worthy of veneration and renown, than those who have burst the shackles of habitual vice." [2]

No Man is much regarded.—" But the truth is, that no man is much regarded by the rest of the world. He that considers how little he dwells upon the condition of others, will learn how little the attention of others is attracted by himself. While we see multitudes passing before us, of whom, perhaps, not one appears to deserve our notice, or excite our sympathy, we should remember, that we likewise are lost in the same throng ; that the eye which happens to glance upon us is turned in a moment on him that follows us, and that the utmost which we can reasonably hope or fear is, to fill a vacant hour with prattle, and be forgotten." [3]

The Zeal of an Antiquary.—" Yet, to rouse the zeal of a true antiquary, little more is necessary than to mention a name which mankind have conspired to forget ; he will make his way to remote scenes of action through obscurity and contradiction, as *Tully* sought amidst bushes and brambles the tomb of *Archimedes.*" [4]

Old Men fall into Pupilage.—" Men eminent for spirit and wisdom often resign themselves to voluntary pupilage, and suffer their lives to be modelled by officious ignorance, and their choice to be regulated by presumptuous stupidity." [5]

Public Assemblies.—" All assemblies of jollity, all places of publick entertainment, exhibit examples of strength wasting in riot, and beauty withering in irregularity." [6]

[1] *Rambler*, No. 155.   [2] *Ibid.*   [3] *Ibid.*, No. 159.
[4] *Ibid.*, No. 161.   [5] *Ibid.*, No. 162.   [6] *Ibid.*, No. 178.

Chance governs Nothing.—" In this state of universal uncertainty, where a thousand dangers hover about us, and none can tell whether the good that he pursues is not evil in disguise, or whether the next step will lead him to safety or destruction, nothing can afford any rational tranquillity, but the conviction that, however we amuse ourselves with unideal sounds, nothing in reality is governed by chance, but that the universe is under the perpetual superintendence of Him who created it ; that our being is in the hands of omnipotent Goodness, by whom what appears casual to us, is directed for ends ultimately kind and merciful; and that nothing can finally hurt him who debars not himself from the divine favour." [1]

The Wisdom and Duty of Forgiveness.—" A wise man will make haste to forgive, because he knows the true value of time, and will not suffer it to pass away in unnecessary pain. He that willingly suffers the corrosions of inveterate hatred, and gives up his days and nights to the gloom of malice, and perturbations of stratagem, cannot surely be said to consult his ease. Resentment is an union of sorrow with malignity, a combination of a passion which all endeavour to avoid, with a passisn which all concur to detest." [2]

" Of him that hopes to be forgiven, it is indispensably required that he forgive. It is therefore superfluous to urge any other motive. On this great duty eternity is suspended ; and to him that refuses to practise it, the throne of mercy is inaccessible, and the SAVIOUR of the world has been born in vain." [3]

[1] *Rambler*, No. 184.

[2] *Ibid.*, No. 185. (*The Rambler* written for Christmas Eve, 1751.)

[3] *Ibid.* " I am no preacher ; let this hint suffice,
The Cross once seen is death to every vice ;
Else He that hung there suffered all his pain,
Bled, groaned, and agonized, and died in vain."
(COWPER, *The Progress of Error.*)

The Fallacious Hopes of Youth.—" With hopes like these, he sallies jocund into life ; to little purpose is he told, that the condition of humanity admits no pure and unmingled happiness ; that the exuberant gayety of youth ends in poverty or disease ; that uncommon qualifications and contrarieties of excellence, produce envy equally with applause ; that, whatever admiration and fondness may promise him, he must marry a wife like the wives of others, with some virtues and some faults, and be as often disgusted by her vices, as delighted by her elegance ; that if he adventures into the circle of action, he must expect to encounter men as artful, as daring, as resolute as himself ; that of his children, some may be deformed, and others vitious ; some may disgrace him by their follies, some offend him by their insolence, and some exhaust him by their profusion. He hears all this with obstinate incredulity, and wonders by what malignity old age is influenced, that it cannot forbear to fill his ears with prediction of misery." [1]

The Approach of Death.—" The loss of our friends and companions impresses hourly upon us the necessity of our own departure ; we know that the schemes of man are quickly at an end, that we must soon lie down in the grave with the forgotten multitudes of former ages, and yield our place to others, who, like us, shall be driven a while by hope or fear, about the surface of the earth, and then like us be lost in the shades of death." [2]

His Serious Essays.—" The essays professedly serious, if I have been able to execute my own intentions, will be found exactly conformable to the precepts of Christianity, without any accommodation to the licentiousness and levity of the present age. I therefore look back on this part of my work with pleasure, which no blame or praise of man shall diminish or augment. I shall never envy the honours which wit and learning obtain in any other cause, if I can

[1] *Rambler*, No. 196.　　　　　　[2] *Ibid.*, No. 203.

D

be numbered among the writers who have given ardour
to virtue, and confidence to truth." [1]

The Jealousies of Scholars.—" But discord, who found
means to roll her apple into the banqueting chamber of
the goddesses, has had the address to scatter her laurels
in the seminaries of learning." [2]

Even Criminals have their Admirers.—" Even the robber
and the cut-throat have their followers, who admire their
address and their intrepidity, their stratagems of rapine,
and their fidelity to the gang." [3]

But the Liar has no Friends.—" The liar, and only the
liar, is invariably and universally despised, abandoned,
and disowned ; he has no domestick consolation, which
he can oppose to the censure of mankind ; he can retire to
no fraternity, where his crimes may stand in the place of
virtues ; but is given up to the hisses of the multitude,
without friend and without apologist." [4]

" There is no crime more infamous than the violation
of truth. It is apparent that men can be social beings no
longer than they believe each other. When speech is employed only as the vehicle of falsehood, every man must
disunite himself from others, inhabit his own cave, and
seek prey only for himself." [5]

No Man but expects to live another Year.—" Though
every funeral that passes before their eyes evinces the
deceitfulness of such expectations, since every man who
is born to the grave thought himself equally certain of
living at least to the next year ; the survivor still continues to flatter himself, and is never at a loss for
some reason why his life should be protracted, and the
voracity of death continue to be pacified with some other
prey." [6]

" But however we may be deceived in calculating the

---

[1] *Rambler*, No. 208. (The conclusion of *The Rambler*.)
[2] *Adventurer*, No. 45.   [3] *Ibid.*, No. 50.   [4] *Ibid.*
[5] *Idler*, No. 20.   [6] *Adventurer*, No. 69.

strength of our faculties, we cannot doubt the uncertainty
of that life in which they must be employed : we see every
day the unexpected death of our friends and our enemies,
we see new graves hourly opened for men older and
younger than ourselves, for the cautious and the careless,
the dissolute and the temperate, for men who like us were
providing to enjoy or improve hours now irreversibly cut
off ; we see all this, and yet, instead of living, let year
glide after year in preparations to live." [1]

Torpid Despondency.—" From torpid despondency can
come no advantage ; it is the frost of the soul, which binds
up all its powers, and congeals life in perpetual sterility.
He that has no hopes of success, will make no attempts ;
and where nothing is attempted, nothing can be done." [2]

The Different Arts of Gallantry.—" Thus love is uniform,
but courtship is perpetually varying ; the different arts
of gallantry, which beauty has inspired, would of themselves be sufficient to fill a volume ; sometimes balls and
serenades, sometimes tournaments and adventures, have
been employed to melt the hearts of ladies, who in
another century have been sensible of scarce any other
merit than that of riches, and listened only to jointures
and pin-money." [3]

The Virtuous not always Happy.—" But surely the
quiver of Omnipotence is stored with arrows, against
which the shield of virtue, however adamantine it has
been boasted, is held up in vain : we do not always suffer
by our crimes ; we are not always protected by our
innocence." [4]

A Consolation.—" While affliction thus prepares us for
felicity, we may console ourselves under its pressures,
by remembering, that they are no particular marks of
divine displeasure ; since all the distresses of persecution
have been suffered by those, ' of whom the world was not

[1] *Adventurer*, No. 108.   [2] *Ibid.*, No. 81.
[3] *Ibid.*, No. 95.   [4] *Ibid.*, No. 120.

worthy ' ; and the Redeemer of Mankind himself was ' a man of sorrows and acquainted with grief.' " [1]

Some read for Style, and some for Argument.—" They read for other purposes than the attainment of practical knowledge ; and are no more likely to grow wise by an examination of a treatise of moral prudence, than an architect to inflame his devotion by considering attentively the proportions of a temple." [2]

The Idle and Listless.—" It is naturally indifferent to this race of men what entertainment they receive, so they are but entertained. They catch, with equal eagerness, at a moral lecture, or the memoirs of a robber ; a prediction of the appearance of a comet, or the calculation of the chances of a lottery." [3]

A Charge against the Great.—" The waste of the lives of men has been very frequently charged upon the Great, whose followers linger from year to year in expectations, and die at last with petitions in their hands." [4]

Thieves of Time.—" He who cannot persuade himself to withdraw from society, must be content to pay a tribute of his time to a multitude of tyrants ; to the loiterer, who makes appointments which he never keeps ; to the consulter, who asks advice which he never takes ; to the projector, whose happiness is to entertain his friends with expectations which all but himself know to be vain ; to the economist, who tells of bargains and settlements ; to the politician, who predicts the fate of battles and breach of alliances ; to the usurer, who compares the different funds ; and to the talker, who talks only because he loves to be talking." [5]

Life's Heaviest Burdens.—" Money and time are the heaviest burdens of life, and the unhappiest of all mortals are those who have more of either than they know how to use." [6]

[1] *Adventurer*, No. 120.   [2] *Ibid.*, No. 137.   [3] *Idler*, No. 3.
[4] *Ibid.*, No. 14.   [5] *Ibid.*   [6] *Ibid.*, No. 30.

Sleep the Leveller.—" It is far more pleasing to consider, that sleep is equally a leveller with death ; that the time is never at a great distance, when the balm of rest shall be diffused alike upon every head, when the diversities of life shall stop their operation, and the high and the low shall lie down together." [1]

Of Monastick Institutions.—" And perhaps retirement ought rarely to be permitted, except to those whose employment is consistent with abstraction, and who, though solitary, will not be idle ; to those whom infirmity makes useless to the commonwealth, or to those who have paid their due proportion to society, and who, having lived for others, may be honourably dismissed to live for themselves." [2]

" It cannot be denied, that a just conviction of the restraint necessary to be laid upon the appetites has produced extravagant and unnatural modes of mortification, and institutions, which, however favourably considered, will be found to violate nature without promoting piety." [3]

On the Death of his Mother.—" These are the calamities by which Providence gradually disengages us from the love of life. Other evils fortitude may repel, or hope may mitigate; but irreparable privation leaves nothing to exercise resolution or flatter expectation. The dead cannot return, and nothing is left us here but languishment and grief." [4]

Of Middle-aged Men.—" From the vexation of pupilage men commonly set themselves free about the middle of life, by shutting up the avenues of intelligence, and resolving to rest in their present state." [5]

Our Common Humanity.—" We are all naked till we are dressed, and hungry till we are fed ; and the general's triumph, and sage's disputation, end, like the humble labours of the smith or ploughman, in a dinner or in sleep." [6]

[1] *Idler*, No. 32.   [2] *Ibid.*, No. 38.   [3] *Ibid.*, No. 52.
[4] *Ibid.*, No. 41.   [5] *Ibid.*, No. 44.   [6] *Ibid.*, No. 51.

Vestigia nulla retrorsum.—" Some may safely venture farther than others into the regions of delight, lay themselves more open to the golden shafts of pleasure, and advance nearer to the residence of the Syrens ; but he that is best armed with constancy and reason is yet vulnerable in one part or other ; and to every man there is a point fixed, beyond which, if he passes, he will not easily return. It is certainly most wise, as it is most safe, to stop before he touches the utmost limit, since every step of advance will more and more entice him to go forward, till he shall at last enter into the recesses of voluptuousness, and sloth and despondency close the passage behind him." [1]

It is necessary to Hope.—" Yet it is necessary to hope, though hope should always be deluded ; for hope itself is happiness, and its frustrations, however frequent, are yet less dreadful than its extinction." [2]

Avoid Scrupulosity.—" Of these learned men, let those who aspire to the same praise imitate the diligence, and avoid the scrupulosity. Let it be always remembered that life is short, that knowledge is endless, and that many doubts deserve not to be cleared." [3]

" *What have ye done ?* "—" He that compares what he has done with what he has left undone, will feel the effect which must always follow the comparison of imagination with reality ; he will look with contempt on his own unimportance, and wonder to what purpose he came into the world ; he will repine that he shall leave behind him no evidence of his having been, that he has added nothing to the system of life, but has glided from youth to age among the crowd, without any effort for distinction." [4]

Cunning.—" The whole power of cunning is privative ; to say nothing, and to do nothing, is the utmost of its reach. Yet men thus narrow by nature, and mean by

[1] *Idler*, No. 52.
[2] *Ibid.*, No. 58.
[3] *Ibid.*, No. 65.
[4] *Ibid.*, No. 88.

art, are sometimes able to rise by the miscarriage of bravery and the openness of integrity ; and, by watching failures and snatching opportunities, obtain advantages which belong properly to higher characters." [1]

Life's Last Hour.—" To life must come its last hour, and to the system of being its last day, the hour at which probation ceases, and repentance will be vain ; the day in which every work of the hand, and imagination of the heart, shall be brought to judgment, and an everlasting futurity shall be determined by the past." [2]

And now let me offer to the reader some shorter sentences and phrases which I have taken from the Essays *passim* :—

" To be lulled in the evening by soothing serenades, or wakened in the morning by sprightly gratulations."

" The dogmatical legions of the present race."

" (Richardson) taught the passions to move at the command of Virtue."

" Pedantry is the unseasonable ostentation of learning."

" The distempered ease of lolling in a chariot."

" This epidemical conspiracy for the destruction of paper."

" Few listen without a desire of conviction to those who advise them to spare their money."

" We are all naturally credulous in our own favour."

" The rower in time reaches the port ; the lexicographer at last finds the conclusion of his alphabet."

" The vacuities of recluse and domestic leisure."

" A vehement assertor of uncontroverted truth."

" Just praise is only a debt, but flattery is a present."

" The student wastes away in meditation, and the soldier perishes on the ramparts."

" Sufficient to awake the most torpid risibility."

" Those that spin out life in trifles and die without a memorial."

[1] *Idler*, No. 92.   [2] *Ibid.*, No. 103.

Here are some more from other works of Johnson, and from the pages of Boswell :

" Poetry has not often been worse employed than in dignifying the amorous fury of a raving girl."

" He never exchanged praise for money, nor opened a shop of condolence or congratulation."

" Pope's [page] is a velvet lawn, shaven by the scythe, and levelled by the roller."

" He meets with no basilisks that destroy with their eyes, his crocodiles devour their prey without tears, and his cataracts fall from the rocks without deafening the neighbouring inhabitants." [1]

" But it is a sad thing to pass through the quagmire of parsimony to the gulf of ruin."

" He is without skill in inebriation."

(Of Collins).—" He delighted to rove through the meanders of enchantment."

" The unauthorized loquacity of common fame."

(Of Gray's notion that he could not write but at certain times).—" A fantastick foppery, to which my kindness for a man of learning and virtue wishes him to have been superior."

(Of the same poet).—" Criticism disdains to chase a schoolboy to his commonplaces."

" Tyburn itself is not safe from the fury of innovation."

(Of an anxious author).—" Sir, there is not a young sapling upon Parnassus more severely blown about by every wind of criticism."

(To a foppish physician who said Johnson must remember him by the fine coat he wore on a former occasion). —" Sir, had you been dipt in Pactolus I should not have noticed you."

" The Scholar wanders about the world without pomp or terror."

[1] Preface to Lobo's *Voyage to Abyssinia* (written when Johnson was twenty-four).

" The rest, whose minds have no impression but that of the present moment, are either corroded by malignant passions or sit stupid in the gloom of perpetual vacancy."

" I came hither, not to measure fragments of temples, or trace choked aqueducts, but to look upon the various scenes of the present world."

(Of Shakespeare's plays).—" Scenes from which a hermit might estimate the transactions of the world, and a confessor predict the progress of the passions."

" The teachers of morality ; they discourse like angels, but they live like men."

" They wandered in gardens of fragrance, and slept in fortresses of security."

" He that races against Time has an antagonist not subject to casualities." [1]

" Time is, of all modes of existence, most obsequious to the imagination."

We read, and are struck by, such passages as these ; but when we ask what is the secret of their power, or their attraction, the explanation is not easy. Sometimes it is their sententiousness, sometimes their wit, sometimes their sarcasm ; but I think the true answer is given by Boswell : " His mind was so full of imagery, that he might have been perpetually a poet." [2]

It is in " imagery " that Johnson excels, in picturesqueness of phrase, in apt and concentrated and vivid expressions. This is Johnson's predominant quality, in which, as a prose writer, he has never since been surpassed. There may be many who have approached him—at least there are two men, one of them an author and both statesmen, who have given reminders and after-tastes of Johnson's curious and indefinable felicitousness. Disraeli,

[1] Horace Walpole, writing to Mason, 14th April 1781, characterizes this sentence as " a piece of bombast nonsense " !

[2] Boswell's *Life of Johnson* (Birkbeck Hill), iv. 428.

in addition to wit and satire, had this power of imagery, and often recalls the style of Johnson :

" In imagination I shook thrones and founded empires." [1]

" To feel fame a juggle and posterity a lie." [2]

" He does not mingle in the path of callous bustle. [3]

" A race of serfs, who are called labourers, and who burn ricks." [4]

(Of the benches occupied by Peel's followers).—" There the gang is still assembled, and there the thong of the whip still sounds." [5]

(Of men ennobled by Pitt).—" He made peers of second-rate squires and fat graziers. He caught them in the alleys of Lombard Street, and clutched them from the counting-houses of Cornhill."

(Of Peel).—" He never quotes a passage that has not previously received the meed of parliamentary approbation."

For Lord Randolph Churchill his son and biographer has justly claimed that he could boast an armoury of " wit, abuse, epigrams, *imagery*, argument." [6] From that armoury I select a few shafts which seem to be tipped with a Johnsonian point :

(Of Mr Gladstone).—" The forest laments that Mr Gladstone may perspire." [7] " The man for whom no flattery is too fulsome, no homage too servile." [8] " The first servant of the Crown has to be watched night and day by Alguazils armed to the teeth." [9]

(Ridicule of Mr W. H. Smith).—" I suppose that in the minds of the lords of suburban villas, of the owners of

---

[1] *Contarini Fleming.*   [2] *Henrietta Temple.*
[3] *Ibid.*   [4] *Coningsby.*   [5] *Sybil.*
[6] *Lord Randolph Churchill* (Winston Spencer Churchill), i. 277.
[7] *Ibid.*, 283.   [8] *Ibid.*, 284.
[9] *Ibid.*, 285. I wonder how many of the Tories of Blackpool had ever before heard of " Alguazils."

vineries and pineries, the mud cabin represents the climax of physical and social degradation." [1]

" Imagery " is a faculty which gives its owner the power of description ; and yet description and expression are but its outward and visible signs. It is not conferred except on those who have spiritual insight, who can see the contradictions and resemblances of things, and have a true and instinctive sense of values ; it implies also something else of importance—a keen perception of the ridiculous. By his spoken or written word the man that has " imagery " will always be able to reach the ear and the mind and the heart of his fellow-man.

[1] *Lord Randolph Churchill* (Winston Spencer Churchill), i. 345.

III

JOHNSON ON PASTORAL

" Pastorals are pretty enough—for those that like them—but to
me Thyrsis is one of the most insipid fellows I ever conversed with,
and as for Corydon, I do not choose his company." Goldsmith,
Citizen of the World, Letter 97.

WITH one exception, I do not propose to examine
the essays that Johnson has written on literary
subjects,[1] my purpose being to ascertain his
views on men and the ways of men rather than on books.
But his estimate of Pastoral poetry is peculiarly characteristic of his prejudices and his common sense, and at the
same time illustrates that distaste for country life of
which more will appear in a succeeding chapter. It also
presents him in a humorous light ; for when Johnson
writes of Pastoral poetry (as also when in the *Life of
Cowley* he writes of Metaphysical poetry) he is not only
very humorous himself, but the reader must feel that there
is something equally humorous in the association of the
writer with his subject :

> " The unwieldy elephant
> To make them mirth, used all his might and wreathed
> His lithe proboscis."

Pastoral poetry, like Allegories and Oriental tales, was
one of those compositions which the eighteenth-century

---

[1] "On Milton" (*Ramblers*, Nos. 86, 88, 90, 94, 139, 140), "Spenser"
(No. 121), "The English Historians" (No. 122), "The Unities and
Tragi-Comedy" (No. 156), "Shakespeare's ' Mean Expressions '"
(No. 158), ",Biography and Autobiography" (*Rambler*, No. 60, *Idler*,
No. 84), "Translations" (*Idlers*, Nos. 68, 69), "Virgil's Eclogues"
(*Adventurer*, No. 92). The essays on Milton should be read and
compared with the *Life*, and the 158th *Rambler* with the *Preface*
to Shakespeare ; the others are well worth attentive study.

author was expected to attempt. It was still usual to write verses about shepherds and shepherdesses, nymphs and swains, to sing of Strephon and Chloe, Alexis and Clorinda, dividing the " fleecy care " of their bleating flock. Johnson often refers to this species of poetry, and always in a vein of ridicule for its modern [1] exponents.

If his ethical speculations were limited by his orthodoxy, in æsthetics he allowed himself a more independent range. Of the Pastoral he has given us his theory in *Ramblers* Nos. 36 and 37 ; we may disagree with this theory, but we must acknowledge it to be original, and worthy of attention. *Rambler* No. 36 gives " the reasons why pastorals delight " ; *Rambler* No. 37 states " the true principles of pastoral poetry."

The Pastoral delights because " it exhibits a life, to which we have been always accustomed to associate peace, and leisure, and innocence," it transports us " to elysian regions, where we are to meet with nothing but joy, and plenty, and contentment ; where every gale whispers pleasure, and every shade promises repose." [2] " In child-hood we turn our thoughts to the country, as to the region of pleasure ; we recur to it in old age as a port of rest, and perhaps with that secondary and adventitious glad-ness, which every man feels on reviewing those places, or recollecting those occurrences, that contributed to his youthful enjoyments, and bring him back to the prime of life, when the world was gay with the bloom of novelty, when mirth wantoned at his side, and hope sparkled before him."

Rather strange, and scarcely acceptable to " nature-poets," are his reasons for affirming the range of pastoral

[1] And as for the ancients, Virgil, said Johnson, " ventured to copy " Theocritus. " And, perhaps, where he excels *Theocritus,* he sometimes obtains his superiority by deviating from the pastoral character " (*Adventurer,* No. 92).

[2] *Rambler,* No. 36.

to be narrow : " For though Nature itself, philosophic-
ally considered, be inexhaustible, yet its general effects
on the eye and on the ear are uniform, and incapable of
much variety of description. Poetry cannot dwell upon
the minuter distinctions, by which one species differs
from another, without departing from that simplicity of
grandeur which fills the imagination ; nor dissect the
latent qualities of things, without losing its general power
of gratifying every mind by recalling its conceptions.
However, as each age makes some discoveries, and those
discoveries are by degrees generally known, as new plants
or modes of culture are introduced, and by little and
little become common, pastoral might receive, from time
to time, small augmentations, and exhibit once in a
century a scene somewhat varied."

This sameness of Nature is reflected in the lives of
the country-folk. " The state of a man confined to the
employments and pleasures of the country, is so little
diversified, and exposed to so few of those accidents
which produce perplexities, terrours, and surprises, in
more complicated transactions, that he can be shown but
seldom in such circumstances as attract curiosity. His
ambition is without policy, and his love without intrigue.
He has no complaints to make of his rival, but that he is
richer than himself ; nor any disasters to lament, but a
cruel mistress, or a bad harvest. The conviction of the
necessity of some new source of pleasure induced *Sanna-*
zarius to remove the scene from the fields to the sea, to
substitute fishermen for shepherds, and derive his sentiments from the piscatory life." [1] Johnson considered
there was not anything necessarily objectionable in this
novel Pastoral of the marine. True, the sea is generally

---

[1] Pope writes of Theocritus : " The subjects of his Idyllia are
purely pastoral ; but he is not so exact in his persons, having
introduced reapers and fishermen as well as shepherds " (*A*
Discourse on Pastoral Poetry).

an " object of terrour," but a poet " may display all the pleasures, and conceal the dangers of the water, as he may lay his shepherd under a shady beech, without giving him an ague, or letting a wild beast loose upon him."

This seems to be no better than a negative qualification for the sea Pastoral. Unluckily it had two positive disadvantages. Firstly, the sea has even less variety than the land : " When he has once shown the sun rising or setting upon it, curled its waters with the vernal breeze, rolled the waves in gentle succession to the shore, and enumerated the fish sporting in the shallows, he has nothing remaining but what is common to all other poetry, the complaint of a nymph for a drowned lover, or the indignation of a fisher that his oysters are refused, and Mycon's accepted."

Secondly, the greater part of mankind lives in ignorance of maritime pleasures : " The sea is only known as an immense diffusion of waters, over which men pass from one country to another, and in which life is frequently lost. They have, therefore, no opportunity of tracing in their own thoughts the descriptions of winding shores and calm bays, nor can look on the poem in which they are mentioned, with other sensations than on a sea chart, or the metrical geography of *Dionysius*."

Such are the attractions and limitations of the Pastoral. In *Rambler* No. 37 Johnson inquires after " some more distinct and exact idea of this kind of writing." " If we search the writings of Virgil " (from whose opinion, he says, it will not appear very safe to depart), " it will be found *a poem in which any action or passion is represented by its effects upon a country life*." And therefore there is no need to introduce into Pastoral the notion of a past " golden age." This " golden age " theory has been introduced because, " according to the custom of modern life, it is improbable that shepherds should be capable of harmonious numbers or delicate sentiments." It is responsible for various absurdities. " Some have thought it necessary that the imaginary manners of the golden age should be universally preserved,[1] and have therefore believed that nothing more could be admitted in pastoral, than lilies and roses, and rocks and streams, among which are heard the gentle whispers of chaste fondness, or the soft complaints of amorous impatience." Others tell us that, " to support the character of the shepherd, it is proper that all refinement should be avoided, and that some slight instances of ignorance should be interspersed. Thus the shepherd in Virgil is supposed to have forgot the name of Anaximander, and in Pope the term Zodiack is too hard for a rustick apprehension." " Other writers, having the mean and despicable condition of a shepherd always before them, conceive it necessary to degrade the language of pastoral by obsolete terms and rustick words, which they very learnedly call Dorick. . . . Spenser begins one of his pastorals with studied barbarity :

> " ' *Diggon Davie*, I bid her good-day :
> Or, *Diggon* her is, or I mis-say.
> DIG.   Her was her while it was day-light,
> But now her is a most wretched wight.'

What will the reader imagine to be the subject on which speakers like these exercise their eloquence ? Will he not be somewhat disappointed when he finds them met together to condemn the corruptions of the Church of Rome ? Surely at the same time that a shepherd learns theology, he may gain some acquaintance with his native language."

Johnson returns to his argument : " Pastoral being the

[1] Johnson may have been referring to Pope. " If we would copy nature, it may be useful to take this idea along with us, that pastoral is an image of what they call the golden age. So that we are not to describe our shepherds as shepherds at this day really are, but as they may be conceived then to have been ; when the best of men followed the employment " (*A Discourse on Pastoral Poetry*, written when Pope was sixteen years of age).

representation of an action or passion, by its effects upon a country life, has nothing peculiar but its confinement to rural imagery, without which it ceases to be pastoral. . . . It is therefore improper to give the title of a pastoral to verses, in which the speakers, after the slight mention of their flocks, fall to complaints of errours in the church, and corruptions on the government, or to lamentations of the death of some illustrious person, whom, when once the poet has called a shepherd, he has no longer any labour upon his hands, but can make the clouds weep, and lilies wither, and the sheep hang their heads, without art or learning, genius or study." [1]

Such is Johnson's *theory* of Pastoral. He took occasion to trace its *history*, from Theocritus to Pope, in his *Life of Ambrose Philips*, which contains this characteristic sentence : "At the revival of learning in Italy, it was soon discovered that a dialogue of imaginary swains might be composed with little difficulty ; because the conversation of shepherds excludes profound or refined sentiment ; and, for images and descriptions, Satyrs and Fauns, and Naiads and Dryads, were always within call ; and woods and meadows, and hills and rivers, supplied variety of matter, which, having a natural power to soothe the mind, did not quickly cloy it." The subject of Pastoral poetry never failed to provoke Johnson to a pleasant irony.

---

[1] Goldsmith could parody such " lamentations " :

" *On the Death of the Right Honourable X X*

" Ye muses, pour the pitying tear
   For Pollio snatched away :
O had he liv'd another year !
   He had not died to-day. . . .

How sad the groves and plains appear,
   And sympathetic sheep ;
Ev'n pitying hills would drop a tear !
   If hills could learn to weep."
          (*Citizen of the World*, Letter 106.)

To return to his theory—that pastoral, to be correct,
can have only a limited scope, which is not understood by
poets who idealize the denizens of rural scenes, or represent
them as debating politics or religion. It is concerned with
"the state of a man confined to the employments and
pleasures of the country." Tennyson's *Northern Farmer*
would have come within the definition ; in his last illness
he calls for his ale, depreciates the Parson, and wonders
how the Squire will get on without him. Mr Thomas,
Hardy has written numerous " pastorals " that might
satisfy Johnson's definition. One is called *Friends Beyond*,
and enumerates the tenants of Mellstock churchyard :

" William Dewy, Tranter Reuben, Farmer Ledlow late at
    plough,
  Robert's kin, and John's, and Ned's,
And the Squire, and Lady Susan. . . ."

When these ghosts talk, they discuss pure country topics
—their crops, their herds, their household stores—and how
free they now feel from those old earthly cares. Even in
death they are remote from London town.

Here it might be asked why Pastoral should be limited
to the country life of country-folk, why it may not sometimes treat of how rural sights and sounds influence the
townsman, or those who are " capable of harmonious
numbers or delicate sentiments," or who may have had to
flee to the country from urban pestilence, or because they
had become bandits, or exiles.

" Hath not old custom made this life more sweet
  Than that of painted pomp ? Are not these woods
  More free from peril than the envious court ? "

Cannot a man be a " shepherd " if he be the owner of a
town house ? May not even an habitual resort to a week-
end cottage qualify him to carry a crook—as well as a
golf-club ?

It can only be answered that Johnson was a Londoner. Had he been a contumacious noble, ordered by his sovereign to retire to his estates, he would have ill consoled himself with elegant moralizing about sermons in stones, and books in the running brooks. Of those who, by their own choice, " pass their days in retreats distant from the theatres of business," and compute time " not by the succession of consuls, but of harvests," he had a poor opinion. For the " sportsman," now regarded with respect and even with veneration, he felt a contempt. He knew that the countryman was not a figure of romance, and that the Golden Age was not to be found lingering in the country-side. " Pastorella fondly conceived that she could dwell for ever by the side of a bubbling fountain, content with her swain and her fleecy care." [1] She shared Savage's expectations of moral felicity : "He could not bear to debar himself from the happiness which was to be found in the calm of a cottage, or lose the opportunity of listening, without intermission, to the melody of the nightingale, which he believed to be heard from every bramble, and which he did not fail to mention as a very important part of the happiness of a country life." [2] The Cockney who, in this belief, went ruralizing was doomed to disappointment. Ned Drugget, the industrious trader, wished " that he might have been so happy as to have renewed his uncle's lease of a farm, that he might have lived without noise and hurry in a pure air, in the artless society of honest villagers, and the contemplation of the works of nature." [3] Ned only moved as far as Islington ; but had he penetrated farther into the heart of the country he might have been as disillusioned as Mr Dick Shifter, a student in the Temple, who " concealed the place of his retirement that none might violate his obscurity ; and promised himself

[1] *Adventurer*, No. 34.
[2] *Lives of the Poets* (Savage).
[3] *Idler*, No. 16.

many a happy day when he should hide himself among the trees, and contemplate the tumults and vexations of the town." [1] On his second day in the country " He walked out, and passed from field to field, without observing any beaten path, and wondered that he had not seen the shepherdesses dancing, nor heard the swains piping to their flocks. At last, he saw some reapers and harvestwomen at dinner. Here, said he, are the true *Arcadians*, and advanced courteously towards them, as afraid of confusing them by the dignity of his presence. They acknowledged his superiority by no other token than that of asking him for something to drink." The Princess in *Rasselas* was equally disappointed with the shepherds she met in the Nile valley : " They were so rude and ignorant, so little able to compare the good with the evil of their occupation, and so indistinct in their narratives and descriptions, that very little could be learned from them. But it was evident that their hearts were cankered with discontent ; that they considered themselves as condemned to labour for the luxury of the rich, and looked up with stupid malevolence toward those that were placed above them." [2]

Such were the disgusts experienced by those who travelled in vain search of Arcadian simplicity and guilelessness. On the poets, by whom these travellers were misled, Johnson had no mercy. If there was anything he hated more than insipidity, it was insincerity or *cant*— cant, the vice of an insincere mind ; and the Pastoral poets were as insipid in expression as they were insincere in thought.[3] Again and again in the *Lives* we find terse

---

[1] *Idler*, No. 71. [2] *Rasselas*, ch. xix.

[3] Goldsmith's Chinese Philosopher must have been a philosopher after Johnson's own heart. " But the most usual manner is this: Damon meets Menalcas, who has got a most gloomy countenance. The shepherd asks his friend, whence that look of distress : to which the other replies, that Pollio is no more. ' If that be the case then,' cries Damon, ' let us retire to yonder bower, at some distance off, where the cypress and the jessamine add fragrance

sentences, full of pungent wit, written in ridicule of this convention :

Of Ambrose Philips : " The Pastorals, which by the writer of *The Guardian* were ranked as one of the four genuine productions of the rustick Muse, cannot surely be despicable. That they exhibit a mode of life which did not exist, nor ever existed, is not to be objected : the supposition of such a state is allowed to Pastoral."

Of Shenstone : " I cannot but regret that it " (his *Pastoral Ballad*) " is pastoral ; an intelligent reader, acquainted with the scenes of real life, sickens at the mention of the *crook*, the *pipe*, the *sheep*, and the *kids*, which it is not necessary to bring forward to notice, for the poet's art is selection, and he ought to shew the beauties without the grossness of the country life."

Of Lyttelton : " The verses cant of shepherds and flocks, and crooks dressed with flowers." " Of his *Progress of Love* it is sufficient blame to say it is pastoral."

Of Pope : " It seems natural for a young poet to initiate himself by Pastorals, which, not professing to imitate real life, require no experience ; and, exhibiting only the simple operation of unmingled passions, admit no subtle reasoning or deep enquiry."

Of Hammond : " Where there is fiction, there is no passion : he that describes himself as a shepherd, and his

to the breeze ; and let us weep alternately for Pollio, the friend of shepherds, and the patron of every muse.' ' Ah ! ' returns his fellow shepherd, ' what think you rather of that grotto by the fountain side ? The murmuring stream will help to assist our complaints ; and a nightingale, on a neighbouring tree, will join her voice to the concert.' When the place is thus settled they begin : the brook stands still to hear their lamentations ; the cows forget to graze ; and the very tygers start from the forest with sympathetic concern. By the tombs of our ancestors, my dear Fum, I am quite unaffected in all this distress : the whole is liquid laudanum to my spirits ; and a tyger, of common sensibility, has twenty times more tenderness than I " (*Citizen of the World*, Letter 106).

Næra or Delia as a shepherdess, and talks of goats and lambs, feels no passion.''

Of Milton: " Nothing can less display knowledge, or less exercise invention, than to tell how a shepherd has lost his companion, and must now feed his flocks alone, without any judge of his skill in piping ; and how one god asks another god what is become of Lycidas, and how neither god can tell.''

And now let Prior come up for judgment. The scene is Thrale's villa at Streatham. " Mrs Thrale disputed with him on the merit of Prior. He attacked him powerfully ; said he wrote of love like a man who had never felt it ; his love verses were college verses ; and he repeated the song, ' Alexis shunn'd his fellow swains,' etc., in so ludicrous a manner, as to make us all wonder how any one could have been pleased with such fantastical stuff. Mrs Thrale stood to her gun with great courage, in defence of amorous ditties, which Johnson despised, till he at last silenced her by saying, ' My dear Lady, talk no more of this. Nonsense can be defended but by nonsense.' '' [1] A very diverting performance must this recitation have been, at which we would give much to have been present, and we may speculate whether the great Doctor, on finishing the last line,

" He bow'd, obey'd, and dy'd,"

fell prone on the hearth-rug of Thrale's library.

And yet *The Despairing Shepherd* is a very pretty piece, whose essential charm was, perhaps, beyond Johnson's faculty of appreciation. We can imagine the pretty verses being sung to the spinet, or the harp, to a pretty air, and, at the end, a bewigged beau adjusting his spyglass to ogle the fair singer, and murmuring, " 'Pon my life, *vastly* pretty ! '' before indulging gracefully in a pinch of snuff. But, after all, the verses *are* " nonsense '' ; for if Clorinda

[1] Boswell's *Life of Johnson* (Birkbeck Hill), ii. 78.

reached a high level of absurdity in pardoning this
universally beloved shepherd for "breathing his vows,"
Alexis was still more sublimely ridiculous in bowing
before expiring. Pastoral had once been the accepted vehicle of true
emotion. When Spenser's shepherd makes his lament,

" But now, ye Shepherd Lasses, who shall lead
Your wandering Troups, or sing your Virelayes ?
Or who shall dight your Bowres, sith she is dead
That was the Lady of your Holy-days ?
Let now your Bliss be turned into Bale,
And into plaints convert your joyous Plays,
And with the same fill every Hill and Dale,"

we can believe in his grief, in spite of his pastoral habili-
ments and accoutrements. Prior's " swain " is an unreal
creature, a Dresden-china shepherd, we cannot believe
that *he* died for love.

From Prior to Crabbe is a far cry, for Prior was born
soon after the Restoration, and Crabbe died in the reign
of William IV. Yet they were both contemporary with
Johnson, who was twelve years old when Prior died.
Sir Joshua Reynolds introduced Crabbe to Johnson, and
Johnson revised *The Village*. "Its sentiments as to the
false notions of rustick happiness and rustick virtue were
quite congenial with his own." [1] Boswell says that the
following verses are, almost wholly, Johnson's improvements on Crabbe's original composition :—

" On Mincio's banks, in Cæsar's bounteous reign,
If Tityrus found the golden age again,
Must sleeping bards the flattering dream prolong,
Mechanick echoes of the Mantuan song ?
From Truth and Nature shall we widely stray,
Where Vergil, not where Fancy, leads the way ? " [2]

[1] Boswell's *Life of Johnson* (Birkbeck Hill), iv. 175.
[2] *The Village*, Book I. 15-20.

To whatever extent Johnson may have improved on
Crabbe, there can be no doubt that he thoroughly approved Crabbe's true and realistic presentation of country
life. And there are two lines of Crabbe that follow, and
sum up much of Johnson's criticism of Pastoral poetry :

" Yes, thus the Muses sing of happy swains,
   Because the Muses never knew their pains." [1]

Johnson thought that Pastoral poetry was insincere and
tedious and nonsensical.[2] No doubt he did much to put it
out of fashion ; in any case it was a part of the Classical
tradition that became neglected and forgotten in the
Romantic movement. And yet one of the great Victorians
had the courage to revert to Pastoral :

" Here, too, our shepherd-pipes we first assay'd.
   Ah me ! this many a year
   My pipe is lost, my shepherd's holiday ! . . .
   He loved his mates ; but yet he could not keep,
   For that a shadow lower'd on the fields,
   Here with the shepherds and the silly sheep."

Those ingenious parodists, who compose imaginary
dialogues upon modern events between Johnson and
modern personages, might agreeably exercise their wits
by writing a Johnsonian criticism of Matthew Arnold's
Thyrsis.

[1] " We must therefore use some illusion to render a pastoral
delightful ; and this consists in exposing the best side only of a
shepherd's life, and in concealing its miseries " (Pope, *A Discourse
on Pastoral Poetry*).

[2] " Nor will a man, after the perusal of thousands of these
performances, find his knowledge enlarged with a single view of
nature not produced before, or his imagination amused with
any new application of those views to moral purposes " (*Rambler*,
No. 36).

IV

JOHNSON THE MORALIST

" Others in virtue placed felicity,
    But virtue joined with riches and long life ;
    In corporal pleasure he, and careless ease ;
    The Stoic last in philosophic pride,
    By him called virtue, and his virtuous man,
    Wise, perfect in himself, and all possessing,
    Equal to God, oft shames not to prefer,
    As fearing God nor man, contemning all
    Wealth, pleasure, pain or torment, death and life—
    Which, when he lists, he leaves, or boasts he can."
                    Paradise Regained, Book IV. 297-306.

MACAULAY calls Johnson " the old philosopher,"
but to this title Johnson has no claim ; let us
rather call him a " sage." [1] His search for truth
was strictly limited by his creed, and by his own prejudices and prepossessions. After narrating a discussion
on Liberty and Necessity, Freewill and Predestination,
Boswell observes : " His supposed orthodoxy here cramped
the vigorous powers of his understanding. He was confined by a chain which early imagination and long habit
made him think massy and strong, but which, had he
ventured to try, he could at once have snapt asunder." [2]
And it was not only on the Freewill controversy that his
understanding was cramped. Sir Leslie Stephen says :

[1] Since this was written, Professor S. Alexander, in the first of
two interesting essays on " Dr Johnson as a Philosopher," contributed to *The Cornhill Magazine* of October and November 1923,
has stated, " he is rather the wise man or sage than the philosopher." It is remarkable that in neither of these essays does
Professor Alexander once refer to Johnson's Essays.

[2] Boswell's *Life of Johnson* (Birkbeck Hill), ii. 104.

73

" Johnson's love of truth in the ordinary affairs of life was combined with an indifference, or, we may almost say, an aversion, to speculative truth." [1] " Johnson was little fitted for abstract speculation. He was an embodiment of sturdy prejudice, or, in other words, of staunch beliefs which had survived their logical justification." [2] " Speculation, in short, though he passed for a philosopher, was simply abhorrent to him. . . . He has made up his mind once for all that religion is wanted, and that the best plan is to accept the established creed." [3]

But Johnson, though no philosopher, was in his Essays a great exponent of religion and morals. Thereby he has incurred the blame of modern critics. Thus Mr A. B. Walkley censures "the ' moralistic ' trend of American criticism, that vitiated so much of our English criticism (notably Sam Johnson's) in the eighteenth century." [4] Yes, it is true ; Johnson will always point the moral. The doctrine of " Art for Art's sake " would simply have infuriated him ; I cannot conceive any one of his contemporaries so hardy as to expound it in his presence. " It is justly considered as the greatest excellence of art, to imitate nature ; but it is necessary to distinguish those parts of nature, which are most proper for imitation." [5] " If the world be promiscuously described, I cannot see of what use it can be to read the account : or why it may not be safe to turn the eye immediately upon mankind as upon a mirrour which shows all that presents itself without discrimination. It is therefore not a sufficient vindication of a character, that it is drawn as it appears ; for many characters ought never to be drawn : nor of a narrative, that the train of events is agreeable to observation and experience ; for that observation which is called know-

[1] *English Thought in the Eighteenth Century*, i. 59.
[2] *Ibid.*, ii. 206.   [3] *Ibid.*, ii. 375.
[4] " On American Civilization," *The Times*, 12th July 1922.
[5] *Rambler*, No. 4.

ledge of the world, will be found much more frequently to make men cunning than good." [1] A note, in the edition which I possess of Johnson's *Works*, states that " this excellent paper was occasioned by the popularity of *Roderick Random*, and *Tom Jones*, which appeared about this time."

But, if Johnson is to be depreciated on this account —that he insisted on all books having a moral—it is to be noted that the other great English essayists will fall under the same condemnation. " The great Purpose of the whole," says Steele at the conclusion of *The Tatler*, " has been to recommend Truth, Innocence, Honour, and Virtue, as the chief Ornaments of Life ; but I considered that Severity of Manners was absolutely necessary to him that would censure others, and for that Reason, and that only, chose to talk in a Mask. I shall not carry my Humility so far as to call myself a vicious Man ; but at the same Time must confess, my Life is at best but pardonable." [2]   And of Addison, Johnson himself writes that *The Tatler* and *The Spectator* " taught with great justness of argument and dignity of language the most important duties and sublime truths." [3]   " It is justly observed by Tickell that he [Addison] employed wit on the side of virtue and religion." [4]   His own moral aim is emphasized by Johnson again and again : " As it has been my principal design to inculcate wisdom or piety, I have allotted few papers to the idle sports of imagination." [5]   " My purpose being to consider the moral discipline of the mind, and to promote the increase of virtue rather than of learning." [6] He specially composed a prayer that God might bless *The Rambler*, " that in this undertaking thy Holy Spirit may

[1] *Rambler*, No. 4. Not only the novelist, but the poet, "ought always to consult the interests of virtue " (*Rambler*, No. 37).

[2] *Tatler*, No. 271.

[3] *Lives of the Poets* (Addison).   [4] *Ibid.*

[5] *Rambler*, No. 208.   [6] *Ibid.*, No. 8.

not be withheld from me, but that I may promote Thy glory, and the salvation of myself and others." [1]

He entertained the same desire for the *Lives of the Poets*: " Last week I published the *Lives of the Poets*, written, I hope, in such a manner as may lead to the promotion of piety." [2] And thus he criticizes Shakespeare : " His first defect is that to which may be imputed most of evil in books or in men. He sacrifices virtue to convenience, and is so much more careful to please than to instruct, that he seems to write without any moral purpose." [3]

And be it noted that Fielding, too, makes the same claim for *Tom Jones* in his dedication to Lord Lyttelton: " I declare that to recommend Goodness and Innocence hath been my sincere Endeavour in this History."

Johnson, then, came forward as a professed moralist ; but, as a rule, he was content to inculcate the minor virtues. He wrote of Addison : " His delight was more to excite merriment than detestation ; and he detects follies rather than crimes." Of Johnson it might be said that he " detected " the minor vices or crimes, rather than the major, though follies also were often his mark. " Those who exalt themselves into the chair of instruction . . . have not sufficiently considered how much of life passes in little incidents, cursory conversation, slight business, and casual amusements ; and therefore they have endeavoured only to inculcate the more awful virtues, without condescending to regard those petty qualities, which grow important only by their frequency." [4] On this principle he has written a fine essay on " The Folly of Anger," in which, after glancing at the effects of " anger operating upon power "—" the subversion of cities, the desolation of countries, the massacre of nations "—he continues : " But this gigantick and enormous species of anger falls

[1] Boswell's *Life of Johnson* (Birkbeck Hill), i. 202.
[2] *Ibid.*, iii. 380n.   [3] *Preface to Shakespeare.*
[4] *Rambler*, No. 72.

not properly under the animadversion of a writer, *whose chief aim is the regulation of common life*, and whose precepts are to recommend themselves by their general use. Nor is this essay intended to expose the tragical or fatal effects even of private malignity. The anger which I propose now for my subject, is such as makes those who indulge it *more troublesome than formidable, and ranks them rather with hornets and wasps, than with basilisks and lions.*" [1] "These sudden bursts of rage generally break out upon small occasions; for life, unhappy as it is, cannot supply great evils as frequently as the man of fire thinks it fit to be enraged." [2] The essay deals, therefore, with the man who, "by a steady perseverance in his ferocity, may fright his children, and harass his servants." [3] This was the spirit in which Johnson took upon himself "the office of a periodical monitor." [4] He was, in Sir Leslie Stephen's words, "a practical moralist in a vein peculiar to the time." [5]

In his religion Johnson accepted, and maintained against all opponents, the "established creed" of the Church of England. He exalts religion above philosophy, and mocks at "the wild enthusiastick virtue of the Stoicks," which "pretended to an exemption from the sensibilities of unenlightened mortals," while they "proclaimed themselves exalted, by the doctrine of their sect, above the reach of those miseries which embitter life to the rest of the world. They therefore removed pain, poverty, loss of friends, and violent death, from the catalogue of evils; and passed, in their haughty style, a kind of irreversible decree, by which they forbad them to be counted any longer among the objects of terrour or anxiety, or to give any disturbance to the tranquillity of a wise man." [6]

[1] *Rambler*, No. 11.   [2] *Ibid.*
[3] *Ibid.*   [4] *Ibid.*, No. 15.
[5] *English Thought in the Eighteenth Century*, ii. 367.
[6] *Rambler*, No. 32.

And thus he concludes that pathetic essay which he wrote on the death of his mother: " Surely there is no man who, thus afflicted, does not seek succour in the *gospel*, which has brought *life and immortality to light*. The precepts of *Epicurus*, who teaches us to endure what the laws of the universe make necessary, may silence, but not content us. The dictates of *Zeno*, who commands us to look with indifference on external things, may dispose us to conceal our sorrow, but not assuage it. Real alleviation of the loss of friends, and rational tranquillity in the prospect of our own dissolution, can be received only from the promises of Him in Whose hands are life and death, and from the assurance of another and better state, in which all tears will be wiped from the eyes, and the whole soul shall be filled with joy. *Philosophy may infuse stubbornness, but Religion only can give patience.*" [1]

" If, instead of wandering after the meteors of philosophy, which fill the world with splendour for a while, and then sink and are forgotten, the candidates of learning fixed their eyes upon the permanent lustre of moral and religious truth, they would find a more certain direction to happiness. A little plausibility of discourse, and acquaintance with unnecessary speculations, is dearly purchased, when it excludes those instructions which fortify the heart with resolution, and exalt the spirit to independence." [2] I will add a passage from his *Life of Milton* :

" The ancient epick poets, wanting the light of Revelation, were very unskilled teachers of virtue ; their principal characters may be great but they are not amiable. The reader may rise from their works with a greater degree of active or passive fortitude, and sometimes of prudence ; but he will be able to carry away few precepts of justice, and none of mercy." [3]

Thus Johnson, himself no philosopher, joins issue with

[1] *Idler*, No. 41. [2] *Rambler*, No. 180.
[3] *Lives of the Poets* (Milton).

the philosophers.[1] But he not only accepts the consolations of religion ; he submits to its stern commands, and
trembles at its terrors. The call of conscience, the necessity of conversion and of remorse, the consequences of
the Fall of Man, hell-fire and damnation—all these were
parts of Johnson's creed. "That every man should
regulate his actions by his own conscience, without any
regard to the opinions of the rest of the world, is one of
the first precepts of moral prudence."[2] "With respect
to original sin, the inquiry is not necessary ; for whatever
is the cause of human corruption, men are evidently and
confessedly so corrupt, that all the laws of heaven and
earth are insufficient to restrain them from crimes."[3]
"Religion informs us that misery and sin were produced
together. The depravation of human will was followed
by a disorder of the harmony of nature ; and by that
Providence which often places antidotes in the neighbourhood of poisons, vice was checked by misery, lest
it should swell to universal and unlimited dominion."[4]
"No corruption is great but by long negligence, which
can scarcely prevail in a mind regularly and frequently
awakened by periodical remorse."[5] "Whether action
may be yet of use in churches, where the preacher addresses
a mingled audience, may deserve inquiry. . . . Yet as
all innocent means are to be used for the propagation of

[1] Art, as well as philosophy, was as nothing in comparison with
religion. *Rambler* No. 94 ("On Milton's Accommodation of Sound
to Sense") ends with these words : "He had indeed a greater and
a nobler work to perform ; a single sentiment of moral or religious
truth, a single image of life or nature, would have been cheaply
lost for a thousand echoes of the cadence to the sense ; and he
who had undertaken to *vindicate the ways of God to man*, might
have been accused of neglecting his cause, had he lavished much
of his attention upon syllables and sounds."
[2] *Rambler*, No. 23.
[3] Boswell's *Life of Johnson* (Birkbeck Hill), iv. 124.
[4] *Idler*, No. 89.   [5] *Rambler*, No. 155.

truth, I would not deter those who are employed in preaching to common congregations, from any practice which they may find persuasive ; for, compared with the conversion of sinners, propriety and elegance are less than nothing." [1] " The secret horrour of the last is inseparable from a thinking being, whose life is limited, and to whom death is dreadful. . . . To life must come its last hour, and to this system of being its last day, the hour at which probation ceases, and repentance will be vain ; the day in which every work of the hand, and imagination of the heart, shall be brought to judgment, and an everlasting futurity shall be determined by the past." [2] " That to please the Lord and Father of the universe, is the supreme test of created and dependent beings, as it is easily proved, has been universally confessed ; and, since all rational agents are conscious of having neglected or violated the duties prescribed to them, the fear of being rejected, or punished by God, has always burdened the human mind." [3] " ' As I cannot be *sure* that I have fulfilled the conditions on which salvation is granted, I am afraid I may be one of those who shall be damned ' (looking dismally). Dr ADAMS. 'What do you mean by damned ? ' JOHNSON (passionately and loudly). ' Sent to Hell, Sir, and punished everlastingly.' Dr ADAMS. ' I don't believe that doctrine.' . . . Mrs ADAMS. ' You seem, Sir, to forget the merits of our Redeemer.' JOHNSON. 'Madam, I do not forget the merits of my Redeemer ; but my Redeemer has said that he will set some on his right hand and some on his left.' He was in gloomy agitation, and said, ' I'll have no more on't.' " [4]

[1] *Idler*, No. 90. Johnson much disliked " action," *supra*, p. 21.
[2] *Ibid.*, No. 103. [3] *Rambler*, No. 110.
[4] Boswell's *Life of Johnson* (Birkbeck Hill), iv. 299, 300. Dr Birkbeck Hill has likened him to Mr Fearing in *The Pilgrim's Progress* : " When he came to the Hill Difficulty, he made no stick at that, nor did he much fear the Lions ; for you must know that his troubles were not about such things as these ; his fear was about his acceptance at last."

Johnson's fears of death, and of damnation, were accentuated by his sense of the miseries of earthly life, and the depràvity of contemporary mankind :

" The controversy about the reality of external evils is now at an end. That life has many miseries, and that these miseries are, sometimes at least, equal to all the powers of fortitude, is now universally confessed. . . . The cure for the greatest part of human miseries is not radical, but palliative. Infelicity is involved in corporeal nature, and interwoven with our being." [1]

" The general lot of mankind is misery." [2]

" Thus life is languished away in the gloom of anxiety, and consumed in collecting resolutions which the next morning dissipates." [3]

" Our state may indeed be more or less embittered, as our duration may be more or less contracted ; yet the utmost felicity which we can ever attain will be little better than alleviation of misery, and we shall always feel more pain from our wants than pleasure from our enjoyments." [4]

" In youth we have nothing past to entertain us, and in age, we derive little from retrospect but hopeless sorrow." [5]

" The depravity of mankind is so easily discoverable, that nothing but the desert or the cell can exclude it from notice." [6]

" The greater part of mankind are corrupt in every condition, and differ in high and in low stations, only as they have more or fewer opportunities of gratifying their desires, or as they are more or less restrained by human censures." [7]

" Life is to most such as could not be endured without frequent intermissions of existence : Homer therefore thought it an office worthy of the goddess of wisdom to lay Ulysses asleep when landed on Phæacia." [8]

[1] *Rambler*, No. 32. [2] *Lives of the Poets* (Savage).
[3] *Rambler*, No. 134. [4] *Ibid.*, No. 165. [5] *Ibid.*, No. 203.
[6] *Ibid.*, No. 175. [7] *Ibid.*, No. 172. [8] *Adventurer*, No. 39.

F

" The evils inseparably annexed to the present condition of man are so numerous and afflictive, that it has been, from age to age, the task of some to bewail, and of others to solace them." [1]

" No man is happy, but as he is compared with the miserable; for such is the state of the world, that we find in it absolute misery, but happiness only comparative; we may incur as much pain as we can possibly endure, though we can never obtain as much happiness as we might possibly enjoy." [2]

" There is, indeed, no topick on which it is more superfluous to accumulate authorities, nor any assertion of which our own eyes will more easily discover, or our sensations more frequently impress the truth, than, that misery is the lot of man, that our present state is a state of danger and infelicity." [3]

" The present life is to all a state of infelicity." [4]

And even in *The Idler*, which generally treats of topics lighter and more trifling than those of *The Rambler*, we have the following :—

" The general condition of life is so full of misery, that we are glad to catch delight without enquiring whence it comes, or by what power it is bestowed." [5]

Did ever another moralist give expression to such an Iliad of woe, to such pessimism and despondency ? If Johnson was a " philosopher," truly he belonged to the school of philosophy which his old fellow-collegian, Oliver Edwards, had in mind : " You are a philosopher, Dr Johnson. I have tried too in my time to be a philosopher ; but, I don't know how, cheerfulness was always breaking in." [6] We know that his gloom was due to bodily infirmities, and to " a life radically wretched," and that in his

---

[1] *Adventurer*, No. 111.   [2] *Ibid.*
[3] *Ibid.*, No. 120.   [4] *Ibid.* No. 138.
[5] *Idler*, No. 18.
[6] Boswell's *Life of Johnson* (Birkbeck Hill), iii. 305.

solitude he was prone to a morbid melancholy and to an
ever-present apprehension of becoming insane. As to
the universal depravity that (as he imagined) surrounded
him, all moralists have been inclined to think their own
age the worst in the history of the world. Johnson was
too much infected with the spirit of Juvenal:

" Nona ætas agitur pejoraque sœcula ferri
Temporibus, quorum sceleri non invenit ipsa
Nomen et a nullo posuit natura metallo."

And so he writes : " That we are fallen upon an age in
which corruption is barely not universal, is universally
confessed. Venality sculks no longer in the dark, but
snatches the bribe in publick ; and prostitution issues
forth without shame, glittering with ornaments of successful wickedness. Rapine preys on the publick without
opposition, and perjury betrays it without inquiry.
Irreligion is not only avowed, but boasted ; and the
pestilence that used to walk in the darkness, is now
destroying at noon-day." [1]

He was lonely, and out of tune with his time. His style
is said to have derived from seventeenth-century models,
and his politics dated from before 1688. And even from
the Revolution there had been a decline. " Whiggism, at
the time of the Revolution, he said, was accompanied with
certain principles, but latterly, as a mere party distinction
under Walpole and the Pelhams, was no better than the
politicks of stock-jobbers, and the religion of infidels." [2]

It would not be difficult to make out a case of peculiar
depravity against any given century. Our own has lately
had to bear some hard knocks. But, justly or unjustly

[1] Dedications, *The Evangelical History of Jesus Christ*, 1758.
[2] Boswell's *Life of Johnson* (Birkbeck Hill), ii. 117. In his old
age Johnson admitted the " necessity " of the Revolution : " ' What
we did at the Revolution was necessary ; but it broke our constitution.' OGLETHORPE. ' My father did not think it necessary ' "
(*Ibid.*, iv. 170-171, 22nd March 1783).

(and I think to a great extent unjustly), the eighteenth has specially incurred the charge of being false and wicked. Walpole and Newcastle were pre-eminently managers, and availed themselves of very mean arts of government ; and, besides the borough-mongering politicians who gave and took bribes, the rakes, fribbles, speculators, and neglectful patrons were of a sordid type. For half-a-century the kings were foreigners ; the divinity that had hedged the king was gone, and there was nothing to compensate for the ancient reverence, for the Church was lethargic, and the tone of bishops and clergy was servile and time-serving. As for the men of pleasure, the Georgian Lovelace was as material and callous as the Rangers and Dorilants of the Restoration. Let Johnson's Mysargurus [1] speak for himself from his stool of repentance in the Fleet :

" As I entered into the world very young, with an elegant person and a large estate, it was not long before I disentangled myself from the shackles of religion ; for I was determined to the pursuit of pleasure, which according to my notions consisted in the unrestrained and unlimited gratifications of every passion and every appetite ; and as this could not be obtained under the frowns of a perpetual dictator, I considered religion as my enemy ; and proceeding to treat her with contempt and derision, was not a little delighted, that the unfashionableness of her appearance, and unanimated uniformity of her notions, afforded opportunities for the sallies of my imagination.

" Conceiving now that I was sufficiently qualified to laugh away scruples, I imparted my remarks to those among my female favourites, whose virtue I intended to attack ; for I was well assured that pride would be able to make but a weak defence, when religion was subverted ; nor was my success below my expectation ; the love of pleasure is too strongly implanted in the female breast,

[1] Dr Birkbeck Hill was of opinion that the papers signed Mysargurus were not written by Johnson.

to suffer them scrupulously to examine the validity of arguments designed to weaken restraint; all are easily led to believe that whatever thwarts their inclination must be wrong : little more, therefore, was required, than, by the addition of some circumstances, and the exaggeration of others, to make merriment supply the place of demonstration ; nor was I so senseless as to offer arguments to such as could not attend to them, and with whom a repartee or catch would more effectually answer the same purpose." [1]

And persons of lower degree were fond of mean pretences that were scarcely less odious. Read the 84th *Adventurer*, the story of the nobleman's butler and the broker's clerk, the lady who kept a cook-shop and the law-writer, how they travelled together for four days in the stage-coach, what airs they gave themselves, and how they tried to impose upon one another as persons of wealth, rank and importance, " assuming a character, which was to end with the day, and claiming upon false pretences honours which must perish with the breath that paid them." Far off, indeed, were the days of the Canterbury pilgrims !

So Johnson, an honest man, had cause for bitterness ;

[1] *Adventurer*, No. 34. Goldsmith also describes these Lovelaces : " Besides the country squire, there is also another set of men, whose whole employment consists in corrupting beauty : these the silly part of the fair sex call amiable ; the more sensible part of them, however, give them the title of abominable. You will probably demand, what are the talents of a man thus caressed by the majority of the opposite sex ? What talents, or what beauty is he possessed of, superior to the rest of his fellows ? To answer you directly, he has neither talents nor beauty ; but then he is possessed of impudence and assiduity " (*Citizen of the World*, Letter 9). " As it is said of some men, that they make their business their pleasure, these sons of darkness may be said to make their pleasure their business. They might conquer their corrupt inclinations with half the pains they are at in gratifying them " (*Spectator*, No. 203).

he was poor and afflicted, and all around him he saw vice or insincerity. But his was far too brave a spirit to succumb to this depression. " I cannot omit to mention," writes Boswell,[1] " that I never knew any man who was less disposed to be querulous than Johnson. Whether the subject was his own situation, or the state of the publick, or the state of human nature in general, though he saw the evils, his mind was turned to resolution, and never to whining or complaint." He could apply " consolations to the timorous " : " Evil is uncertain in the same degree as good, and for the reason that we ought not to hope too securely, we ought not to fear with too much dejection. The state of the world is continually changing, and none can tell the result of the next vicissitude. Whatever is afloat in the stream of time may, when it is very near us, be driven away by an accidental blast, which shall happen to cross the general course of the current. The sudden accidents by which the powerful are depressed, may fall upon those whose malice we fear ; and the greatness by which we expect to be overborne, may become another proof of the false flatteries of fortune." [2] " Yet it is certain likewise that many of our miseries are merely comparative : we are often made unhappy, not by the presence of any real evil, but by the absence of some fictitious good." [3] And he could draw from evil a still higher comfort : " The miseries of life may, perhaps, afford some proof of a future state, compared as well with the mercy as the justice of God." [4]

But mark how his strong sense of humour, the true test of a man's essential sanity, could rescue him from his moods of dejection ; for none could laugh more heartily than Johnson at his own " dolorous declamations." Thus begins his 109th *Rambler*, purporting to come from

---

[1] Boswell's *Life of Johnson* (Birkbeck Hill), ii. 357.
[2] *Rambler*, No. 29.
[3] *Adventurer*, No. 111.　　　　[4] *Ibid.*, No. 120.

his correspondent Florentulus, to "gratify you with an imitation of your own syllables of sadness ":

"Sir,

"Though you seem to have taken a view sufficiently extensive of the miseries of life, and have employed much of your speculation on mournful subjects, you have not yet exhausted the whole stock of human infelicity. . . .

"I cannot but imagine the start of attention awakened by this welcome hint; and at this instant see the Rambler snuffing his candle, rubbing his spectacles, stirring his fire, locking out interruption, and settling himself in his easy chair, that he may enjoy a new calamity without disturbance. For whether it be that continued sickness or misfortune has acquainted you only with the bitterness of being ; or that you imagine none but yourself able to discover what I suppose has been seen and felt by all the inhabitants of the world ; whether you intend your writings as antidotal to the levity and merriment with which your rivals endeavour to attract the favour of the publick ; or fancy that you have some particular powers of dolorous declamation, and *warble out your groans* with uncommon elegance or energy ; it is certain that, whatever be your subject, melancholy for the most part bursts in upon your speculation, your gayety is quickly overcast, and though your readers may be flattered with hopes of pleasantry, they are seldom dismissed but with heavy hearts."

Surely this is very pleasant fooling, and surely a man's mind must be sound when he can treat his own indulgence in bad spirits as a foible to be ridiculed.

I shall only mention three other aspects of Johnson the Moralist—his contempt for riches, his idea of duty, and his attitude towards the doctrine that virtue is a mean between two extremes. All three illustrate his courage, his independence, and his lofty spirit.

"Poverty," Johnson admits, "is an evil always in our

view, an evil complicated with so many circumstances of uneasiness and vexation, that every man is studious to avoid it. Some degree of riches is therefore required, that we may be exempt from the gripe of necessity." [1] And yet, " of riches, as of everything else, the hope is more than the enjoyment. . . . No sooner do we sit down to enjoy our acquisitions, than we find them insufficient to fill up the vacuities of life." [2] On those who make riches their standard and *summum bonum* Johnson can inflict the lash; some of the characters he describes are certainly not spared. " *Tetrica* had a large fortune bequeathed to her by an aunt, which made her very early independent, and placed her in a state of superiority to all about her." Her maid " informed her that ladies, such as she, had nothing to do but to take pleasure their own way; that she wanted nothing from others, and had therefore no reason to value their opinion; that money was everything." [3] Tetrica becomes insolent and selfish. Melissa is more amiable; she loses fortune, but gains philosophy. " I have always thought the clamours of women unreasonable, who imagine themselves injured because the men who followed them upon the supposition of a greater fortune, reject them when they are discovered to have less. I have never known any lady who did not think wealth a title to some stipulations in her favour: and surely what is claimed by the possession of money is justly forfeited by its loss. She that has once demanded a settlement has allowed the importance of fortune; and when she cannot show pecuniary merit, why should she think her cheapener obliged to purchase ? " [4] Mrs Busy, the frugal country widow, when recommended to give her children a proper education, replied " that she never saw bookish or finical people grow rich, and that she was good for nothing herself till she had forgotten the nicety

[1] *Rambler*, No. 38.   [2] *Idler*, No. 73.
[3] *Rambler*, No. 74.   [4] *Ibid.*, No. 75.

of the boarding-school." She is a notable manager; in
fact " the only things neglected about her are her children,
whom she has taught nothing but the lowest household
duties." [1] Perdita was obsequious to her aunt, who left
her a considerable fortune, " and having received, from
the concurrent opinion of all mankind, a notion, that to
be rich was to be great and happy, I thought I had obtained my advantages at an easy rate." [2] Mercator, a
London tradesman, writes of his early experiences : " My
beginning was narrow, and my stock small ; I was, therefore, a long time brow-beaten and despised by those, who
having more money thought they had more merit than
myself." [3] Mrs Deborah Ginger, a City lady, married a
husband who was at first diligent and civil, and prospered
accordingly : " Thus every day increased our wealth and
our reputation. My husband was often invited to dinner
openly on the *Exchange* by hundred thousand pounds
men ; and whenever I went to any of the halls, the wives
of the aldermen made me low courtesies. . . . You will
easily believe that I was well enough pleased with my
condition ; for what happiness can be greater than that
of growing every day richer and richer ? " [4] " My master,"
writes Misocapelus, the son of a country gentleman (and
apprentice to a haberdasher), " who had no conception of
any virtue, merit, or dignity, but that of being rich, had
all the good qualities which naturally arise from a close
and unwearied attention to the main chance ; his desire
to gain wealth was so well tempered by the vanity of showing it, that, without any other principle of action, he lived
in the esteem of the whole commercial world ; and was
always treated with respect by the only men whose good
opinion he valued or solicited, those who were universally
allowed to be richer than himself." [5] On his vacation,

---

[1] *Rambler*, No. 138.   [2] *Adventurer*, No. 74.
[3] *Ibid.*, No. 102.
[4] *Idler*, No. 47.   [5] *Rambler*, No. 116.

Misocapelus, being snubbed by a Templar and a Guardsman, makes this pathetic observation : " As I knew that neither of these gentlemen had more money than myself, I could not discover what had depressed me in their presence." But his mother, who was a citizen's daughter, administered comfort " by telling me, that perhaps these showy talkers were hardly able to pay every one his own ; that he who has money in his pocket need not care what any man says of him ; that, if I minded my trade, the time will come when lawyers and soldiers would be glad to borrow out of my purse ; and that it is fine, when a man can set his hands to his sides, and say he is worth forty thousand pounds every day of the year." [1] I will add a remark made by Johnson upon Pope :   " The great topick of his ridicule is poverty ; the crimes with which he reproaches his antagonists are their debts, their habitation in the Mint, and their want of a dinner. He seems to be of an opinion not very uncommon in the world, that to want money is to want everything." [2]

Johnson does not attack riches and the pursuit of riches as bad in themselves.   " There are few ways," he said, " in which a man can be more innocently employed than in getting money." [3]   He would probably have agreed with Addison that it was perilous for a trader to break away from his occupation, and that " the very first step out of business is into vice or folly." [4]   What angered him in rich people was their lack of ideals, their commonplace character, their illiberality of mind, the torpor of their self-satisfaction. He found them at this work of acquisition in the country as well as in the City. They live " with no other wish than that of adding acre to acre, and filling one bag after another." [5]

[1] *Rambler*, No. 116.
[2] *Lives of the Poets* (Pope).
[3] Boswell's *Life of Johnson* (Birkbeck Hill), ii. 323.
[4] *Spectator*, No. 411.   [5] *Rambler*, No. 39.

" Ergo paratur
Altera villa tibi, cum rus non sufficit unum,
Et proferre libet fines, majorque videtur
Et melior vicina seges."

He put profusion before avarice, just as he preferred
rashness to cowardice. In fact he had little commendation
for the neutral safe virtues, for the μεσότης, the golden
mean between extremes; he considered there was more
hope for ὑπερβολή than for ἔλλειψις. "It may be laid
down as an axiom that it is more easy to take away
superfluities than to supply defects; and therefore he
that is culpable, because he has passed the middle point
of virtue, is always accounted a fairer object of hope,
than he who fails by falling short. The one has all that
perfection requires, and more, but the excess may be easily
retrenched; the other wants the qualities requisite to
excellence, and who can tell how he shall obtain them?
We are certain that the horse may be taught to keep pace
with his fellows, whose fault is that he leaves them behind.
*We know that a few strokes of the axe will lop a cedar; but
what arts of cultivation will elevate a shrub?* " [1]   As for
rashness and cowardice, "the one is never mentioned
without some kind of veneration, and the other always
considered as a topick of unlimited and licentious censure,
on which all the virulence of reproach may be lawfully
exerted. The same distinction is made, by the common
suffrage, between profusion and avarice, and, perhaps,
between many other opposite vices." [2]   "That there is a
middle path, which it is every man's duty to find, is
unanimously confessed: but it is likewise acknowledged
that this middle path is so narrow, that it cannot be easily
discovered, and so little beaten, that there are no certain
marks by which it can be followed: the care, therefore, of
all those who conduct others has been, that whenever they

[1] *Rambler*, No. 25.   [2] *Ibid.*

decline into obliquities, they should tend towards the side of safety. It can, indeed, raise no wonder that temerity has been generally censured; for it is one of the vices with which few can be charged, and which therefore great numbers are ready to condemn. *It is the vice of noble and generous minds*, the exuberance of magnanimity, and the ebullition of genius; and is therefore not regarded with much tenderness, because it never flatters us by that appearance of softness and imbecility which is commonly necessary to conciliate compassion." [1] To use a modern expression, Johnson advises his readers " to live dangerously "; and certainly he practised what he preached. In No. 100 of *The Idler* he points the moral by the story of Mr Tim Warner, who, having determined to marry, " drew upon a page of his pocket-book a scheme of all female virtues and vices, with the vices which border upon every virtue, and the virtues which are allied to every vice; . . . and having estimated the good and evil of every quality, employed his own diligence, and that of his friends, to find the lady in whom nature and reason had reached that happy mediocrity which is equally remote from exuberancy and deficience." [2] His addresses were accepted by Miss Gentle, " a good sort of woman," equally remote from ὑπερβολή and ἔλλειψις; but his marriage was not a happy one.

Let us contrast with Johnson a whole-hearted admirer of the Golden Mean—both in morals and in manners. " The sure characteristic of a sound and strong mind," writes Lord Chesterfield to his son, " is, to find, in every thing, those certain bounds, *quos ultra citrave nequit consistere rectum*. These boundaries are marked out by a very fine line, which only good sense and attention can discover; *it is much too fine for vulgar eyes*. In Manners, this line is good breeding; beyond it, is troublesome ceremony; short of it, is unbecoming negligence and inattention.

[1] *Rambler*, No. 129.   [2] *Idler*, No. 100.

In Morals, it divides ostentatious Puritanism from criminal Relaxation, Superstition from Impiety ; and, in short, every virtue from its kindred vice or weakness. I think you have sense enough to discover the line : keep it always in your eye, and learn to walk upon it ; rest upon Mr Harte, and he will poize you, till you are able to go alone. By the way, there are fewer people who walk well upon that line than upon the slack rope ; and therefore, a good performer shines so much the more." [1]

Very neat, and full of good sense, is this chapter of Georgian Ethics, and not wholly alien from the Nico-machæan system ; but we know how Johnson character-ized Lord Chesterfield's letters.

Johnson's doctrine on man's virtue and duty was that each of us has been given a " post," a " rank," a " station " in this life which he must maintain. It is the antique Roman notion of a sentinel keeping his post, and dying at it if need be. Thus of the passionate man : " The first reflection upon his violence must show him that he is mean enough *to be driven from his post* by every petty incident, that he is the mere slave of casualty, and that his reason and virtue are in the power of the wind." [2] " It is true that no diligence can ascertain success ; death may intercept the swiftest career ; but he who is cut off in the execution of an honest undertaking, has at least *the honour of falling in his rank*, and has fought the battle, though he missed the victory." [3] Of envy : " To avoid depravity like this, it is not necessary that any one should aspire to heroism or sanctity, but only that he should resolve *not to quit the rank which nature assigns him*, and wish to maintain the dignity of a human being." [4] Of the snare of retirement : " These ought to consider themselves as appointed the guardians of mankind, they are placed in an evil world, to exhibit publick examples of good life : and may be said,

[1] Lord Chesterfield's *Letters to his Son*, No. 142.
[2] *Rambler*, No. 11.   [3] *Ibid.*, No. 134.   [4] *Ibid.*, No 183.

where they withdraw to solitude, *to desert the station which Providence assigned them.*" [1]

But a man has not only to perform the duty of a soldier in life's battle, he must also fulfil the part of a good citizen in the commonwealth—ἄνθρωπος φύσει πολιτικὸν ζῷον. He points out the great fault of men of learning: "Despised, as useless to common purposes, as unable to conduct the most trivial affairs, and unqualified to perform those offices by which the concatenation of society is preserved, and mutual tenderness excited and maintained." [2] "Mankind is one vast republick, where every individual receives many benefits from the labours of others, which, by labouring in his turn for others, he is obliged to repay; where the united efforts of all are not able to exempt all from misery, none have a right to withdraw from their lack of vigilance, or to be indulged in idle wisdom or solitary pleasures." [3] And so it is good even for "the virgin whom the last summer released from her governess" to come up for the London season, however disappointing may be her experiences, for, "to know the world is necessary, since we were born for the help of one another." [4] "She that brings to *London* a mind well prepared for improvement, though she misses her hope of uninterrupted happiness, will gain in return an opportunity of adding knowledge to vivacity, and enlarging innocence to virtue." [5]

So Johnson, it is clear, was no admirer of "a fugitive and cloistered virtue, unexercised and unbreathed."

[1] *Adventurer*, No. 126.
[2] *Rambler*, No. 24.
[3] *Idler*, No. 19.
[4] *Ibid.*, No. 80.
[5] *Ibid.*

V

JOHNSON THE OBSERVER OF MANNERS

1. AUTHORS, CRITICS, PATRONS

" Deign on the passing world to turn thine eyes,
And pause awhile from Letters, to be wise ;
There mark what ills the scholar's life assail,
Toil, envy, want, the patron, and the gaol."

The Vanity of Human Wishes.

CARLYLE described Johnson as " an English plebeian and moving rag and dust mountain, coarse proud irascible imperious." Carlyle himself was born a Scotch peasant, but the social origins of Johnson are not so clearly defined. His father, Michael Johnson, was a bookseller, but Stebbing Shaw, the historian of Staffordshire, stated that Michael was the first of the family to emerge from " the obscure occupation of a day-labourer." Johnson himself was not much interested in his own family history, and once remarked : " I can hardly tell who was my grandfather " ; but a modern investigator [1] has discovered that this grandfather was styled a " yeoman," that Johnson's father nearly married (in fact took out the licence to marry)

---

[1] Mr Aleyn Lyell Reade (see his *Johnsonian Gleanings*). Mr Reade has noted that (in *Who's Who* for 1907) Dr Joseph W. Johnson, of Beaulieu Manor, Maidstone, was stated to be a descendant of Dr Johnson, Archdeacon of Leicester and founder of Uppingham (1584), and a collateral descendant of Samuel Johnson. Mr Reade has written a book of 115 pages about Francis Barber, Johnson's negro servant (*Johnsonian Gleanings*, Part II.). Is there any other great man in the history of the world whose valet has been thought worthy of a biography ?

the daughter of a prominent Derby tradesman, that his
great-uncle Henry Ford was " of Clifford Inn, Gent.," and
other facts that go to disprove the " day-labourer " theory.
We should not have held Johnson in less respect had he
been born in a cottage ; but, before we consider his descriptions of the social life of his times, it is natural to
ask what opportunities he had had of observing it, and in
what society he had mixed both in his earlier and later
years. " Johnson was so far fortunate," says Boswell [1]
(and let us remember, once for all, that Boswell was the
most veracious of biographers), " that the respectable
character of his parts, and his own merit, had, from his
earliest years, secured him a kind reception in the best
families of Lichfield." Amongst these kind friends of the
youthful Johnson Boswell mentions Mr Howard (a lawyer),
Dr Swinfen,[2] Capt. Garrick (father of David), Dr James,
a physician of repute,[3] and especially Gilbert Walmsley,
Registrar of the Prerogative Court of Lichfield, whose
character was eulogized by Johnson at the conclusion of
his *Life of Edmund Smith* (*alias* Neale).[4] And in most of
these families " he was in the company of ladies, particularly
at Mr Walmsley's, whose wife and sisters-in-law, of the
name of Aston, and daughters of a Baronet, were remarkable for good breeding ; so that the notion which has been
industriously circulated and believed, that he never was
in good company till late in life, and consequently had
been confirmed in coarse and ferocious manners by long
habits, is wholly without foundation. Some of the ladies
have assured me, they recollected him well when a young

[1] Boswell's *Life of Johnson* (Birkbeck Hill), i. 80.

[2] " A gentleman of a very ancient family in Staffordshire," and
the father of Mrs Desmoulins, later an inmate of Johnson's home.

[3] Was he the inventor of " James's powders," so dear to Horace
Walpole and other gouty martyrs ?

[4] *Lives of the English Poets.* Johnson there writes of Walmsley :
" He was of an advanced age, and I was only not a boy ; yet he
never received my notions with contempt."

man, as distinguished for his complaisance." [1] May we not conclude that his " coarse and ferocious " manners dated from his later London life of poverty, disappointment and solitude ?

When he came to London in 1737, besides beccming the friend of Savage, he received much kindness and attention from Henry Hervey, a son of the 3rd Earl of Bristol, whose acquaintance he had probably made when Hervey was in the army and quartered at Lichfield. [2] *The Rambler* gained him Langton's friendship, and Langton made him acquainted with Topham Beauclerk. [3] His circle of friends in the year 1752 (when he lost his wife) is given by Boswell [4]; they range in social rank from the Earl of Orrery to Mrs Gardiner, " wife of a tallow-chandler on Snow-hill, not in the learned way, but a worthy good woman," and include physicians, city merchants, authoresses, printers and booksellers. " Nothing can be more erroneous than the notion which some persons have entertained, that Johnson was then a retired authour, ignorant of the world ; and, of consequence, that he wrote only from his imagination when he described characters and manners. He said to me, that before he wrote that work [*The Rambler*], he had been ' running about the world,' as he expressed it, more than almost anybody ; and I have heard him relate, with much satisfaction, that several of the characters in *The Rambler* were drawn so naturally, that when it first circulated in numbers, a club in one of the towns in Essex imagined themselves to be severally exhibited in it, and were much incensed against a person who, they suspected, had thus made them objects of publick notice." [5] " Why, Sir, I am a man of the world. I live in the world, and I take, in some degree, the colour of the world as it moves along." [6]

[1] Boswell's *Life of Johnson* (Birkbeck Hill), i. 82.
[2] *Ibid.*, 106.   [3] *Ibid.*, 247, 248.
[4] *Ibid.*, 242.   [5] *Ibid.*, 215, 216.   [6] *Ibid.*, 427.

G

I must quote one more passage from Boswell in order
to emphasize the range and variety of Johnson's friends
and connections : " Volumes would be required to contain a list of his numerous and various acquaintance,
none of whom he ever forgot ; and could describe and
discriminate them all with precision and vivacity. He
associated with persons the most widely different in
manners, abilities, rank and accomplishments. He was at
once the companion of the brilliant Colonel Forrester of
the Guards, who wrote *The Polite Philosopher*, and of the
awkward and uncouth Robert Levet ; of Lord Thurlow,
and Mr Sastres, the Italian master ; and has dined one
day with the beautiful, gay, and fascinating Lady Craven,
and the next with good Mrs Gardiner, the tallow-chandler,
on Snow-hill." [1]

So it was that in all sorts of society Johnson was at
ease, and could hold his own. He knew when to speak, and
when to refrain from speech. After King George III.
had paid him a well-turned compliment in the library of
Buckingham House, he was asked if he made any reply :
" ' No, Sir. When the King had said it, it was to be so.
It was not for me to bandy civilities with my Sovereign.'
Perhaps no man who had spent his whole life in courts
could have shewn a more nice and dignified sense of true
politeness, than Johnson did in this instance." [2] True
it is that at times his manners offended, but we must
try to realize that the fine gentleman of exquisite breeding whom we associate with the era of Chesterfield and
Horace Walpole, like the chaste knights of the troubadour
period, were the exception rather than the rule. There
was much formality and ceremony, but at table the
standard of behaviour was not high. Chesterfield himself
has described the *bêtises* of an awkward diner: " There
he holds his knife, fork, and spoon, differently from other

people ; eats with his knife to the great danger of his
mouth, picks his teeth with his fork, and puts his spoon,
which has been in his throat twenty times, into the dishes
again. If he is to carve, he can never hit the joint ; but,
in his vain endeavours to cut through the bone, scatters
the sauce in everybody's face. He generally daubs himself
with soup and grease, though his napkin is commonly
stuck through a button-hole, and tickles his chin. When
he drinks, he infallibly coughs in his glass, and besprinkles
the company. Besides all this, he has strange tricks and
gestures ; such as snuffing up his nose, making faces,
putting his fingers in his nose, or blowing it and looking
afterwards in his handkerchief, so as to make the company
sick." [1] Compared with such offences, Johnson's voracity
and perspirations are not very alarming. Whenever the
occasion demanded it, he could exhibit an elaborate,
perhaps an over-elaborate and over-studied, politeness.
That he had the heart and instinct of a gentleman
appears again and again from his correspondence. [2]

It is therefore clear that Johnson was familiar, and at
his ease, with the inhabitants of the City and of the Court
end of London. Of course he also knew the life of a
university. Was he equally at home with country folk ?
Macaulay answered the question in the negative : " He
was no master of the great science of human nature. He
had studied, not the genus man, but the species Londoner.
Nobody was ever so thoroughly conversant with all the
forms of life and all the shades of moral and intellectual
character which were to be seen from Islington to the
Thames, and from Hyde-Park corner to Mile-end Green.
But his philosophy stopped at the first turnpike-gate. Of
the rural life of England he knew nothing ; and he took
it for granted that everybody who lived in the country

[1] Lord Chesterfield's *Letters to his Son*, No. 59.
[2] *E.g.* his letter to Dr Burney when the latter was a young and
obscure man. Boswell's *Life of Johnson* (Birkbeck Hill), i. 286.

was either stupid or miserable." [1] Macaulay denies any value to Johnson's "remarks on society beyond the bills of mortality."

Now it is true that Johnson, like nearly all the wits of his age, preferred London to the country. [2] One good reason for this preference was that in London not only society, but solitude, was obtainable. In the country the visitor was at the mercy of every caller. " The country," wrote Mr Spectator, " is not a place for a person of my temper, who does not love jollity, and what they call good-neighbourhood. A man that is out of humour when an unexpected guest breaks in upon him, and does not care for sacrificing an afternoon to every chance-comer ; that will be the master of his own time, and the pursuer of his own inclinations ; makes but a very unsociable figure in this kind of life. I shall therefore retire into the town, if I may make use of that phrase, and get into the crowd again as fast as I can, in order to be alone. I can there raise what speculations I please upon others, without being observed myself, and at the same time enjoy all the advantages of company with all the privileges of solitude." [3] Johnson makes Imlac the scholar express the same sentiment—" in a city populous as Cairo, it is possible to obtain at the same time the gratifications of society and the secrecy of solitude." [4] The cultured Londoner had a horror of the " good-neighbourhood " that must be practised in the country — the receiving and returning of visits, the prolonged meals and drinking bouts, the conversation of sportsmen. [5] One of Thackeray's characters, George

---

[1] Macaulay's essay on *Croker's Boswell*.

[2] " For who would leave, unbrib'd, Hibernia's land,
    Or change the rocks of Scotland for the Strand ? "
was Juvenal's, not Johnson's, sentiment.

[3] *Spectator*, No. 131.   [4] *Rasselas*, ch. xii.

[5] A much-to-be-pitied victim of " good-neighbourhood " was Mr B—— in *Pamela*. On his wedding day " three mad rakes " looked in on him for dinner. " They have nothing to do " (writes

Warrington, complains of this unutterable and insufferable boredom: "Mr Johnson talked of coming, but he
put us off once or twice. I suppose our house was dull. I
know that I myself would be silent for days, and fear that
my moodiness must often have tried the sweetest-tempered
woman in the world who lived with me. I did not care for
field-sports. The killing one partridge was so like killing
another, that I wondered how men could pass days after
days in the pursuit of that kind of slaughter. Their
fox-hunting stories would begin at four o'clock, when
the tablecloth was removed, and last till supper-time. I
sat silent, and listened : day after day I fell asleep : no
wonder I was not popular with my company." [1]

It must be admitted that Johnson entertained a poor
opinion of country life and country pursuits ; it is not
so certain that he was as ignorant of them as Macaulay
has asserted. Granted that he was not greatly interested
in agriculture, and that he felt a contempt for " sport,"
but that he was well qualified to depict certain rustic
types will appear from many characters he has drawn in
his Essays, of which I shall give examples in later pages.

Let us turn for the moment from the country to a species
of human beings, principally urban, of whom Johnson's
knowledge was unquestioned and unrivalled. Johnson
knew authors as only a professional author could know
them. They were a very numerous tribe. " The authors
of *London* were formerly computed by *Swift* at several

Pamela) " but to travel round the country, and beat up their
friends' quarters all the way ; and it is all one to them whether
they stay a night or a month at a place."

[1] *The Virginians*, vol. ii., ch. xxxvii. Becky Sharp, also, was
bored with the country. " What news was there to tell," she writes
to Amelia Sedley, " of the sayings and doings of Humdrum Hall,
as I have christened it, and what do you care whether the turnip
crop is good or bad ; whether the fat pig weighed thirteen stone
or fourteen ; and whether the beasts thrive well on mangel-
wurzel ? " (*Vanity Fair*, ch. xi.).

thousands, and there is not any reason for suspecting that their number has decreased."[1]   They suffered the hardships of a "race of beings equally obscure and equally indigent, who, because their usefulness is less obvious to vulgar apprehensions, live unrewarded and die unpitied."[2] Miss Burney is our authority that Johnson had never set foot in Grub Street.   "He acknowledged he had never paid his respects to it himself.   'However,' says he, 'you and I, Burney, will go together; we have a very good right to go, so will visit the mansions of our progenitors, and take up our own freedom together.'"[3]   But he knew, none better, the denizens of that sad thoroughfare.   This is Murphy's account of his indolent course of life in the year 1756 : "He rose about two, and then received the visits of his friends.   Authors, long since forgotten, waited on him as their oracle, and he gave responses in the chair of criticism.   He listened to the complaints, the schemes, and the hopes and fears, of a crowd of inferior writers, 'who,' he said, in the words of Roger Ascham, 'lived, *men knew not how, and died obscure,* men marked not when.' He believed, that he could give a better history of Grub Street than any man living.   His house was filled with a succession of visitors till four or five in the evening. During the whole time he presided at his tea-table."[4] But this history of Grub Street would have been a melancholy record.   "To be sincere," writes the Citizen of the World to his friend Fum Hoam, "were I to send you an account of the lives of the western poets, either ancient or modern, I fancy you would think me employed in collecting materials for a history of human wretchedness."[5]   He wrote truly, for this was the lot of Savage : "During a considerable part of the time in which he was

[1] *Rambler,* No. 145.   [2] *Ibid.*
[3] *Diary and Letters of Madame d'Arblay,* July 1780.
[4] *An Essay on the Life and Genius of Dr Johnson.*
[5] Goldsmith's *Citizen of the World,* Letter 83.

employed upon this performance" (*The Tragedy of Sir Thomas Overbury*), " he was without lodging, and often without meat ; nor had he any other conveniences for study than the fields or the streets allowed him ; there he used to walk and form his speeches, and afterwards step into a shop, beg for a few moments the use of the pen and ink, and write down what he had composed upon paper which he had picked up by accident."[1] Later in his career Savage " lodged as much by accident as he dined, and passed the night sometimes in mean houses, which are set open at night to any casual wanderers, sometimes in cellars among the riot and filth of the meanest and most profligate of the rabble ; and sometimes, when he had not money to support even the expenses of these receptacles, walked about the streets till he was weary, and lay down in the summer upon a bulk, or in the winter, with his associates in poverty, among the ashes of a glass-house."[2] Of Lewis, who translated for him many of the mottoes of the *Ramblers*, Johnson gave this account : " Sir, he lived in London, and hung loose upon society."[3] In 1775 he wrote to Mrs Thrale of two poor men who had helped him with his *Dictionary* : " Peyton and Macbean are both starving, and I cannot keep them " ; and when next year Peyton died, " tears have been shed for the sufferings, and wonder excited by the fortitude of those who neither did nor suffered more than Peyton."[4] Johnson was generous to his needy fellow-craftsmen. In his early London days he collected a sum in sixpences to redeem from pawn the clothes of Samuel Boyse, who was said to be " well known by his ingenious productions."[5] Boyse's Life is included in *The Lives of the Poets of Great*

[1] *Lives of the Poets* (Savage).   [2] *Ibid.*
[3] Boswell's *Life of Johnson* (Birkbeck Hill), i. 226.
[4] Piozzi *Letters*, quoted in Boswell's *Life of Johnson* (Birkbeck Hill), ii. 379n.
[5] Boswell's *Life of Johnson* (Birkbeck Hill), iv. 408n.

Britain and Ireland to the time of Dean Swift. By Mr Cibber.[1] This was the manner of his existence : his clothes being in pawn, " he sat up in bed with the blanket wrapt about him, through which he had cut a hole large enough to admit his arm, and placing the paper upon his knee, scribbled in the best manner he could the verses he was obliged to make. . . . Whenever his distresses so pressed as to induce him to dispose of his shirt, he fell upon an artificial method of supplying one. He cut some white paper in strips, which he tied round his wrists, and in the same manner supplied his neck. In this plight he frequently appeared abroad, with the additional inconvenience of wanting breeches." And when he died, " the remains of this son of the Muses were with very little ceremony hurried away by the parish officers, and thrown amongst common beggars." [2]

Johnson's life from 1737, when he first came to London, till 1763, when Boswell knew him, can never be written.

[1] Johnson said they were written by Robert Shiels. See *Six Essays on Johnson* (Raleigh), p. 119.

[2] These quotations from the *Life of Boyse*, with many others of peculiar interest, appear in Sir Walter Raleigh's *Six Essays on Johnson*, pp. 123-125. This mode of life has been depicted by Goldsmith :

" Where the Red Lion, flaring o'er the way,
Invites each passing stranger that can pay ;
Where Calvert's butt, and Parsons' black champagne,
Regale the drabs and bloods of Drury-Lane ;
There, in a lonely room, from bailiffs snug,
The muse found Scroggen stretch'd beneath a rug :
A window, patch'd with paper, lent a ray,
That dimly show'd the state in which he lay ; . . .
The morn was cold, he views with keen desire
The rusty grate unconscious of a fire ;
With beer and milk arrears the frieze was scor'd,
And five crack'd tea cups dress'd the chimney board ;
A night-cap deck'd his brows, instead of bay,
A cap by night—a stocking all the day ! "
(*Citizen of the World*, Letter 30.)

What would we not give for a full account of it ? We get glimpses from his conversation, as recorded by Boswell, Miss Burney, or Mrs Thrale, and some hints from the *Lives of the Poets.* Had he but written his " History of Grub Street " we should have known much more, for he shared all the vicissitudes of poor authors,

" Et hunc inopem vidistis Athenæ."

But of one of them he has given a revealing sketch in an essay called " The Revolutions of a Garret." [1] The previous tenants of this apartment had been a tailor of doubtful honesty, a young woman of doubtful chastity, and a coiner. The coiner was " wanted " and disappeared, but as a lodger he had been unexceptionable, and the landlady wondered " why any body should be hanged for making money when such numbers are in want of it." However, like Mrs Bardell, she once more hopefully placed the bill in the window. " At last a short meagre man, in a tarnished waistcoat, desired to see the garret, and when he had stipulated for two long shelves, and a larger table, hired it at a lower rate. When the affair was completed, he looked round him with great satisfaction, and repeated some words which the woman did not understand. In two days he brought a great box of books, took possession of his room, and lived very inoffensively, except that he frequently disturbed the inhabitants of the next floor by unseasonable noises. He was generally in bed at noon, but from evening to midnight he sometimes talked aloud with great vehemence, sometimes stamped as in rage, sometimes threw down his poker, then clattered his chairs, then sat down in deep thought, and again burst out into loud vociferations ; sometimes he would sigh as oppressed with misery, and sometimes shake with convulsive laughter. When he encountered any of the family,

[1] *Rambler*, No. 161.

he gave way or bowed, but rarely spoke, except that
as he went upstairs he often repeated,

'"Ὃς ὑπέρτατα δώματα ναίει'
' This habitant th'aërial regions boast ' ;

hard words, to which his neighbours listened so often,
that they learned them without understanding them.
What was his employment she did not venture to ask
him, but at last heard the printer's boy inquire for the
author.

" My landlady was often advised to beware of this
strange man, who, though he was quiet for the present,
might perhaps become outrageous in the hot months ;
but, as she was punctually paid, she could not find any
sufficient reason for dismissing him, till one night he
convinced her, by setting fire to his curtains, that it was
not safe to have an author for her inmate."

No doubt this poor fellow was engaged on his *Irene*,
and Johnson could sympathise with him. But he could
tolerate, and find a good word for, " secondary writers "
—compilers, translators and even " plagiaries." " Yet
are not even these writers to be indiscriminately censured
and rejected. Truth like beauty varies its fashions, and
is best recommended by different dresses to different
minds ; and he that recalls the attention of mankind to
any part of learning which time has left behind it,
may be truly said to advance the literature of the age." [1]
" Even the abridger, compiler, and translator, though
their labours cannot be ranked with those of the diurnal
historiographer, yet must not be rashly doomed to anni-
hilation." [2] Journalists had their uses, " if it be pleasing
to hear of the preferment and dismission of statesmen,
the birth of heirs, and the marriage of beauties, the humble
author of journals and gazettes must be considered as a
liberal dispenser of beneficial knowledge." [3] But he could

[1] *Idler*, No. 85.   [2] *Rambler*, No. 145.   [3] *Ibid.*

be severe on the sensational journalist: " In Sir Henry Wotton's jocular definition, *an ambassador is said to be a man of virtue sent abroad to tell lies for the advantage of his country* ; a news-writer is a man *without virtue, who writes lies at home for his own profit.* To these compositions is required neither genius nor knowledge, neither industry nor sprightliness ; but contempt of shame and indifference to truth are absolutely necessary. He who by a long familiarity with infamy has obtained these qualities, may confidently tell to-day what he intends to contradict to-morrow ; he may affirm fearlessly what he knows that he shall be obliged to recant, and may write letters from *Amsterdam* or *Dresden* to himself.

" . . . Scarcely anything awakens attention like a tale of cruelty. The writer of news never fails in the intermission of action to tell how the enemies murdered children and ravished virgins ; and, if the scene of action be somewhat distant, scalps half the inhabitants of a province.

" Among the calamities of war may be justly numbered the diminution of the love of truth, by the falsehoods which interest dictates, and credulity encourages. A peace will equally leave the warrior and relator of wars destitute of employment ; and I know not whether more is to be dreaded from streets filled with soldiers accustomed to plunder, or from garrets filled with scribblers accustomed to lie." [1] In *The Idler*, No. 5, he compresses this argument into seven words: " A bloody battle makes a vendible narrative."

Poverty was the general lot of authors, but they had their other peculiar trials. They began by being too sanguine : " A man of lively fancy no sooner finds a hint moving in his mind, than he makes momentaneous excursions to the press, and to the world, and, with a little encouragement from flattery, pushes forward into future

[1] *Idler*, No. 30.

ages, and prognosticates the honours to be paid him, when envy is extinct, and faction forgotten, and those, whom partiality now suffers to obscure him, shall have given way to the triflers of as short duration as themselves." [1]

But then comes the bitter disillusionment: "He is seldom contented to wait long without the enjoyment of his new praises. With an imagination full of his own importance, he walks out like a monarch in disguise to learn the various opinions of his readers. Prepared to feast upon admiration ; composed to encounter censures without emotion ; and determined not to suffer his quiet to be injured by a sensibility too exquisite of pleasure or blame, but to laugh with equal contempt at vain objections and injudicious commendations, he enters the places of mingled conversation, sits down to his tea in an obscure corner, and while he appears to examine a file of antiquated journals, catches the conversation of the whole room. He listens, but hears no mention of his book, and therefore supposes that he has disappointed his curiosity by delay ; and that as men of learning would naturally begin their conversation with such a wonderful novelty, they had digressed to other subjects before his arrival. The company disperses, and their places are supplied by others equally ignorant, or equally careless. The same expectation hurries him to another place, from which the same disappointment drives him soon away. His impatience then grows violent and tumultuous, he ranges over the town with restless curiosity, and hears in one quarter of a cricket-match, in another of a pick-pocket ; is told by some of an unexpected bankruptcy ; by others of a turtle-feast ; is sometimes provoked by importunate enquiries after the white bear, and sometimes with praises of the dancing dog ; he is afterwards entreated to give his judgment upon a wager about the height of the Monument ;

[1] *Rambler*, No. 2.

invited to see a foot-race in the adjacent villages ; desired to read a ludicrous advertisement ; or consulted about the most effectual method of making enquiry after a favourite cat. The whole world is busied in affairs, which he thinks below the notice of reasonable creatures, and which are nevertheless sufficient to withdraw all regard from his labours and his merits." [1] He is, in short, overlooked and neglected, and " there is nothing more dreadful to an author than neglect, compared with which reproach, hatred, and opposition, are names of happiness ; yet this worse, this meanest fate, every one who dares to write has reason to fear." [2] And maybe he deserves this neglect. " But though it should happen that an author is capable of excelling, yet his merit may pass without notice, huddled in the variety of things, and thrown into the general miscellany of life. He that endeavours after fame by writing, solicits the regard of a multitude fluctuating in pleasures or immersed in business, without time for intellectual amusements ; he appeals to judges, prepossessed by passions, or corrupted by prejudices, which preclude their approbation of any new performance. Some are too indolent to read any thing, till its reputation is established ; others too envious to promote that fame which gives them pain by its increase." [3]

So an author may be neglected, even though he deserve recognition. But even supposing he win renown, will it last ? " If we look back into past times, we find innumerable names of authors once in high reputation, read perhaps by the beautiful, quoted by the witty, and commented on by the grave ; but of whom we now know only that they once existed." [4] Yes, and fame may vanish even in an author's lifetime : " The regard of the publick is not to be kept but by tribute, and the remembrance of

<hr>

[1] *Rambler*, No. 146. [2] *Ibid.*, No. 2.
[3] *Ibid.* [4] *Ibid.*, No. 21.

past service will quickly languish, unless successive performances frequently revive it. Yet in every new attempt there is new hazard, and there are few who do not at some unlucky time injure their own characters by attempting to enlarge them." [1]

Was it surprising that authors were vain and sensitive? " I have heard of one that, having advanced some erroneous doctrines in philosophy, refused to see the experiments by which they were confuted. . . . Of all mortals none seem to have been more infected with this species of vanity, than the race of writers, whose reputation arising solely from their understanding, gives them a very delicate sensibility of any violence attempted on their literary honour." [2] For such nervous and irritable folk " perhaps the best advice would be, that they should keep out of the way of one another." [3]

The unhappy race of authors, besides suffering from hardships, disappointments and neglect, and from their own sensitiveness, were attacked by enemies in the shape of critics. " Yet there is a certain race of men, that either imagine it their duty, or make it their amusement, to hinder the reception of every work of learning or genius, who stand as sentinels in the avenues of fame, and value themselves upon giving IGNORANCE and ENVY the first notice of a prey." [4] And this is the genesis of the critic : " Criticism is a study by which men grow important and formidable at a very small expense. The power of invention has been conferred by nature upon few, and the labour of learning those sciences which may by mere labour be obtained is too great to be willingly endured ; but every man can exert such judgment as he has upon the works of others ; and he whom nature has made weak, and idleness keeps ignorant, may yet support his

[1] *Rambler*, No. 21.   [2] *Ibid.*, No. 31.
[3] *Lives of the Poets* (Rowe).
[4] *Rambler*, No. 3.

vanity by the name of a Critick." [1] He enlarges on their fallibility: " In trusting therefore to the sentence of a critick, we are in danger not only from that vanity which exalts writers too often to the dignity of teaching what they are yet to learn, from that negligence which sometimes steals upon the most vigilant caution, and that fallibility to which the condition of nature has subjected every human understanding; but from a thousand extrinsick and accidental causes, from every thing which can excite kindness or malevolence, veneration or contempt." [2] Here is a neat hit, from his argument as to the sufficiency of the English language: " The more airy and elegant studies of philology and criticism have little need of any foreign help. Though our language, not being very analogical, gives few opportunities for grammatical researches, yet we have not wanted authors who have considered the principles of speech ; and with critical writings we abound sufficiently, to enable pedantry to impose rules which can be seldom observed, and vanity to talk of books which are seldom read." [3]

Critics can be severe and cruel. " Much mischief is done in the world with very little interest or design. He that assumes the character of a critick, and justifies his claim by perpetual censure, imagines that he is hurting none but the author, and him he considers as a pestilent animal, whom every other being has a right to

[1] *Idler*, No. 60. Goldsmith gives this definition : " A critic is a being possessed of all the vanity, but not the genius of a scholar : incapable, from his native weakness, of lifting himself from the ground, he applies to contiguous merit for support, makes the sportive sallies of another's imagination his serious employment, pretends to take our feelings under his care, teaches where to condemn, where to lay the emphasis of praise, and may, with as much justice, be called a man of taste, as the Chinese, who measures his wisdom by the length of his nails " (*Citizen of the World*, Letter 20).

[2] *Rambler*, No. 93.   [3] *Idler*, No. 91.

persecute." [1] " Among the principal of comick calamities, may be reckoned the pain which an author, not yet hardened into insensibility, feels at the onset of a furious critick, whose age, rank, or fortune, gives him confidence to speak without reserve; who heaps one objection upon another, and obtrudes his remarks, and enforces his corrections, without tenderness or awe." [2] They can also be petty and pedantic : " Some seem always to read with the microscope of criticism, and employ their whole attention upon minute elegance, or faults scarcely visible to common observation. The dissonance of a syllable, the recurrence of the same sound, the repetition of a particle, the smallest deviation from propriety, the slightest defect in construction or arrangement, swell before their eyes into enormities. As they discern with great exactness, they comprehend but a narrow compass, and know nothing of the justness of the design, the general spirit of the performance, the artifice of connexion, or the harmony of the parts ; they never conceive how small a proportion that which they are busy in contemplating bears to the whole, or how the petty inaccuracies with which they are offended, are absorbed and lost in general excellence." [3]

They mislead the public and prevent it from appreciating good literature. " If a new performance happens not to fall into the hands of some who have courage to tell, and authority to propagate their opinion, it often remains long in obscurity, and perishes unknown and unexamined. A few, a very few, commonly constitute the taste of the time ; the judgment which they have once pronounced, some are too lazy to discuss, and some too timorous to contradict ; it may however be, I think, observed, that their power is greater to depress than exalt, as mankind are more credulous of censure than of praise." [4]

As to the author's remedy against these ills : " *Vida*, a

[1] *Idler*, No. 3.   [2] *Rambler*, No. 176.
[3] *Ibid*.   [4] *Adventurer*, No. 138.

man of considerable skill in the politicks of literature, directs his pupil wholly to abandon his defence, and even when he can irrefutably refute all objections, to suffer tamely the exultations of his antagonist."[1] But this policy of "taking it lying down" was not likely to please Johnson. "When the book has once been dismissed into the world, and can be no more retouched, I know not whether firmness and spirit may not sometimes be of use to overpower arrogance and repel brutality. Softness, diffidence, and moderation, will often be mistaken for imbecility and dejection ; they lure cowardice to the attack by the hopes of easy victory, and it will soon be found that he whom every man thinks he can conquer, shall never be at peace."[2]

Luckily for the author, the critic is sometimes placable. "I have heard how some have been pacified with claret and a supper, and others laid asleep with the soft notes of flattery."[3]

But though Johnson could resent the cruelty, and ridicule the incompetence, of critics, he recognized their proper function. Every author, by publishing, invites criticism ; he could have avoided it by refraining from writing. "There is indeed some tenderness due to living writers, when they attack none of those truths which are of importance to the happiness of mankind, and have committed no other offence than that of betraying their own ignorance or dullness. I should think it cruelty to crush an insect that had provoked me only by buzzing in my ear; and would not willingly interrupt the dream of harmless stupidity, or destroy the jest which makes its author laugh. Yet I am far from thinking this tenderness universally necessary ; for he that writes may be considered as a kind of general challenger, whom every one has a right to attack, since he quits the common rank of life, steps forward beyond the lists, and offers his merit

[1] *Rambler*, No. 176.   [2] *Ibid.*   [3] *Ibid.*, No. 3.

H

to the public judgment. To commence author is to claim praise, and no man can justly aspire to honour but at the hazard of disgrace." [1] In his *Life of Pope* he points the same moral. He excuses the *Dunciad*: " In this design there was petulance and malignity enough, but I cannot think it very criminal. An author places himself uncalled before the tribunal of Criticism, and solicits fame at the hazard of disgrace. Dulness or deformity are not culpable in themselves, but may be very justly reproached when they pretend to the honour of wit or the influence of beauty. If bad writers were to pass without reprehension, what should restrain them ? *impune diem consumpserit ingens Telephus* ; and upon bad writers only will censure have much effect. The satire, which brought Theobald and Moore into contempt, dropped impotent from Bentley, like the javelin of Priam." [2]

For, after all, the critic had this task—" neither to depreciate, nor dignify by partial representations, but to hold out the light of reason, whatever it may discover ; and to promulgate the determinations of Truth, whatever she shall dictate." [3]

These are Johnson's general observations on critics, but in two amusing papers,[4] he has described a member of the tribe, whom he calls Dick Minim. Dick, while apprenticed to a brewer, inherited from an uncle " a large fortune in the stocks," and, " being now at liberty to follow his genius, he resolved to be a man of wit and humour." He first frequented the theatres, and, when they were shut, " he retired to *Richmond* with a few select writers." Fortified by study, he felt himself able to express his views on the great authors : it must be acknowledged that, if some of these views were sound, some were not very original. " His opinion was, that *Shakespear*, committing himself wholly to the impulse of nature, wanted that correctness

---

[1] *Rambler*, No. 94.   [2] *Lives of the Poets* (Pope).
[3] *Rambler*, No. 93.   [4] *Idler*, Nos. 60 and 61.

which learning would have given him, and that *Jonson*, trusting to learning, did not sufficiently cast his eye on nature. He blamed the *stanza* of *Spenser*, and could not bear the *hexameters* of *Sidney*. *Denham* and *Waller*, he held the first reformers of *English* numbers ; and thought that if *Waller* could have obtained the strength of *Denham*, or *Denham* the sweetness of *Waller*, there had been nothing wanting to complete a poet. He often expressed his commiseration of *Dryden's* poverty, and his indignation at the age which suffered him to write for bread ; he repeated with rapture the first lines of *All for Love*, but wondered at the corruption of taste which could bear anything so unnatural as rhyming tragedies. In *Otway* he found uncommon powers of moving the passions, but was disgusted by his general negligence, and blamed him for making a conspirator his hero ; and never concluded his disquisition, without remarking how happily the sound of the clock is made to alarm the audience. *Southern* would have been his favourite, but that he mixes comick with tragick scenes, intercepts the natural course of the passions, and fills the mind with a wild confusion of mirth and melancholy. The versification of *Rowe* he thought too melodious for the stage, and too little varied in different passions. He made it the great fault of *Congreve*, that all his persons were wits, and that he always wrote with more art than nature. He considered *Cato* rather as a poem than a play, and allowed *Addison* to be the complete master of allegory and grave humour, but paid no great deference to him as a critick. He thought the chief merit of *Prior* was in his easy tales and lighter poems, though he allowed that his *Solomon* had many noble sentiments elegantly expressed. In *Swift* he discovered an inimitable vein of irony, and an easiness which all would hope and few would attain. *Pope* he was inclined to degrade from a poet to a versifier, and thought his numbers rather luscious than sweet."

Mr Minim gradually grew in repute. " He was now an

acknowledged critick, and had his own seat in a coffee-house, and headed a party in the pit." At last he attained such a position that youths of promising parts were brought to receive his directions for the prosecution of their studies. " He then puts on a very serious air ; he advises the pupil to read none but the best authors, and, when he finds one congenial to his own mind, to study his beauties, but avoid his faults, and, when he sits down to write, to consider how his favourite author would think at the present time on the present occasion."

Plainly Johnson represents Minim as a pretentious fool, and so it is worth noticing that he makes this critic approve of academies. "Minim professes great admiration of the wisdom and munificence by which the academies of the continent were raised ; and often wishes for some standard of taste, for some tribunal, to which merit may appeal from caprice, prejudice, and malignity. He has formed a plan for an academy of criticism, where every work of imagination may be read before it is printed, and which shall authoritatively direct the theatres what pieces to receive or reject, to exclude or revive.

" Such an institution would, in *Dick's* opinion, spread the fame of *English* literature over *Europe*, and make *London* the metropolis of elegance and politeness, the place to which the learned and ingenious of all countries would repair for instruction and improvement, and where nothing would any longer be applauded or endured that was not conformed to the nicest rules, and finished with the highest elegance."

I do not remember any other essay in which Johnson discusses this subject ; but, as an academy is being set up (and is to be magnificently housed) in the United States, I will here add two passages from his *Lives of the Poets*, which, as I venture to think, still represent the views of nine out of ten Englishmen, and English Men of Letters. The first is from the *Life of Roscommon*, who

" formed the plan of a society for refining our language and fixing its standard." On this Johnson observes: " In this country an academy could be expected to do but little. If an academician's place were profitable, it would be given by interest; if attendance were gratuitous, it would be rarely paid, and no man would endure the least disgust. Unanimity is impossible, and debate would separate the assembly. But suppose the philological decree made and promulgated, what would be its authority? In absolute governments, there is sometimes a general reverence paid to all that has the sanction of power and the countenance of greatness. How little this is the state of our country needs not to be told. We live in an age in which it is a kind of publick sport to refuse all respect that cannot be enforced. The edicts of an English academy would probably be read by many, only that they might be sure to disobey them."

The other pronouncement is from the *Life of Swift*, upon Swift's " Proposal for correcting, improving, and ascertaining the English Tongue ": " The certainty and stability which, contrary to all experience, he thinks attainable, he proposes to secure by instituting an academy; the decrees of which every man would have been willing, and many would have been proud, to disobey, and which, being renewed by successive elections, would in a short time have differed from itself."

Besides " pride, envy, want," there was another ill that assailed the author—the patron. The power of the patron, it is true, was on the decline; he was beginning to be no longer indispensable. " A writer of real merit, now, may easily be rich," wrote Goldsmith [1] (1760), " if his heart be set only on fortune; and for those who have no merit, it is but fit that such should remain in merited obscurity. He may now refuse an invitation to dinner, without fearing to incur his patron's displeasure, or to

[1] *Citizen of the World*, Letter 84.

starve by remaining at home." "A man goes to a book-seller," said Johnson (1773), "and gets what he can. We have done with patronage."[1] The author, fortunately for himself, could now look to a list of benevolent sub-scribers, or even to the general reading public. But in 1747, when Johnson wrote the *Plan* of his *Dictionary*, he addressed it to a very eminent patron, Philip Dormer, Earl of Chesterfield, then one of his Majesty's Secretaries of State. Whether Chesterfield deliberately neglected Johnson is open to question. Great men, and especially great men in office, sometimes from the multiplicity of their engagements, and sometimes through the inadvert-ence of their private secretaries, have often incurred such a charge unjustly. Sometimes they have been wearied or disgusted by the arrogance of the applicant ; both Savage and Chatterton were apt to bite the hand that fed them. Be that as it may, Chesterfield will always be made famous, or the opposite of famous, by the celebrated letter of 7th February 1755—a composition of undeniable force, but (to my mind) a little too much laboured and theatrical, a little too much of a conscious *beau geste*.[2] "When we think our excellencies overlooked by the world," wrote Johnson,[3] "or desire to recall the attention of the publick to some particular performance, we sit down with great composure and write a letter to ourselves." A letter to an unappreciative patron was perhaps capable of administering equal comfort.[4]

Johnson wrote an excellent *Rambler*[5] on the "Meanness and Mischief of Indiscriminate Dedication," but I do not

---

[1] Boswell's *Life of Johnson* (Birkbeck Hill), v. 59.

[2] In 1790 Boswell published this letter separately at the price of half-a-guinea.

[3] *Rambler*, No. 193.

[4] In a letter to *The Morning Post* of 15th March 1924 the Hon Stephen Coleridge has raised the question whether Johnson eve. actually *sent* the famous letter to Lord Chesterfield.

[5] *Rambler*, No. 136.

consider that his dedication of the *Plan* to Chesterfield
should make him obnoxious to criticism on this score.
When he congratulated himself that his undertaking
" had been thought by your Lordship of importance
sufficient to attract your favour," and describes it as
" a design that you, my Lord, have not thought unworthy
to share your attention with treaties and with wars," he
wrote sincerely, and in the confidence of the great man's
steady support. *The Rambler* censures those authors who
" scatter praise or blame without regard to justice. . . .
Nothing has so much degraded literature from its natural
rank, as the practice of indecent and promiscuous dedication ; for what credit can he expect who professes himself the hireling of vanity, however profligate, and, without
shame or scruple, celebrates the worthless, dignifies the
mean, and gives to the corrupt, licentious, and oppressive the ornaments which ought only to add grace to
truth, and loveliness to innocence ? Every other kind of
adulation, however shameful, however mischievous, is less
detestable than the crime of counterfeiting characters,
and fixing the stamp of literary sanction upon the dross
and refuse of the world." But not every dedication is to
be condemned. " To censure all dedications as adulatory
and servile, would discover rather envy than justice.
Praise is the tribute of merit, and he that has incontest-
ably distinguished himself by any publick performance,
has a right to all the honours which the publick can
bestow. To men thus raised above the rest of the community, there is no need that the book or its author should
have any particular relation ; that the patron is known
to deserve respect, is sufficient to vindicate him that pays
it. . . . I know not whether great relaxation may not be
indulged, and whether hope as well as gratitude may not
unblamably produce a dedication ; but let the writer who
pours out his praises only to propitiate power, or attract
the attention of greatness, be cautious lest his desire

betray him to exuberant eulogies." It is possible that Johnson was here justifying himself.

He represented patronage as one of the causes of an author's failure. " Miscarriages of this kind are likewise frequently the consequence of that acquaintance with the great, which is generally considered as one of the chief privileges of literature and genius. A man who has once learned to think himself exalted by familiarity with those whom nothing but their birth, or their fortunes, or such stations as are seldom gained by moral excellence, set above him, will not be long without submitting his understanding to their conduct ; he will suffer them to prescribe the course of his studies, and employ him for their own purposes either of diversion or interest." [1]

This bitterness of dependence was tasted by Eubulus, [2] who had obtained " the reputation of a great genius " at the university, and of " a pretty fellow " in London, but became reduced in his circumstances through foolishly offending his wealthy uncle. Eubulus at first had hopes of preferment from the good offices of his own youthful friends, but from indolence or selfishness these all disappointed him. " My resolution was now to ingratiate myself with men whose reputation was established, whose high stations enabled them to prefer me, and whose age exempted them from sudden changes of inclination. I was considered as a man of parts, and therefore easily found admission to the table of Hilarius, the celebrated orator, renowned equally for the extent of his knowledge, the elegance of his diction, and the acuteness of his wit. Hilarius received me with an appearance of great satisfaction, produced me to all his friends, and directed me to that part of his discourse in which he most endeavoured to display his imagination. I had now learned my own interest enough to supply him opportunities for smart remarks and gay sallies, which I never failed to echo and

[1] *Rambler*, No. 21.   [2] *Ibid.*, Nos. 26 and 27.

applaud. Thus I was gaining every hour on his affections, till unfortunately, when the assembly was more splendid than usual, his desire of admiration prompted him to turn his raillery upon me. I bore it for some time with great submission, and success encouraged him to redouble his attacks ; at last my vanity prevailed over my prudence, I retorted his irony with such spirit, that Hilarius, unaccustomed to resistance, was disconcerted, and soon found means of convincing me that his purpose was not to encourage a rival, but to foster a parasite.

" I was then taken into the familiarity of Argutio, a nobleman eminent for judgment and criticism. He had contributed to my reputation by the praises which he had often bestowed upon my writings, in which he owned that there were proofs of a genius that might rise to high degrees of excellence, when time, or information, had reduced its exuberance. He therefore required me to consult him before the publication of any new performance, and commonly proposed innumerable alterations, without sufficient attention to the general design, or regard to my form of style, and mode of imagination. But these corrections he never failed to press as indispensably necessary, and thought the least delay of compliance an act of rebellion. The pride of an author made this treatment insufferable, and I thought any tyranny easier to be borne than that which took from me the use of my understanding.

" My next patron was Eutyches the statesman, who was wholly engaged in publick affairs, and seemed to have no ambition but to be powerful and rich. I found his favour more permanent than that of the others ; for there was a certain price at which it might be bought ; he allowed nothing to humour, or to affection, but was always ready to pay liberally for the service that he required. His demands were, indeed, very often such as virtue could not easily consent to gratify ; but virtue is not to be consulted when men are to raise their fortunes by the favour of the great. His measures were censured ; I wrote in his defence, and was recompensed with a place, of which the profits were never received by me without the pangs of remembering that they were the reward of wickedness —a reward which nothing but that necessity which the consumption of my little estate in these wild pursuits had brought upon me, hindered me from throwing back in the face of my corrupter.

" At last my uncle died without a will, and I became heir to a small fortune. I had resolution to throw off the splendour which reproached me to myself, and retire to an humbler state, in which I am now endeavouring to recover the dignity of virtue, and hope to make some reparation for my crime and follies, by informing others, who may be led after the same pageants, that they are about to engage in a course of life, in which they are to purchase, by a thousand miseries, the privilege of repentance."

About this degrading relationship Johnson also composed an allegory called " The Conduct of Patronage," [1] in which he has personified Truth, Hope, Liberality, Fortune, Justice, the Sciences, Caprice, Flattery, Suspicion, Infamy, Reputation, Impudence, Pride and other portentous abstractions. I will inflict upon the reader only the concluding paragraph : " The SCIENCES, after a thousand indignities, retired from the palace of PATRONAGE, and having long wandered over the world in grief and distress, were led at last to the cottage of INDEPENDENCE, the daughter of FORTITUDE ; where they were taught by PRUDENCE and PARSIMONY to support themselves in dignity and quiet."

It will be noticed that this allegory, and the confessions of Eubulus, point the same moral.

It may be here not out of place to say a few words on Johnson's allegories, for in his day to write allegories or

[1] *Rambler*, No. 91.

visions [1] was one of an author's accomplishments. *The Idler* contains no allegories, but *The Rambler* has several, one being contributed by Miss Catherine Talbot and one by the learned Mrs Carter. Both Steele and Addison wrote allegories, and it was necessary for Johnson to sustain the tradition. Moreover, he may have been emulous of Addison ; he praised Addison's " elegant fictions and refined allegories," [2] and according to Murphy,[3] " Johnson used to say the essay on *The Burthens of Mankind* (in *The Spectator*, No. 558) was the most exquisite he had ever read." Boswell includes the " allegorical and oriental tales " among the glories of *The Rambler*,[4] but, for my part, I can but agree with Sir Leslie Stephen that the allegories are " unendurably frigid." Sir Leslie Stephen adds " and clumsy," but a good deal of ingenuity has been lavished on them, an ingenuity misspent and misapplied. Tedious indeed are the personifications, and tedious their pedigrees, connections, and employments. " CRITICISM . . . was the eldest daughter of LABOUR and of TRUTH : she was, at her birth, committed to the care of JUSTICE, and brought up by her in the palace of WISDOM. Being soon distinguished by the celestials, for her uncommon qualities, she was appointed the governess of FANCY, and empowered to beat time to the chorus of the Muses, when they sung before the throne of Jupiter." [5] Poor Criticism ! let us hope she appreciated the distinction ! " LABOUR was the son of NECESSITY " (it follows that Necessity was the grandmother of Criticism), " the nurseling of HOPE, and the pupil of ART ; he had the strength of his mother, the spirit of his nurse, and the dexterity of his

[1] I think the principal difference between an " allegory " and a " vision " is that in the case of a vision the writer must first imagine himself to be asleep.

[2] *Lives of the Poets* (Addison).

[3] *Essay on the Life and Genius of Dr Johnson.*

[4] Boswell's *Life of Johnson* (Birkbeck Hill), i. 214.

[5] *Rambler*, No. 3.

governess." [1] As Queen Victoria would have said, "We are not amused"; and in any volume of Johnson's selected essays I think it would be a mistake to insert specimens of the allegories.

It was also a literary convention that an essayist should besprinkle his pages with Oriental tales. Goldsmith included in an authors' club "Mr Tibbs, a very *useful hand*, he writes receipts for the bite of a mad dog, and throws off an eastern tale to perfection." [2] He has introduced us to another author who "generally began" such narratives as follows :—" Eben-bo-bolo, who was the son of Ban, was born on the foggy summits of Benderabassi. His beard was whiter than the feathers which veil the breast of the Penguin ; his eyes were like the eyes of doves, when washed by the dews of the morning ; his hair, which hung like the willow weeping over the glassy stream, was so beautiful that it seemed to reflect its own brightness, and his feet were as the feet of a wild deer which fleeth to the tops of the mountains." [3]

There is wit in this ridicule, but Johnson had to follow the fashion. And there is something very incongruous about this typical Englishman, with his robust common sense, sitting down to compose these flowery fables. And yet Johnson was not wholly alien from the Oriental. He was contemplative and he was melancholy. "Vanity of vanities, saith the preacher, all is vanity," and Johnson wrote a poem on the Vanity of Human Wishes. This is the moral of *Rasselas*, from the splendid opening, "Ye who listen with credulity to the whispers of fancy, and pursue with eagerness the phantoms of hope," to the concluding paragraph : "Of these wishes that they had formed they well knew that none could be obtained."

"His Oriental tales," wrote Murphy, "are in the true

[1] *Rambler*, No. 33.   [2] *Citizen of the World*, Letter 29.
[3] *Ibid.*, Letter 33.

style of eastern magnificence." At the least, they attest
the variety of his genius. Each begins with a fine simplicity. " Obidah, the son of Abensina, left the caravan-
serai early in the morning, and pursued his journey through
the plains of Indostan." [1] " In the reign of *Jenghiz Can*,
conqueror of the East, in the city of *Samarcand*, lived
Nouradin the merchant, renowned through all the regions
of *India*, for the extent of his commerce, and the integrity
of his dealings." [2] " *Seged*, lord of *Ethiopia*, to the inhabitants of the world : To the sons of *presumption*, humility
and fear ; and to the daughters of *sorrow*, content and
acquiescence." [3] These stories nearly all exemplify the
uncertainty and transience of human prosperity, a topic
congenial to Johnson :

> " At length his sov'reign frowns—the train of state
> Mark the keen glance, and watch the sign to hate.
> Where'er he turns, he meets a stranger's eye,
> His suppliants scorn him, and his followers fly."

But, especially in the East, the favourites of fortune
had reason to be fearful : the rich man was at the mercy
of the governor, the governor was the creature of the
Sultan's caprice, and the Sultan himself might be the
victim of his own Prætorian Guard. " Many of those who
surrounded the Bassa were sent only to watch and report
his conduct ; every tongue was muttering censure, and
every eye was searching for a fault. At last the letters
of revocation arrived, the Bassa was carried in chains to
Constantinople, and his name was mentioned no more.
. . . In a short time the second Bassa was deposed. The
Sultan that had advanced him was murdered by the
Janizaries, and his successor had other views and different
favourites." [4] " The sun grew weary of gilding the palaces
of *Morad*, the clouds of sorrow gathered round his head,

[1] *Rambler*, No. 65.
[2] *Ibid.*, No. 120.
[3] *Ibid.*, No. 204.
[4] *Rasselas*, ch. xxiv.

and the tempest of hatred roared around his dwelling. *Morad* saw ruin hastily approaching. The first that forsook him were his poets; their example was followed by all those whom he had rewarded for contributing to his pleasures, and only a few, whose virtue had entitled them to favour, were now to be seen in his hall or chambers. He felt his danger, and prostrated himself at the foot of the throne." [1]

At this kind of writing Johnson was " a very useful hand." But he could poke fun at it. How else are we to regard the romance of Anningait and Ajut, [2] which showed how " love, that extends his dominion wherever humanity can be found, perhaps exerts the same power in the *Greenlander's* hut as in the palaces of eastern monarchs." [3] Anningait thus celebrated Ajut: " Her fingers were white as the teeth of the morse, and her smile grateful as the dissolution of the ice; that he would pursue her, though she should pass the snows of the midland cliffs, or seek shelter in the caves of the eastern cannibals. . . . Night is the time of ease and felicity, of revels and gayety; but what will be the flaming lamp, the delicious seal, or the soft oil, without the smile of *Ajut* ? "

As I have somewhat digressed from Johnson's views on authors to consider a species of composition which exhibits Johnson himself in the character of a professional scribe, I will conclude this chapter with some of his utterances on amateurs.

He called his own age " *the age of Authors*, [4] for, perhaps,

[1] *Rambler*, No. 190.   [2] *Ibid.*, Nos. 186 and 187.
[3] Captain Macheath, too, boasted that his love would triumph over the cold of Greenland :

> " Were I laid on Greenland's coast,
>   And in my arms embraced my lass,
>   Warm amidst eternal frost
>   Too soon the half-year's night would pass."

[4] *Adventurer*, No. 115.

there never was a time in which men of all degrees of
ability, of every kind of education, of every profession
and employment, were posting with ardour so general to
the press. The province of writing was formerly left to
those, who by study, or appearance of study, were supposed to have gained knowledge unattainable by the busy
part of mankind, but in these enlightened days, every
man is qualified to instruct every other man ; and he
that beats the anvil, or guides the plough, not content
with supplying corporal necessities, amuses himself in
the hours of leisure with providing intellectual pleasures
for his countrymen." Women, as well as men, were
affected. " In former times, the pen, like the sword, was
considered as consigned by nature to the hands of men ;
the ladies contented themselves with private virtues and
domestick excellence ; and a female writer, like a female
warriour, was considered as a kind of eccentric being,
that deviated, however illustriously, from her due sphere
of motion, and was, therefore, rather to be gazed at with
wonder, than countenanced by imitation. But as the
times past are said to have seen a nation of Amazons,
who drew the bow and wielded the battle-axe, formed
encampments and wasted nations, the revolution of years
has now produced a generation of Amazons of the pen,
who with the spirit of their predecessors have set masculine
tyranny at defiance, asserted their claim to the regions of
science, and seem resolved to contest the usurpations of
virility."

Johnson points out what small inducements these
writers have to write : " The cause, therefore, of this
epidemical conspiracy for the destruction of paper, must
remain a secret : nor can I discover, whether we owe it to
the influences of the constellations, or the intemperature
of seasons : whether the long continuance of the wind at
any single point, or intoxicating vapours exhaled from
the earth, have turned our nobles and our peasants, our

soldiers and traders, our men and women, all into wits, philosophers, and writers.

" It is, indeed, of more importance to search out the cure than the cause of this intellectual malady ; and he would deserve well of this country, who, instead of amusing himself with conjectural speculations, should find means of persuading the peer to inspect his steward's accounts, or repair the rural mansion of his ancestors, who could replace the tradesman behind his counter, and send back the farmer to the mattock and the flail."

In *The Idler*, No. 2, he returns to this plague of writing : " But surely I may be allowed to complain, that, in a nation of authors, not one has thought me worthy of notice after so fair an invitation. At the time when the rage of writing has seized the old and young, when the cook warbles her lyrics in the kitchen, and the thrasher vociferates his heroicks in the barn ; when our traders deal out knowledge in bulky volumes, and our girls forsake their samplers to teach kingdoms wisdom; it may seem very unnecessary to draw any more from their proper occupations, by affording new opportunities of literary fame.

" I should be indeed unwilling to find that, for the sake of corresponding with *The Idler*, the smith's iron had cooled on the anvil, or the spinster's distaff stood unemployed. I solicit only the contributions of those who have already devoted themselves to literature, or, without any determinate intention, wander at large through the expanse of life, and wear out the day in hearing at one place what they utter at another."

Now let Johnson leave these generalities, and offer a specimen of an amateur author. *Idler* No. 55 is a diverting history of a gentleman who, " having been long a student," thought himself " qualified in time to become an author." " I deliberated three years which part of knowledge to illustrate by my labours. Choice is more often determined by accident than by reason : I walked abroad one morning with a curious lady, and, by her inquiries and observations, was invited to write the natural history of the county in which I reside. . . .

" Seven years I was employed in collecting animals and vegetables, and then found that my design was imperfect. The subterranean treasures of the place had been passed unobserved, and another year was to be spent in mines and coal-pits. What I had already done supplied a motive to do more. I acquainted myself with the black inhabitants of metallic caverns, and, in defiance of damps and floods, wandered through the gloomy labyrinths, and gathered fossils from every fissure. . . .

" The book was at last finished, and I did not doubt but my labour would be repaid by profit, and my ambition satisfied with honours. I considered that natural history is neither temporary nor local, and that, though I limited my inquiries to my own county, yet every part of the earth has productions common to all the rest. Civil history may be partially studied, the revolutions of one nation may be neglected by another ; but after that in which all have an interest, all must be inquisitive. No man can have sunk so far into stupidity, as not to consider the properties of the ground on which he walks, of the plants on which he feeds, or the animals that delight his ear, or amuse his eye ; and therefore I computed that universal curiosity would call for many editions of my book, and that in five years I should gain fifteen thousand pounds by the sale of thirty thousand copies.

" When I began to write, I insured the house ; and suffered the utmost solicitude when I entrusted my book to the carrier, though I had secured it against mischances by lodging two transcripts in different places. At my arrival, I expected that the patrons of learning would contend for the honour of a dedication, and resolved to maintain the dignity of letters by a haughty contempt of pecuniary solicitations.

I

" I took lodgings near the house of the Royal Society, and expected every morning a visit from the president. I walked in the Park, and wondered that I overheard no mention of the great naturalist. At last I visited a noble earl, and told him of my work : he answered, that he was under an engagement never to subscribe. I was angry to have that refused which I did not mean to ask, and concealed my design of making him immortal. I went next day to another, and, in resentment of my late affront, offered to prefix his name to my new book. He said, coldly, that *he did not understand those things* ; another thought *there were too many books* ; and another *would talk with me when the races were over.*

" Being amazed to find a man of learning so indecently slighted, I resolved to indulge the philosophic pride of retirement and independence. I then sent to some of the principal booksellers the plan of my book, and bespoke a large room in the next tavern, that I might more commodiously see them together, and enjoy the contest, while they were outbidding one another. I drank my coffee, and yet nobody was come ; at last I received a note from one, to tell me that he was going out of town ; and from another, that natural history was out of his way. At last there came a grave man, who desired to see the work, and, without opening it, told me, that a book of that size *would never do.*

" I then condescended to step into shops, and mentioned my work to the masters. Some never dealt with authors ; others had their hands full ; some never had known such a dead time ; others had lost by all that they had published for the last twelve-month. One offered to print my work, if I could procure subscriptions for five hundred, and would allow me two hundred copies for my property. I lost my patience, and gave him a kick ; for which he has indicted me.

" I can easily perceive that there is a combination

among them to defeat my expectations ; and I find it so general, that I am sure it must have been long concerted. I suppose some of my friends, to whom I read the first part, gave notice of my design, and, perhaps, sold the treacherous intelligence at a higher price than the fraudulence of trade will now allow me for my book.

" Inform me, Mr *Idler*, what I must do ; where must knowledge and industry find their recompense, thus neglected by the high, and cheated by the low ? I sometimes resolve to print my book at my own expense, and, like the Sybil, double the price ; and sometimes am tempted, in emulation of *Raleigh*, to throw it into the fire, and leave this sordid generation to the curses of posterity. Tell me, dear *Idler*, what I shall do."

The " curious lady " who was responsible for this author's ill-fated enterprise may be imagined indulging in a subtle smile when reflecting on the consequences of her " inquiries and observations." But Johnson could sympathize, though his sympathy might be ironically expressed : " If, as it has sometimes happened in general combinations against merit, he cannot persuade the world to buy his books, he may present them to his friends ; and if his friends are seized with the epidemical infatuation, and cannot find his genius, or will not confess it, let him then refer his cause to posterity, and reserve his labours for a future age." [1] Though an editor, he retained humane feelings : " I am afraid that I may be taxed with insensibility by many of my correspondents, who believe their contributions unjustly neglected. And, indeed, when I sit before a pile of papers, of which each is the production of laborious study, and the offspring of a fond parent, I, who know the passions of an author, cannot remember how long they have lain in my boxes unregarded, without imagining to myself the various changes of sorrow,

[1] *Rambler*, No. 10.

impatience, and resentment, which the writers must have felt in the tedious interval. . . .

"I know well how rarely an author, fired with the beauties of his new composition, contains his raptures in his own bosom, and how naturally he imparts to his friends his expectations of renown ; and as I can easily conceive the eagerness with which a new paper is snatched up, by one who expects to find it filled with his own production, and perhaps has called his companions to share the pleasure of a second perusal, I grieve for the disappointment which he is to feel at the fatal inspection. His hopes, however, do not yet forsake him ; he is certain of giving lustre the next day. The next day comes, and again he pants with expectation, and having dreamed of laurels and Parnassus, casts his eye upon the barren page, with which he is doomed never more to be delighted." [1]

But underlying this kindly humour is the contempt of an author, whose authorship was his trade, for the amateur. If a man " quits the common rank of life, steps forward beyond the lists, and offers his merit to the public judgment," by the public judgment he must abide. Doctor *major* would have heartily agreed with Doctor *minor* in the following sentiment:—" For my own part, were I to buy a hat, I would not have it from a stocking-maker, but a hatter ; were I to buy shoes, I should not go to the tailor's for that purpose. It is just so with regard to wit : did I, for my life, desire to be well served, I would apply only to those who made it their trade, and lived by it. You smile at the oddity of my opinion ; but be assured, my friend, that wit is in some measure mechanical ; and that a man, long habituated to catch at even its resemblance, will at last be happy enough to possess the substance : by a long habit of writing, he acquires a justice of thinking, and a mastery of manner, which

[1] *Rambler*, No. 56.

holiday-writers, even with ten times his genius, may vainly attempt to equal." [1]

Johnson knew all the disappointments and trials of authors. Were they, after all, more miserable than other men ? *The Adventurer*, No. 138, discusses this question. On the one hand, authors have the feeling of anticipating fame and fortune ; and writing itself is " no unpleasing employment, when one sentiment readily produces another, and both ideas and expressions present themselves at the first summons." On the other hand, there are difficulties of execution ; ideas may vanish, or present themselves in an embarrassing confusion ; sometimes the author tires of his own composition, sometimes the public disregards it. But " upon the whole, as the author seems to share all the common miseries of life, he appears to partake likewise of its lenitives and abatements."

2. The Londoner in the Country

"Roma domusque subit, desideriumque locorum,
Quidquid et amissa restat in Urbe mei."
OVID, *Tristia*.

OUR generation has seen a sort of revolution in the conditions of travelling since that winter morning, some five and twenty years ago, when an enormous crowd blocked Northumberland Avenue to stare at a dozen intrepid motorists starting on a great adventure—a drive from London to Brighton. But ninety years have passed since the real revolution, which was brought about by the steam engine and the railway.

The railway, it has been said, made a greater difference to our lives in three decades than all the improvements and inventions of the previous three centuries. That is

[1] *Citizen of the World*, Letter 93.

one reason why the eighteenth century interests us ; it was the end of the pre-railway era, and therefore the manner of life in Dr Johnson's time, especially in the country, was in some respects more different from that of the nineteenth or twentieth century than from that of the Tudors. The gulf between town and country yawned much wider, and the London wit, if far removed from his club and coffee-house, was as home-sick as Ovid at Tomi. He was oppressed, too, by the thought of the weary leagues that separated him from the only place where life was worth living :

" Bosporos et Tanais superant, Scythiæque paludes."

To begin with, travelling was not only dangerous, but unutterably long and tedious. " When a tiresome and vexatious journey of four days had brought me to the house," writes Cornelia.[1] And Serotinus, of his visit to his native village, " but my horses felt none of their master's ardour, and I was shaken four days upon rugged roads." [2] London, we realize, was distant not only in space, but in time. And the farther the traveller proceeded, the more outlandish were the inhabitants. One of Addison's most amusing *Spectators* purports to be a letter from a barrister, who, while riding the Western Circuit in 1711, noted as he proceeded westward the ever-increasing antiquity of costume. " Not far from Salisbury I took notice of a justice of peace's lady, who was at least ten years behind-hand in her dress. . . . The greatest beau at our next country sessions was dressed in a most monstrous flaxen periwig, that was made in King William's reign." At last he reaches Cornwall : " We fancied ourselves in King Charles the Second's reign, the people having made little variations in their dress since that time. The smartest of the Country Squires appear still in the Monmouth cock."

[1] *Rambler,* No. 51.
[2] *Ibid.,* No. 165.

But, he concludes, " I am informed there are greater curiosities in the northern circuit than on the western ; and that a fashion makes its progress much slower into Cumberland than into Cornwall." [1]

But let us venture even beyond Cumberland, to a still more northern portion of King George's dominions, beyond the coach routes, into a region where we must travel with pack-horses. We may now find ourselves far behind the civilization of the Restoration, or even of the Middle Ages. Are we even in Christendom ? Or are we exploring the haunt of some primitive Congo tribe ? The scene is Auchnasheal, about ten miles from Fort Augustus in the Highlands ; the brave travellers are Boswell and Johnson ; they have three horses for themselves and their servant Joseph, one more to carry their portmanteaux, and two Highlanders to walk in attendance. " We had a considerable circle about us, men, women, and children, all M'Craas, Lord Seaforth's people. Not one of them could speak English. I observed to Dr Johnson, it was much the same as being with a tribe of Indians. JOHNSON. ' Yes, Sir, but not so terrifying.' . . . There was great diversity in the faces of the circle around us : some were as black and wild in their appearance as any American savages whatever. One woman was as comely almost as the figure of Sappho, as we see it painted." [2] Such were the inhabitants of the Highlands of Scotland in 1773. Do we not admire the courage that animated a Londoner of sixty-four, a man of sedentary habits, to leave his club and his home and his pleasant quarters at Thrale's villa, and make such a journey ?

In the Highlands and the Hebrides Johnson suffered discomfort and encountered danger ; but I think he did not frequently experience boredom, for he was constantly on the move. Boredom was the affliction of the Londoner

[1] *Spectator*, No. 129.
[2] Boswell's *Life of Johnson* (Birkbeck Hill), v. 142, 143.

who went not so far afield. A Londoner endured boredom
when he spent his long vacation with persons who were
of his own rank and education, but who seemed to their
guest to have become atrophied by the rural routine. On
the sufferings thereby occasioned to women of fashion
Johnson wrote one of his best *Ramblers*,[1] "The Lady's
Misery in a Summer Retirement." It is the end of May,
when in George the Second's reign the London Season
ended : " The season of the year is now come, in which
the theatres are shut, and the card-tables forsaken ; the
regions of luxury are for a while unpeopled, and pleasure
leads out her votaries to groves and gardens, to still
scenes and erratick gratifications. Those who have passed
many months in a continual tumult of diversion, who
have never opened their eyes in the morning, but upon
some new appointment ; nor slept at night without a
dream of dances, musick, and good hands, or of soft sighs
and humble supplications ; must now retire to distant
provinces, where the syrens of flattery are scarcely to be
heard, where beauty sparkles without praise or envy, and
wit is repeated only by the echo." He feels for " the
condition of my fair readers, who are now preparing to
leave all that has so long filled up their hours, all from
which they have been accustomed to hope for delight ;
and who, till fashion proclaims the liberty of returning
to the seats of mirth and elegance, must endure the
rugged 'squire, the sober housewife, the loud huntsman,
or the formal parson, the roar of obstreperous jollity,
or the dulness of prudential instruction ; without any
retreat, but to the gloom of solitude, where they will yet
find greater inconveniences, and must learn, however
unwillingly, to endure themselves. . . .

" To them who leave the places of publick resort in the
full bloom of reputation, and withdraw from admiration,
courtship, submission, and applause, a rural triumph can

[1] *Rambler*, No. 124.

give nothing equivalent. The praise of ignorance, and the subjection of weakness, are little regarded by beauties who have been accustomed to more important conquests, and more valuable panegyricks. Nor indeed should the powers which have made havock in the theatres, or borne down rivalry in courts, be degraded to a mean attack upon the untravelled heir, or ignoble contest with the ruddy milkmaid.

" How then must four months be worn away ? Four months, in which there will be no routs, no shows, no ridottos ; in which visits must be regulated by the weather, and assemblies will depend upon the moon! The Platonists imagine, that the future punishment of those who have in this life debased their reason by subjection to their senses, and have preferred the gross gratifications of lewdness and luxury, to the pure and sublime felicity of virtue and contemplation, will arise from the predominance and solicitations of the same appetites, in a state which can furnish no means of appeasing them. I cannot but suspect that this month, bright with sunshine, and fragrant with perfumes ; this month, which covers the meadow with verdure, and decks the gardens with all the mixtures of colorifick radiance ; this month, from which the man of fancy expects new infusion of imagery, and the naturalist new scenes of observation ; this month will chain down multitudes to the *Platonick* penance of desire without enjoyment, and hurry them from the highest satisfactions, which they have yet learned to conceive, into a state of hopeless wishes and pining recollection, where the eye of vanity will look round for admiration to no purpose, and the hand of avarice shuffle cards in a bower with ineffectual dexterity."

One of these rural martyrs was Euphelia, the daughter of " a very fine lady, who has more numerous and more frequent assemblies at her house than any other person

in the same quarter of the town." [1] She was to pay her
first visit to " a rich aunt in a remote county," and had
suffered her head " to be filled with expectation of some
nameless pleasure in a rural life." She was disappointed,
and afterwards, with insolent force, put the blame for her
disappointment on authors—" you produce to the publick
whatever notions you can speciously maintain, or elegantly express, without inquiring whether they are just,
and transcribe hereditary falsehoods from old authors
perhaps as ignorant and careless as yourselves." [2] But to
return to her experiences : the first sight of " a large old
house, encompassed on three sides with woody hills, and
looking from the front on a gentle river," [3] was delightful.
" My aunt came out to receive me, but in a dress so far
removed from the present fashion, that I could scarcely
look upon her without laughter. . . . The night and the
next morning were driven along with inquiries about
our family ; my aunt then explained our pedigree, and
told me stories of my great grandfather's bravery in the
civil wars, nor was it less than three days before I could
persuade her to leave me to myself.   At last economy
prevailed ; she went in the usual manner about her own
affairs, and I was at liberty to range in the wilderness,
and sit by the cascade.

" The novelty of the objects about me pleased me for
a time, but after a few days they were new no longer."
At the time of writing Euphelia had still to live through
four weeks of her visit, and had become the victim of a
terrible *ennui*.   " I go out and return ; I pluck a flower
and throw it away ; I catch an insect, and when I have
examined its colours set it at liberty ; I fling a pebble
into the water, and see one circle spread after another.
When it chances to rain, I walk in the great hall, and
watch the minute-hand upon the dial, or play with a litter

[1] *Rambler*, No. 42.   [2] *Ibid.*, No. 46.
[3] *Ibid.*, No. 42.

of kittens, which the cat happens to have brought at a lucky time." [1]

But the day of release dawns at last. The vacation is over ; "many a mind which has languished some months without emotion or desire now feels a sudden renovation of its faculties. . . . The lady who is hastening to the scene of action flutters her wings, displays her prospects of felicity, tells how she grudges every moment of delay, and, in the presence of those whom she knows condemned to stay at home, is sure to wonder by what arts life can be made supportable throughout a winter in the country, and to tell how often, amidst the ecstasies of an opera, she shall pity those friends whom she has left behind. Her hope of giving pain is seldom disappointed ; the affected indifference of one, the faint congratulations of another, the wishes of some openly confessed, and the silent dejection of the rest, all exalt her opinion of her own superiority." [2]

Now let us note how the sentiments which Johnson has attributed to these ladies are re-echoed by his own authentic utterances. "When one of his friends

---

[1] Does not this *Rambler* remind the reader of Pope's charming lines ?—

"She went, to plain-work, and to purling brooks,
    Old-fashion'd halls, dull aunts, and croaking rooks ;
    She went from opera, park, assembly, play,
    To morning-walks, and prayers three hours a day ;
    To part her time 'twixt reading and bohea,
    To muse, and spill her solitary tea,
    Or o'er cold coffee trifle with her spoon,
    Count the slow clock, and dine exact at noon :
    Divert her eyes with pictures in the fire,
    Hum half a tune, tell stories to the squire ;
    Up to her godly garret after seven,
    There starve and pray, for that's the way to Heaven."

(*Epistle to Mrs Blount on her leaving the Town after the Coronation.*)

[2] *Idler*, No. 80.

endeavoured to maintain that a country gentleman might
contrive to pass his life very agreeably, ' Sir ' (said he),
' you cannot give me an instance of any man who is permitted to lay out his own time, contriving not to have
tedious hours.' " [1] " ' Why, Sir, you find no man, at all
intellectual, who is willing to leave London. No, Sir, when
a man is tired of London, he is tired of life ; for there is
in London all that life can afford.' " [2] " ' Yet, Sir ' (said
I), ' there are many people who are content to live in the
country.' JOHNSON. ' Sir, it is in the intellectual world as
in the physical world ; we are told by natural philosophers
that a body is at rest in the place that is fit for it ; they
who are content to live in the country, are *fit* for the
country.' " [3] " I observed to Dr Johnson, that I had a most
disagreeable notion of the life of country gentlemen ; that
I left Mr Fraser just now, as one leaves a prisoner in a jail.
Dr Johnson said, that I was right in thinking them unhappy ; for that they had not enough to keep their minds
in motion." [4] And here the pupil was in full sympathy
with his master : " I was happy when tea came. Such, I
take it, is the state of those who live in the country.
Meals are wished for from the cravings of vacuity of mind,
as well as from the desire of eating." [5]

Johnson, " whose melancholy mind required the dissipa-
tion of quick successive variety," [6] felt perhaps more than
the ordinary Londoner's distaste for country life. His
contempt for country personages was almost equal to
Addison's, whose Whiggism prompted him to see a
Jacobite in every fox-hunter. When Sir Harry Quickset,
of Staffordshire, Bart., called on Mr Bickerstaffe, the
latter " met him with all the respect due to so venerable
a vegetable," and he describes Sir Harry and his friends

[1] Boswell's *Life of Johnson* (Birkbeck Hill), ii. 194.
[2] *Ibid.*, iii. 178.   [3] *Ibid.*, iv. 338.
[4] *Ibid.*, v. 108.   [5] *Ibid.*, 159.
[6] *Ibid.*, iv. 338.

" as persons of so much state and rusticity," [1] on which
Bishop Hurd, Addison's commentator, makes this very
just remark: " The scene is . . . pleasant enough ; but
why so much pains, here and elsewhere, to throw contempt on *rural Knights* and *Squires* ? A set of men better
stationed on their own estates, than in courts and great
cities ; and more estimable, by far, with all their rustic-
ities, and (what offended Mr Addison and his coadjutor
more) with all their party prejudices, at that time about
them, than their finer sons, whose good-breeding hath
eaten out every other virtue, and made them too polite
to endure the country air, or the conversation of their
neighbours and tenants." Addison made amends by drawing Sir Roger, who was a benevolent man and a good
squire ; but I do not recall in any of Johnson's essays a
precursor of the worthy modern country gentleman:

" A patron of some thirty charities,
A pamphleteer on guano and on grain,
A quarter-sessions chairman, abler none."

And yet there must have been many in his day. We
may smile at Sir Harry Quickset and Sir Giles Wheel-
barrow ; they do not appear to advantage in London,
but we prefer them to " *Thriftless* and *Latterwit*, two
smart fellows, who had estates in the same part of the
Kingdom, which they visited now and then in a frolick,
to take up their rents beforehand, debauch a milk-maid,
make a feast for the village, and tell stories of their own
intrigues, and then rode post back to town to spend their
money." [2]
The rustic was represented by Johnson and other writers
of his age as paying homage to the superiority of his
London visitors. Their wit and elegant manners, it would

[1] *Tatler*, No. 86.
[2] *Rambler*, No. 35.

seem, made them irresistible. The Londoner came with the *prestige* of an archangel:

> " Haste hither, Eve, and, worth thy sight, behold
> Eastward among those trees what glorious Shape
> Comes this way moving ; seems another morn
> Risen on mid-noon."

Sir Roger was grateful to a town lady for a very qualified commendation: " However, I must need say, this accomplished mistress of mine has distinguished me above the rest, and has been known to declare Sir Roger de Coverley was the tamest and most humane of all the brutes in the country. . . . Upon the strength of this slender encouragement of being thought least detestable, I made new liveries, new-paired my coach - horses." [1] So the country-bred Myrtilla was charmed by Flavia : " I was taken, of course, to compliment the stranger, and was, at the first sight, surprised at the unconcern with which she saw herself gazed at by the company she had never known before ; at the carelessness with which she received compliments, and the readiness with which she returned them. I found she had something which I perceived myself to want, and could not but wish to be like her, at once easy and officious, attentive and unembarrassed. I went home and for four days could think and talk of nothing but miss *Flavia*." [2]

The courtier uncle made the same easy impression on his nephew. The youth, while waiting perforce for the privilege of conversation, " was amply rewarded by seeing an exact and punctilious practice of the arts of a courtier, in all the stratagems of endearment, the gradations of respect, and variations of courtesy. . . . I soon discovered that he possessed some science of graciousness and attraction which books had not taught, and of which neither I nor my father had any knowledge ; that he had

[1] *Spectator*, No. 118 (by Steele).   [2] *Rambler*, No. 84.

the power of obliging those whom he did not benefit ; that he diffused, upon his cursory behaviour and most trifling actions, a glow of softness and delicacy by which everyone was dazzled ; and that, by some occult method of captivation, he animated the timorous, softened the supercilious, and opened the reserved. I could not but repine at the inelegance of my own manners, which left me no hopes but not to offend, and at the inefficacy of rustick benevolence, which gained no friends but by real service." [1] The impoverished children, who were sent into the country to be brought up with unkind cousins, excited envy by their good-breeding. " It was unfortunate that our early introduction into polite company, and habitual knowledge of the arts of civility, had given us such an appearance of superiority to the awkward bashfulness of our relations, as naturally drew respect from every stranger." [2] When Eugenio visited his country seat, the first week " was passed in receiving visits from his neighbours, who crowded about him with all the eagerness of benevolence ; some impatient to learn the news of the court and town, that they might be qualified by authentick information to dictate to the rural politicians on the next bowling day." [3] His advice was also sought " in the settlement of their fortunes and the marriage of their children."

So the Londoner was not only acknowledged as *arbiter elegantiarum*, but regarded as an authority on politics and business. True, he was sometimes disappointing. The unlucky wit, Hilarius, brought down to the country by his patron Demochares, became a prey to nerves. The company invited to meet him, " while we waited for dinner, cast their eyes first upon me, and then upon each other, like a theatrical assembly waiting for a show." [4] No wonder that he was a conversational failure, and,

[1] *Rambler*, No. 147.   [2] *Ibid.*, No. 149.
[3] *Ibid.*, No. 142.   [4] *Ibid.*, No. 101.

when the evening was at an end, heard Demochares' guests, " as they walked along the court, murmuring at the loss of the day, and inquiring whether any man would pay a second visit to a house haunted by a wit." And sometimes the affectation of omniscience caused resentment. Ruricola complained of a haughtiness to which " they are indeed too much encouraged by the respect which they receive amongst us for no other reason than that they come from London. For no sooner is the arrival of one of these disseminators of knowledge known in the country, than we crowd about him from every quarter, and by innumerable inquiries flatter him into an opinion of his own importance. He sees himself surrounded by multitudes, who propose their doubts, and refer their controversies to him, as to a being descended from some nobler region, and he grows on a sudden oraculous and infallible, solves all difficulties, and sets all objections at defiance." [1]

Ruricola then gives an account of Mr Frolick's visit to the country—a story which pleasantly exemplifies Johnson's powers of sustained sarcasm, and which I think the reader will find entertaining :

" It is well remembered here, that, about seven years ago, one Frolick, a tall boy, with lank hair, remarkable for stealing eggs, and sucking them, was taken from the school in this parish, and sent up to London to study the law. As he had given amongst us no proofs of a genius designed by nature for extraordinary performances, he was, from the time of his departure, totally forgotten, nor was there any talk of his vices or virtues, his good or his ill fortune, till last summer a report burst upon us, that Mr Frolick was come down in the first post-chaise which this village had seen, having travelled with such rapidity that one of his postilions had broke his leg, and another narrowly escaped suffocation in a quicksand ;

[1] *Rambler*, No. 61.

but that Mr Frolick seemed totally unconcerned, for such things were never heeded at London.

" Mr Frolick next day appeared among the gentlemen at their weekly meeting at the bowling-green, and now were seen the effects of a London education. His dress, his language, his ideas, were all new, and he did not much endeavour to conceal his contempt of everything that differed from the opinions, or practice, of the modish world. He showed us the deformity of our skirts and sleeves, informed us where hats of the proper size were to be sold, and recommended to us the reformation of a thousand absurdities in our clothes, our cookery, and our conversation. When any of his phrases were unintelligible, he could not suppress the joy of confessed superiority, but frequently delayed the explanation, that he might enjoy his triumph over our barbarity.

" When he is pleased to entertain us with a story, he takes care to crowd into it names of streets, squares and buildings, with which he knows we are unacquainted. The favourite topicks of his discourse are the pranks of drunkards, and the tricks put upon country gentlemen by porters and link-boys. When he is with ladies, he tells them of innumerable pleasures to which he can introduce them ; but never fails to hint how much they will be deficient, at their first arrival, in the knowledge of the town. What it is *to know the town*, he has not indeed hitherto informed us, though there is no phrase so frequent in his mouth, nor any science which he appears to think of so great a value, or so difficult attainment.

" But my curiosity has been most engaged by the recital of his own adventures and achievements. I have heard of the union of various characters in single persons, but never met with such a constellation of great qualities as this man's narrative affords. Whatever has distinguished the hero ; whatever has elevated the wit ; whatever has endeared the lover, are all concentred in Mr Frolick, whose

K

life has, for seven years, been a regular interchange of intrigues, dangers, and waggeries, and who has distinguished himself in every character that can be feared, envied, or admired.

" I question whether all the officers of the royal navy can bring together, from all their journals, a collection of so many wonderful escapes as this man has known upon the Thames, on which he has been a thousand and a thousand times on the point of perishing, sometimes by the terrors of foolish women in the same boat, sometimes by his own acknowledged imprudence in passing the river in the dark, and sometimes by shooting the bridge under which he has rencountered mountainous waves, and dreadful cataracts.

" Nor less has been his temerity by land, nor fewer his hazards. He has reeled with giddiness on the top of the Monument ; he has crossed the street amidst the rush of coaches ; he has been surrounded by robbers without number ; he has headed parties at the playhouse ; he has scaled the windows of every toast ; he has been hunted for whole winters by his rivals ; he has slept upon bulks, he has cut chairs, he has bilked coachmen ; he has rescued his friends from the bailiffs, has knocked down the constable, has bullied the justice, and performed many other exploits, that have filled the town with wonder and with merriment.

" But yet greater is the fame of his understanding than his bravery ; for he informs us that he is, at London, the established arbitrator of all points of honour, and the decisive judge of all performances of genius ; that no musical performer is in reputation till the opinion of Frolick has ratified his pretensions ; that the theatres suspend their sentence till he begins to clap or hiss, in which all are proud to concur ; that no publick entertainment has failed or succeeded, but because he opposed or favoured it ; that all controversies at the gaming-table

are referred to his determination ; that he adjusts the
ceremonial at every assembly, and prescribes every
fashion of pleasure or of dress.

" With every man whose name occurs in the papers of
the day, he is intimately acquainted ; and there are very
few posts, either in the state or army, of which he has not
more or less influenced the disposal. He has been very
frequently consulted both upon war and peace ; but the
time is not yet come when the nation shall know how
much it is indebted to the genius of Frolick."

Johnson might well have ended here, leaving us with
no illusions about Mr Frolick. Mr Frolick was a fraud,
but he must have been an amusing fraud, and, admiring
his brilliant powers of fancy, we could have forgiven
him his boasting and vainglory ; moreover, we are indebted to him for furnishing a sort of *locus classicus*
for all those sallies and escapades by which the young
" bloods " of London sought to distinguish themselves in
the year 1750.

Mr Frolick, no doubt, was not such a wild fellow as he
represented himself. We remember that Justice Shallow,
like Mr Frolick, spent some early years in the law ; he
was " once of Clement's Inn ; where, I think, they will
talk of mad Shallow yet," and he would prate " of the
wildness of his youth, and the feats he hath done about
Turnbull-street." Falstaff humoured him : " We have
heard the chimes at midnight, Master Shallow." But
Johnson was a moralist, and felt himself bound, at the
conclusion of this clever *Rambler*, to demolish poor Frolick.
" If he is celebrated by other tongues than his own, I
shall willingly propagate his praise ; but if he has swelled
among us with empty boasts, and honours conferred only
by himself, I shall treat him with rustick sincerity, and
drive him as an impostor from this part of the Kingdom
to some region of more credulity."

I think it would have been a pity to show up Mr

Frolick, and kinder to suffer him to continue infusing a little colour into the drabness of his native parish. But Johnson must finish with a castigation: " The beadle within him was often eager to apply the lash." [1]

3. COUNTRY LIFE : CONVERSATION AND HOUSEKEEPING

"None is so wasteful as the scraping dame,
She loses three for one ; her soul, rest, fame."
GEORGE HERBERT.

IT is clear, then, that Johnson, like Addison, Chesterfield and Goldsmith, looked on the countryman as a dull fellow, whose ideas resembled his clothes in being woefully behind the times. Let us test this judgment a little more closely, and inquire in what particular ways the rustic offended, and how he provoked the scorn of his visitors.

Conversation was Johnson's chief delight, and it was his good fortune to converse habitually with all the great men of his day. His own standard of conversation was high and exacting, and we have noticed [2] what pains he took to talk well, and to talk correctly. In the Essays we find frequent complaints from his imaginary correspondents of the conversation of country-folk. Family pedigrees, and the prowess of ancestors in the Civil Wars, were favourite topics,[3] but such topics, being local, were profoundly boring to the Londoner. The neighbouring gentry, writes Euphelia from her aunt's country house, " came at first with great eagerness to see the fine lady from London, but when we met, we had no common topick on which we could converse ; they had no curiosity after plays, operas, or musick : and I find as little satis-

---

[1] Boswell's *Life of Johnson* (Birkbeck Hill), iii. 81.
[2] *Supra*, p. 20.   [3] *Supra*, p. 138.

faction from their accounts of the quarrels or alliances of families, whose names, when once I can escape, I shall never hear. The women have now seen me, know how my gown is made, and are satisfied ; the men are generally afraid of me, and say little, because they think themselves not at liberty to talk rudely." [1] This economy of male conversation in Euphelia's presence was, at least, a sign of grace ; but it was not always practised. Perdita reports of one of her suitors : " I was then addressed by Mr *Sturdy*, and congratulated by all my friends on the manors of which I was shortly to be lady : but *Sturdy's* conversation was so gross, that after the third visit I could endure him no longer ; and incurred, by dismissing him, the censure of all my friends, who declared that my nicety was greater than my prudence, and that they feared it would be my fate at last to be wretched with a wit." [2] Conversation was universally very coarse, and we know what Sir Robert Walpole declared to be its one acceptable topic ; but Perdita seems to imply that, in this respect, the "wit" was somewhat more particular than the squire.

Euphelia declared that defamation by female tongues was worse in the country, because it assailed not only the living but the dead. On this point she is very witty, and gives such amusing, though possibly exaggerated, instances that I will quote her *in extenso*. Family scandals, if we may believe her, retained their relish, and family quarrels were kept alive, for generations—even for centuries. " It is common to reproach the tea-table and the park, with giving opportunities and encouragement to scandal. I cannot wholly clear them from the charge ; but must, however, observe in favour of the modish prattlers, that, if not by principle, we are at least by accident less guilty of defamation than the country ladies. For having greater numbers to observe and censure, we

[1] *Rambler*, No. 42. [2] *Adventurer*, No. 74.

are commonly content to charge them only with their own faults, or follies, and seldom give way to malevolence, but such as arises from some injury or affront, real or imaginary, offered to ourselves. But in these distant provinces, where the same families inhabit the same houses from age to age, they transmit and recount the faults of a whole succession. I have been informed how every estate in the neighbourhood was originally got, and find, if I may credit the accounts given me, that there is not a single acre in the hands of the rightful owner. I have been told of intrigues between beaus and toasts that have been now three centuries in their quiet graves, and am often entertained with traditional scandal on persons of whose names there would have been no remembrance, had they not committed somewhat that might disgrace their descendants.

" In one of my visits I happened to commend the air and dignity of a young lady, who had just left the company ; upon which two grave matrons looked with great sliness at each other, and the elder asked me whether I had ever seen the picture of Henry the Eighth. You may imagine that I did not immediately perceive the propriety of the question : but after having waited a while for information, I was told that the lady's grandmother had a great-great-grandmother that was an attendant on Anna Bullen, and supposed to have been too much a favourite of the king.

" If once there happens a quarrel between the principal persons of two families, the malignity is continued without end, and it is common for old maids to fall out about some election, in which their grandfathers were competitors ; the heart-burnings of the civil war are not yet extinguished ; there are two families in the neighbourhood who have destroyed each other's game from the time of Philip and Mary ; and when an account came of an inundation, which had injured the plantations of a worthy gentleman, one of the hearers remarked, with exultation, that he might now have some notion of the ravages committed by his ancestors in their retreat from *Bosworth.*

" Thus malice and hatred descend here with an inheritance, and it is necessary to be well versed in history that the various factions of this county may be understood. You cannot expect to be on good terms with families who are resolved to love nothing in common ; and, in selecting your intimates, you are perhaps to consider which party you most favour in the barons' wars. I have often lost the good opinion of my aunt's visitants by confounding the interests of York and Lancaster, and was once censured for sitting silent when William Rufus was called a tyrant. I have however now thrown aside all pretences to circumspection, for I find it impossible in less than seven years to learn all the requisite cautions. At London, if you know your company, and their parents, you are safe ; but you are here suspected of alluding to the slips of great-grandmothers, and of reviving contests which were decided in armour by the redoubted knights of ancient times. I hope therefore that you will not condemn my impatience, if I am weary of attending where nothing can be learned, and of quarrelling where there is nothing to contest, and that you will contribute to divert me while I stay here by some facetious performance." [1]

It is also to be observed that city people, who " married into the county," or, having made their fortunes, purchased estates and became landed gentry, despised the conversation of the squires and their ladies, as much as did more fashionable folk. " I am naturally inclined to hospitality," writes Mercator, " and for some time kept up a constant intercourse of visits with the neighbouring gentlemen ; but though they are easily brought about me by better wine than they can find at any other house, I am not much relieved by their conversation ; they have no

[1] *Rambler*, No. 46.

skill in commerce or the stocks, and I have no knowledge of families or the factions of the country ; so that when the first civilities are over, they usually talk to one another, and I am left alone in the midst of the company." [1] Misocapelus, the " second son of a country gentleman by the daughter of a wealthy citizen of *London*," was his mother's darling, " because I kept my coat clean, and my complexion free from freckles, and did not come home, like my brother, mired and tanned, nor carry corn in my hat to the horse, nor bring dirty curs into the parlour. My mother had not been taught to amuse herself with books, and being much inclined to despise the ignorance and barbarity of the country ladies, disdained to learn their sentiments or conversation, and had made no addition to the notions, which she had brought from the precincts of Cornhill." [2]   Here Johnson kills two birds with one stone, the " barbarous " lady of the country and the illiterate lady from the city.

Country occupations were, in Johnson's view, on a level with country conversation.   Housekeeping cares narrowed women's minds, and deadened their spirits : the useless, aimless routine of sport absorbed the time and energies of men.   Economy, in our day, has sometimes come to signify stinginess, or at least to connote the art of saving.   The fault of niggardliness would have been detestable to the generous soul of Johnson ; but the true meaning of economy is given by the first definition of the word in the *Dictionary* : " The management of a family ; the government of a household."   The proper administration of one's household is a duty, the neglect of which Johnson would have been the first to censure ; but he condemned far more severely a total self-immersion in household cares, a pursuit of the means of living as an end in itself.   The mother who, having forgotten all she herself had ever learnt, sacrificed the liberal education

[1] *Adventurer*, No. 102.   [2] *Rambler*, No. 116.

of her children to their training in οἰκονομική had no more unsparing satirist than Johnson. But let us hear his own description of two such housekeepers, the first of a lady whose activities were shown indoors, and in the garden, while the second extended her sway to farm and field:

The Employments of a Housewife in the Country [1]

" *To the* RAMBLER.

" SIR,

" As you have allowed a place in your paper to Euphelia's letters from the country, and appear to think no form of human life unworthy of your attention, I have resolved, after many struggles with idleness and diffidence, to give you some account of my entertainment in this sober season of universal retreat, and to describe to you the employments of those who look with contempt on the pleasures and diversions of polite life, and employ all their powers of censure and invective upon the uselessness, vanity, and folly, of dress, visits, and conversation.

" When a tiresome and vexatious journey of four days had brought me to the house, where invitation, regularly sent for seven years together, had at last induced me to spend the summer, I was surprised, after the civilities of my first reception, to find, instead of the leisure and tranquillity, which a rural life always promises, and, if well conducted, might always afford, a confused wildness of care, and a tumultuous hurry of diligence, by which every face was clouded, and every motion agitated. The lady, who was my father's relation, was, indeed, very full of the happiness which she received from my visit, and according to the forms of obsolete breeding, insisted that I should recompense the long delay of my company with a promise not to leave her till winter. But, amidst all her kindness and caresses, she very frequently turned her

---

[1] *Rambler*, No. 51.

head aside, and whispered, with anxious earnestness, some order to her daughters, which never failed to send them out with impolite precipitation. Sometimes her impatience would not suffer her to stay behind ; she begged my pardon, she must leave me for a moment ; she went, and returned and sat down again, but was again disturbed by some new care,—dismissed her daughters with the same trepidation, and followed them with the same countenance of business and solicitude.

" However I was alarmed at this show of eagerness and disturbance, and however my curiosity was excited by such busy preparations as naturally promised some great event, I was yet too much a stranger to gratify myself with inquiries ; but finding none of the family in mourning, I pleased myself with imagining that I should rather see a wedding than a funeral.

" At last we sat down to supper, when I was informed that one of the young ladies, after whom I thought myself obliged to inquire, was under a necessity of attending to some affair that could not be neglected. Soon afterward my relation began to talk of the regularity of her family, and the inconvenience of London hours, and at last let me know that they had purposed that night to go to bed sooner than was usual, because they were to rise early in the morning to make cheesecakes. This hint sent me to my chamber, to which I was accompanied by all the ladies, who begged me to excuse some large sieves of leaves and flowers that covered two thirds of the floor, for they intended to distil them when they were dry, and they had no other room that so conveniently received the rising sun.

" The scent of the flowers hindered me from rest, and therefore I rose early in the morning with a resolution to explore my new habitation. I stole unperceived by my busy cousins into the garden, where I found nothing either more great or elegant, than in the same number of acres cultivated for the market. Of the gardener I soon learnt that his lady was the greatest manager in that part of the country, and that I was come hither at the time in which I might learn to make more pickles and conserves, than could be seen at any other house a hundred miles round.

" It was not long before her ladyship gave me sufficient opportunities of knowing her character, for she was too much pleased with her own accomplishments to conceal them, and took occasion, from some sweetmeats which she set next day upon the table, to discourse for two long hours upon robs and gellies ; laid down the best methods of conserving, reserving, and preserving all sorts of fruit ; told us with great contempt of the London lady in the neighbourhood, by whom these terms were very often confounded ; and hinted how much she should be ashamed to set before company, at her own house, sweetmeats of so dark a colour as she had often seen at Mistress Sprightly's.

" It is, indeed, the great business of her life, to watch the skillet on the fire, to see it simmer with the due degree of heat, and to snatch it off at the moment of projection ; and the employments to which she has bred her daughters, are to turn rose-leaves in the shade, to pick out the seeds of currants with a quill, to gather fruit without bruising it, and to extract bean-flower water for the skin. Such are the tasks with which every day, since I came hither, has begun and ended, to which the early hours of life are sacrificed, and in which time is passing away which never shall return.

" But to reason or expostulate are hopeless attempts. The lady has settled her opinions, and maintains the dignity of her own performances with all the firmness of stupidity accustomed to be flattered. Her daughters having never seen any house but their own, believe their mother's excellence on her own word. Her husband is a mere sportsman, who is pleased to see his table well furnished, and thinks a day sufficiently successful, in which he brings home a leash of hares to be potted by his wife.

" After a few days I pretended to want books, but my lady soon told me that none of her books would suit my taste ; for her part she never loved to see young women give their minds to such follies, by which they would only learn to use hard words ; she bred up her daughters to understand a house, and whoever should marry them, if they knew anything of good cookery, would never repent it.

" There are, however, some things in the culinary sciences too sublime for youthful intellects, mysteries with which they must not be initiated till the years of serious maturity, and which are referred to the day of marriage, as the supreme qualification of connubial life. She makes an orange pudding, which is the envy of all the neighbour-hood, and which she has hitherto found means of mix-ing and baking with such secrecy, that the ingredient to which it owes its flavour has never been discovered.   She, indeed, conducts this great affair with all the caution that human policy can suggest. It is never known beforehand when this pudding will be produced ; she takes the in-gredients privately into her own closet, employs her maids and daughters in different parts of the house, orders the oven to be heated for a pie, and places the pudding in it with her own hands, the mouth of the oven is then stopped, and all inquiries are vain.

" The composition of the pudding, however, she has promised Clarinda, that if she pleases her in marriage, she shall be told without reserve. But the art of making English capers she has not yet persuaded herself to dis-cover, but seems resolved that secret shall perish with her, as some alchymists have obstinately suppressed the art of transmuting metals.

" I once ventured to lay my fingers on her book of receipts, which she left upon the table, having intelligence that a vessel of gooseberry wine had burst the hoops. But though the importance of the event sufficiently engrossed her care, to prevent any recollection of the danger to which her secrets were exposed, I was not able to make any use of the golden moments ; for this treasure of hereditary knowledge was so well concealed by the manner of spelling used by her grandmother, her mother, and herself, that I was totally unable to understand it, and lost the opportunity of consulting the oracle, for want of knowing the language in which its answers were returned.

" It is, indeed, necessary, if I have any regard to her ladyship's esteem, that I should apply myself to some of these economical accomplishments ; for I overheard her, two days ago, warning her daughters, by my mournful example, against negligence of pastry, and ignorance in carving : for you saw, said she, that, with all her pretensions to knowledge, she turned the partridge the wrong way when she attempted to cut it, and, I believe, scarcely knows the difference between paste raised, and paste in a dish.

" The reason, Mr Rambler, why I have laid Lady Bustle's character before you, is a desire to be informed whether, in your opinion, it is worthy of imitation, and whether I shall throw away the books which I have hitherto thought it my duty to read, for *The Lady's Closet Opened*, *The Complete Servant Maid*, and *The Court Cook*, and resign all curiosity after right and wrong, for the art of scalding damascenes without bursting them, and preserving the whiteness of pickled mushrooms.

" Lady Bustle has, indeed, by this incessant application to fruits and flowers, contracted her cares into a narrow space, and set herself free from many perplexities with which other minds are disturbed. She has no curiosity after the events of a war, or the fate of heroes in distress ; she can hear, without the least emotion, the ravage of a fire, or devastations of a storm ; her neighbours grow rich or poor, come into the world or go out of it, without regard, while she is pressing the gelly-bag, or airing the store-room ; but I cannot perceive that she is more free from disquiets than those whose understandings take a wider range. Her marigolds, when they are almost cured, are often scattered by the wind, and the rain sometimes falls upon fruit when it ought to be gathered dry. While her artificial wines are fermenting, her whole life is restlessness and anxiety. Her sweetmeats are not always bright, and the maid sometimes forgets the just proportions of salt and pepper, when venison is to be baked. Her conserves mould, her wines sour, and pickles mother ; and, like all the rest of mankind, she is every day mortified with the defeat of her schemes, and the disappointment of her hopes.

" With regard to vice and virtue, she seems a kind of neutral being. She has no crime but luxury, nor any virtue but chastity ; she has no desire to be praised but for her cookery, nor wishes any ill to the rest of mankind, but that whenever they aspire to a feast, their custards may be weyish, and their pie-crusts tough.

" I am now very impatient to know whether I am to look on these ladies as the great pattern of our sex, and to consider conserves and pickles as the business of my life ; whether the censures which I now suffer be just, and whether the brewers of wines, and the distillers of washes, have a right to look with insolence on the weakness of
" CORNELIA."

Such was Lady Bustle. Mrs Busy [1] also was the wife of a sportsman, who recognized her peculiar talents, and allowed her full scope for their exercise. Mrs Busy may be considered as the complement of Lady Bustle ; had they been able to work together, they would have made any landed estate extremely profitable.

[1] *Rambler*, No. 138.

" Mrs *Busy* was married at eighteen from a boarding-school, where she had passed her time, like other young ladies, in needle-work, with a few intervals of dancing and reading. When she became a bride she spent one winter with her husband in town, where, having no idea of any conversation beyond the formalities of a visit, she found nothing to engage her passions ; and when she had been one night at Court, and two at an opera, and seen the Monument, the Tombs, and the Tower, she concluded that *London* had nothing more to show, and wondered that when women had once seen the world, they could not be content to stay at home. She therefore went willingly to the ancient seat, and for some years studied housewifery under Mr *Busy's* mother, with so much assiduity, that the old lady, when she died, bequeathed her a caudle-cup, a soup-dish, two beakers, and a chest of table-linen spun by herself.

" Mr *Busy*, finding the economical qualities of his lady, resigned his affairs wholly into her hands, and devoted his life to his pointers and his hounds. He never visited his estates, but to destroy the partridges and the foxes ; and often committed such depredations in the rage of pleasure, that some of his tenants refused to hold their lands at the usual rent. Their landlady persuaded them to be satisfied, and entreated her husband to dismiss his dogs, with many exact calculations of the ale drank by his companions, and corn consumed by the horses, and remonstrances against the insolence of the huntsman, and the frauds of the groom. The huntsman was too necessary to his happiness to be discarded ; and he had still continued to ravage his own estate, had he not caught a cold and a fever by shooting mallards in the fens. His fever was followed by a consumption, which in a few months brought him to the grave.

" Mrs *Busy* was too much an economist to feel either joy or sorrow at his death. She received the compliments and consolations of her neighbours in a dark room, out of which she stole privately every night and morning to see the cows milked ; and, after a few days, declared that she thought a widow might employ herself better than in nursing grief ; and that, for her part, she was resolved that the fortunes of her children should not be impaired by her neglect.

" She therefore immediately applied herself to the reformation of abuses. She gave away the dogs, discharged the servants of the kennel and stable, and sent the horses to the next fair, but rated at so high a price that they returned unsold. She was resolved to have nothing idle about her, and ordered them to be employed in common drudgery. They lost their sleekness and grace, and were soon purchased at half their value.

" She soon disencumbered herself from her weeds, and put on a riding-hood, a coarse apron, and short petticoats, and has turned a large manor into a farm, of which she takes the management wholly upon herself. She rises before the sun to order the horses to their gears, and sees them well rubbed down at their return from work ; she attends the dairy morning and evening, and watches when a calf falls that it may be carefully nursed ; she walks out among the sheep at noon, counts the lambs, and observes the fences, and, where she finds a gap, stops it with a bush till it can be better mended. In harvest she rides a-field in the waggon, and is very liberal of her ale from a wooden bottle. At her leisure hours she looks goose eggs, airs the wool room, and turns the cheese.

" When respect or curiosity brings visitants to her house, she entertains them with prognosticks of a scarcity of wheat, or a rot among the sheep, and always thinks herself privileged to dismiss them, when she is to see the hogs fed, or to count her poultry in the roost.

" The only things neglected about her are her children, whom she has taught nothing but the lowest household duties. In my last visit I met Mrs *Busy* carrying grains to a sick cow, and was entertained with the accomplishments of her eldest son, a youth of such early maturity, that, though he is only sixteen, she can trust him to sell corn in the market. Her younger daughter, who is eminent for her beauty, though somewhat tanned in making hay, was busy in pouring out ale to the ploughmen, that every one might have an equal share.

" I could not but look with pity on this young family, doomed by the absurd prudence of their mother, to ignorance and meanness ; but, when I recommended a more elegant education, was answered, that she never saw bookish or finical people grow rich, and that she was good for nothing herself till she had forgotten the nicety of the boarding-school."

I will present a few minor sketches of Johnson's rural economists. There was Squire Bluster, whose grandmother " taught him very early to inspect the steward's accounts, to dog the butler from the cellar, and to catch the servants at a junket ; so that he was at the age of eighteen a complete master of all the lower arts of domestic policy, had often on the road detected combinations between the coachman and the ostler, and procured the discharge of nineteen maids for illicit correspondence with cottagers and charwomen." [1] Myrtilla's aunt " knew little beyond her needle and her dairy, and professed to think that nothing more is required of a woman than to see that the house is clean and that the maids go to bed and rise at an early hour." [2] It was the business of Eriphile " every morning to visit all the rooms, in hopes of finding a chair without its cover, a window shut or open contrary to her orders, a spot on the hearth, or a feather on the floor, that the rest of the day may be justifiably spent in taunts of contempt, and vociferations·of anger. She lives for no other purpose but to preserve the neatness

[1] *Rambler*, No. 142. [2] *Ibid.*, No. 84.

L

of a house and gardens, and feels neither inclination to pleasure, nor aspiration after virtue, while she is engrossed by the great employment of keeping gravel from grass, and wainscoat from dust." [1] Sophronia " considered wit as dangerous, and learning as superfluous, and thought that the woman who kept her house clean, and her accounts exact, took receipts for every payment, and could find them at a sudden call, inquired nicely after the condition of her tenants, read the price of stocks once a week, and purchased everything at the best market, could want no accomplishments necessary to the happiness of a wise man." [2] The husband of one of these paragons complained to *The Idler* [3] that his daughters " grow up in total ignorance of everything past, present, and future."

No doubt there was another side to this matter. We may admire the pluck and energy of Mrs Busy; it was not her fault that her own education had been defective, and it would not have been surprising if she had spent the years of her widowhood in idleness and extravagance. And we must remember that in the days of the Georges great households were the scenes of great waste, and the peculations of servants were a very real plague. Sophronia truly observed " how many were ruined by confidence in their servants." "They have no where else " (wrote Steele) " such plentiful diet, large wages, or indulgent liberty. There is no place where they labour less, and yet where they are so little respectful, more wasteful, more negligent, or where they so frequently change their masters." [4] This wastefulness of servants reduced Jack Scatter to a debtors' prison—but Jack had delivered himself over to their depredations; " he abandoned his cellar to the butler, ordered his groom to provide hay and corn at discretion, took his housekeeper's word for the expenses of the kitchen, allowed all his servants to do their work by

[1] *Rambler*, No. 112.   [2] *Ibid.*, No. 113.
[3] *Idler*, No. 13.   [4] *Spectator*, No. 88.

deputies, permitted his domesticks to keep his house open to their relations and acquaintance, and in ten years was conveyed hither." [1] With what satisfaction Matthew Bramble cleansed poor Baynard's house of "those vermin" when the extravagant Mrs Baynard died! "The next step I took was to disband that legion of supernumerary domestics, who had preyed so long upon the vitals of my friend; a parcel of idle drones, so intolerably insolent that they even treated their own master with the most contemptuous neglect." [2]

But Johnson was satirizing a carefulness carried to excess. He has pointed out [3] that by "the common suffrage" profusion is a lesser vice than avarice, and he disdained the "restlessness and anxiety" which expresses itself in a "rigorous and spiteful superintendence of domestic trifles." With this he associated stupidity, indifference to public events, meanness, and ignorance —an ignorance that despised and hated learning, and a pride in futile employments "in which time is passing away which never shall return":

"For loss of catel may recovered be,
But loss of time shendeth us, quod he."

But, worst of all, the education of children was sacrificed. These people whom Johnson satirized were landed gentry, the natural leaders and rulers of the nation. But what chance had Mrs Busy's heir, whose "early maturity" at sixteen years of age qualified him to sell corn in the market, to exhibit the virtues of "a true natural aristocracy"? How was he being trained "to stand upon such elevated ground as to be enabled to take a large view of the wide-spread and infinitely diversified combinations of men and affairs in a large society; to

[1] *Adventurer*, No. 53.
[2] Smollett, *The Expedition of Humphrey Clinker*.
[3] *Supra*, p. 91.

have leisure to read, to reflect, to converse ; to be enabled
to draw the court and attention of the wise and learned
wherever they are to be found ;—to be habituated in
armies to command and to obey " ? These, according to
the Whig political philosopher, were the proper functions
of a governing class. I think the Tory Johnson would
have subscribed to Burke's ideal of a liberal education.

4. COUNTRY LIFE : SPORT, ECCENTRICITY, TYRANNY, YOUNGER SONS, CLERGYMEN

" Every one indulges the full enjoyment of his own choice, and
talks and lives with no other view than to please himself."
Rambler, No. 138.

THE rural occupations, and preoccupations, described in
the previous chapter were mainly those of the female
sex. Johnson, it is evident, thought that women magni-
fied the importance of housekeeping, and were apt to
be " cumbered about much serving." But, before passing to other country pursuits, I think I may already
claim to have shown some cause for doubting Macaulay's
sweeping statement : " Of the rural life of England he
knew nothing." [1] Of the minor economies of rural life,
of the kitchen operations and still-room mysteries of
country houses, Johnson surely appears to have known
a good deal.

Let us now consider Johnson's views on Sport, then
almost monopolized by men. What did he think about
fox-hunting ? The answer is that he had a poor opinion
of it.

Fox-hunting is now (like cricket) a national affair ;
we might almost regard it as an integral part of the
British constitution. Any man who decried it would be
regarded as a crank, a person of subversive disposition.

[1] *Supra*, p. 99.

But a different view was held in the eighteenth century. The " wits " attacked fox-hunting, and for various reasons.

Addison was strongly prejudiced against this sport ; for him " fox-hunter " spelt " Jacobite." " For the honour of his Majesty, and the safety of his government, we cannot but observe, that those who have appeared the greatest enemies to both, are of that rank of men who are commonly distinguished by the title of Fox-hunters." [1] He sarcastically pictures the Jacobite army in 1715 being diverted from its march by a fox which " unluckily crossing the road, drew off a considerable detachment, who clapped spurs to their horses, and pursued him with whoops and halloos, till we had lost sight of them." [2] And so he always ridicules sportsmen. In *The Tatler*, No. 153, he classifies mankind as they resemble musical instruments ; some have the quality of lutes, some of violins or trumpets, but " As for your rural wits, who talk with great eloquence and alacrity of foxes, hounds, horses, quickset hedges and six-bar gates, double ditches, and broken necks, I am in doubt whether I should give them a place in the conversable world. However, if they will content themselves with being raised to the dignity of hunting-horns, I shall desire that for the future they may be known by that name." He also portrays what was then a *lusus naturæ*, or miracle of unwomanliness—a female fox-hunter : " On the other hand I have very frequently the opportunity of seeing a rural Andromache, who came up to town last winter, and is one of the greatest fox-hunters in the country. She talks of hounds and horses, and makes nothing of leaping over a six-bar gate. If a man tells her a waggish story, she gives him a push with her hand in jest, and calls him an impudent dog ; and if her servant neglects his business, threatens to kick him out of the house. I have heard her, in her wrath, call a substantial

[1] *Freeholder*, No. 22.   [2] *Ibid.*, No. 3.

tradesman a lousy cur." [1] I scarcely think this nymph of the chase would have been a welcome attendant to Diana.

Chesterfield thought that sport was beneath a gentleman : " There are some pleasures that degrade a gentleman, as much as some trades could do. Sottish drinking, indiscriminate gluttony, driving coaches, rustic sports, such as fox-chases, horse-races, etc., are, in my opinion, infinitely below the honest and industrious professions of a tailor, and a shoemaker, which are said to *déroger*." [2] By his will, his godson Philip was " to forfeit £5 to the dean and chapter of Westminster if he ever was concerned in the keeping of any racehorse or pack of hounds." [3] Chesterfield's notions of hunting, by the way, were not very British ; he writes to his son : " I suppose you have hunted at Compiegne. The King's hunting there is a fine sight, the French manner of hunting is gentleman-like ; ours is only for bumpkins and boobies." [4] But be it noted that Johnson had a proper contempt for this gentleman-like and Chesterfieldian hunting : " 'The English (said he) are the only nation who ride hard a-hunting. A Frenchman goes out upon a managed horse, and capers in the field, and no more thinks of leaping a hedge than of mounting a breach.' " [5]

Cowper included fox-hunting amongst the temptations of youth :

" Hourly allurements on his passions press,
Safe in themselves, but dangerous in the excess." [6]

[1] *Spectator*, No. 57. An English writer, said Addison, represented country gentlemen " as lying under a kind of curse pronounced to them in the words of Goliath, ' I will give thee to the fowls of the air, and to the beasts of the field ' " (*Spectator*, No. 583).

[2] Lord Chesterfield, *Letters to his Son*, No. 148.

[3] *Dictionary of National Biography*.

[4] *Letters to his Son*, No. 230.

[5] Boswell's *Life of Johnson* (Birkbeck Hill), v. 253.

[6] *The Progress of Error*.

He wrote of the sportsman :

" Charged with the folly of his life's mad scene,
He takes offence, and wonders what you mean." [1]

As for the sporting parson :

" He takes the field. The master of the pack
Cries, ' Well done, saint ! ' and claps him on the back.
Is this the path of sanctity ? Is this
To stand a waymark in the road to bliss ? " [2]

No doubt many serious persons of that age reprehended
a life wholly devoted to sport as unworthy of a rational
educated man. So Chaucer's Clerke censured Walter,
Marquis of Saluce, who was too busy hunting even to
think of marrying :

" I blame him thus, that he considered nought
In time comyng what mighte him betide,
But on his lust present was al his thought,
As for to hauke and hunte on every side ;
Wel neigh al other cures let he slide,
And eek he nolde and that was worst of all
Wedde no wife for aught that might befall."

Johnson is always sarcastic about hunting. " My elder
brother," writes Misocapelus, " was very early initiated in
the chace, and, at an age when other boys are *creeping
like snails unwillingly to school*, he could wind the horn,
beat the bushes, bound over hedges, and swim rivers.
When the huntsman one day broke his leg, he supplied his
place with equal abilities, and came home with the scut
in his hat, amidst the acclamations of the whole village." [3]
But brief was the career of this youthful prodigy : " In
the sixth year of my servitude [*i.e.* apprenticeship] my
brother died of drunken joy, for having run down a fox
that had baffled all the packs of the province." [4] Another

[1] *The Progress of Error.*   [2] *Ibid.*   [3] *Rambler*, No. 116.   [4] *Ibid.*

younger son writes : " I was in my eighteenth year despatched to the university without any rural hcnours. I had never killed a single woodcock, nor partaken one triumph over a conquered fox." [1] Especially does he ridicule those who engage in the sport, not because they enjoy it, but because they consider it the correct thing to do. Misocapelus, having succeeded to his brother's estate, and forsworn City life and his apprenticeship to a haberdasher, " had hopes of being able to distinguish myself, and to support the honour of my family. I therefore bought guns and horses, and, contrary to the expectation of the tenants, increased the salary of the huntsman. But when I entered the field, it was soon discovered, that I was not destined to the glories of the chase. I was afraid of thorns in the thicket, and of dirt in the marsh ; I shivered on the brink of a river while the sportsmen crossed it, and trembled at the sight of a five-bar gate. When the sport and danger were over, I was still equally disconcerted ; for I was effeminate, and could only join a feebly whispering voice in the clamours of their triumph." [2] But there were others, not even country-bred, who " found themselves irresistibly determined toward sylvan honours." Such was Mercator, the successful City man, who after long deliberation gave up business for the life of a squire. " An estate was at length purchased, I transferred my stock to a prudent young man who had married my daughter, went down into the country, and commenced lord of a spacious manor." [3] Mercator as a hare-hunter was a prototype of Mr Punch's " Post-war Sportsman " : " When first I took possession of my estate, I bought guns and nets, filled my kennels with dogs and my stable with horses : but a little experience showed me that these instruments of rural felicity would afford me few gratifications. I never shot but to miss the mark, and, to confess

[1] *Rambler*, No. 153. [2] *Ibid.*, No. 123.
[3] *Adventurer*, No. 102.

the truth, was afraid of the fire of my own gun. I could
discover no musick in the cry of the dogs, nor could divest
myself of pity for the animal whose peaceful and inoffen-
sive life was sacrificed to our sport. I was not, indeed,
always at leisure to reflect upon her danger ; for my
horse, who had been bred to the chase, did not always
regard my choice either of speed or way, but leaped
hedges and ditches at his own discretion, and hurried me
along with the dogs, to the great diversion of my brother
sportsmen. His eagerness of pursuit once incited him
to swim a river ; and I had leisure to resolve in the
water, that I would never hazard my life again for the
destruction of a hare."

It was no fear for his neck that predisposed Johnson
against riding after hounds, for Johnson and fear were
strangers. While Addison suspected the sport as seditious,
Chesterfield contemned it as only fit for country bumpkins,
and Cowper denounced it as sinful, Johnson rejected it
as dull and boring. "Amongst other modes of passing
time in the country, Johnson once or twice tried hunting,
and, mounted on an old horse of Mr Thrale's, acquitted
himself to the surprise of the ' field,' one of whom delighted
him by exclaiming, ' Why, Johnson rides as well, for
ought I see, as the most illiterate fellow in England.'
But a trial or two satisfied him :

" ' He thought at heart like courtly Chesterfield,
Who after a long chase o'er hills, dales, fields,
And what not, though he rode beyond all price,
Asked next day, If men ever hunted twice ? '

"It is very strange, and very melancholy, was his
reflection, that the paucity of human pleasures should
persuade us ever to call hunting one of them. The mode
of locomotion in which he delighted was the vehicular." [1]

[1] *Autobiography of Mrs Piozzi* (Abraham Hayward), ed. 1861,
i. 79.

The glamour and exhilaration of the chase could never capture Johnson's imagination. " Oh, how that beautiful word, Fox," exclaimed Mr Jorrocks in the course of a famous lecture, "gladdens my 'eart, and warms the declinin' embers of my age ! " Johnson and Mr Jorrocks were both typical English characters, though Johnson was a scholar and Mr Jorrocks was an illiterate London grocer ; both belonged to the *genus* John Bull. Yet to Mr Jorrocks were granted faculties of not only physical, but æsthetical, enjoyment, that were denied to Johnson ; for who shall say that this sportsman's joy was devoid of poetical feeling ? " But when the hautumn comes—when the brownin' copse and cracklin' stubble proclaim the farmer's fears are past, then, dash my vig, 'ow I glories in pursuin' of him to destruction, and holdin' him above the bayin' pack ! "

Perhaps Johnson had one more reason for disliking sport. He tells a story [1] of a younger son who went into trade in the City, and, having grown rich, was enabled to buy back a large estate which his extravagant elder brother had been obliged to sell. This gentleman, " as soon as he had settled his economy, began to show his rural sovereignty by breaking the hedges of his tenants in hunting, and seizing the guns or nets of those whose fortunes did not qualify them for sportsmen." [2] Sport, we are reminded, might be practised in an inconsiderate or oppressive way. And so it may here not be out of place to say a word about rural tyrants, as Johnson depicted them.

Contrasting London and country life, he analyses the conditions which made this tyranny possible, and almost inevitable : " In cities, and yet more in courts, the minute discriminations which distinguish one from another are for the most part effaced, the peculiarities of temper and

---

[1] *Rambler*, No. 192.

[2] So Mr Busy " often committed depredations in the rage of pleasure," *supra*, p. 159.

opinion are gradually worn away by promiscuous converse, as angular bodies and uneven surfaces lose their points and asperities by frequent attrition against one another, and approach by degrees to uniform rotundity. The prevalence of fashion, the influence of example, the desire of applause and the dread of censure obstruct the natural tendencies of the mind, and check the fancy in its first efforts to break forth into experiments of caprice.

"Few inclinations are so strong as to grow up into habits, when they must struggle with the constant opposition of settled forms and established customs. But in the country every man is a separate and independent being : solitude flatters irregularity with hopes of secrecy ; and wealth, removed from the mortification of comparison and the awe of equality, swells into contemptuous confidence, and sets blame and laughter at defiance ; the impulses of nature act unrestrained, and the disposition dares to show itself in its true form, without any disguise of hypocrisy, or decorations of elegance. Every one indulges the full enjoyment of his own choice, and talks and lives with no other view than to please himself, without inquiring how far he deviates from the general practice, or considering others as entitled to any account of his sentiments or actions. If he builds or demolishes, opens or encloses, deluges or drains, it is not his care what may be the opinion of those who are skilled in perspective or architecture, it is sufficient that he has no landlord to control him, and that none has any right to examine in what projects the lord of the manor spends his own money on his own grounds.

"For this reason it is not very common to want subjects for rural conversation. Almost every man is daily doing something which produces merriment, wonder, or resentment among his neighbours. This utter exemption from restraint leaves every anomalous quality to operate in its full extent, and suffers the natural character to diffuse itself to every part of life. The pride which, under the check of publick observation, would have been only vented among servants and domesticks, becomes in a country baronet the torment of a province, and, instead of terminating in the destruction of China ware and glasses, ruins tenants, dispossesses cottagers, and harasses villagers with actions of trespass and bills of indictment." [1]

In another essay Johnson examines why people turn to solitary lives: "Some, haughty and impetuous, fly from society only because they cannot bear to repay to others the regard which themselves exact; and think no state of life eligible, but that which places them out of the reach of censure or controul, and affords them opportunities of living in a perpetual compliance with their own inclinations, without the necessity of regulating their actions by any other man's convenience or opinion." [2]

"The torment of a province." Yes, England in the eighteenth century knew such "torments." One who signally merited the description was the notorious Sir James Lowther, the first Earl of Lonsdale and one of Junius' *bêtes noires*. Lowther, according to Alexander Carlyle, was "more detested than any man alive, as a shameless political sharper, a domestic bashaw, and an intolerable tyrant over his tenants and dependants," [3] of whom Lord Albemarle said: "He exacted a serf-like submission from his poor and abject dependants. He professed a thorough contempt for modern refinements. Grass grew in the neglected approaches to his mansion. . . . Awe and silence pervaded the inhabitants (of Penrith) when the gloomy despot traversed the streets." [4]

---

[1] *Rambler*, No. 138.   [2] *Adventurer*, No. 126.
[3] Carlyle, *Autobiography*, pp. 418, 419, quoted in D.N.B. (Sir James Lowther).
[4] Lord Albemarle, *Memoirs of Rockingham*, ii. 70. Lowther treated Boswell with great brutality (Boswell's *Life of Johnson* (Birkbeck Hill), v. 113*n*).

So I conclude that Squire Bluster was not overdrawn in *Rambler* No. 142. Squire Bluster in his bringing-up had been spoilt by his grandmother, who had kept him from school and taught him, amongst other home accomplishments, how to spy meanly on servants. At his " coming of age " celebrations he insulted an aged friend of his father by offering to wager a greater sum than the old gentleman could afford. " His next acts of offence were committed in a contentious and spiteful vindication of the privileges of his manors, and a rigorous and relentless prosecution of every man that presumed to violate his game. As he happens to have no estate adjoining equal to his own, his oppressions are often borne without resistance, for fear of a long suit, of which he delights to count the expenses without the least solicitude about the event ; for he knows, that where nothing but an honorary right is contested, the poorer antagonist must always suffer, whatever shall be the last decision of the law. By the success of some of these disputes, he has so elated his insolence, and, by reflection upon the general hatred which they have brought upon him, so irritated his virulence, that his whole life is spent in meditating or executing mischief. It is his common practice to procure his hedges to be broken in the night, and then to demand satisfaction for damages which his grounds have suffered from his neighbour's cattle. An old widow was yesterday soliciting *Eugenio* to enable her to replevin her only cow then in the pound by Squire *Bluster's* order, who had sent one of his agents to take advantage of her calamity, and persuade her to sell the cow at an under rate. He has driven a day-labourer from his cottage, for gathering blackberries in a hedge for his children, and has now an old woman in the county gaol for a trespass which she committed, by coming into his ground to pick up acorns for her hog.

" Money, in whatever hands, will confer power. Distress

will fly to immediate refuge, without much consideration of remote consequences. *Bluster* has therefore a despotic authority in many families, whom he has assisted, on pressing occasions, with larger sums than they can easily repay. The only visits that he makes are to these houses of misfortune, where he enters with the insolence of absolute command, enjoys the terrours of the family, exacts their obedience, riots at their charge, and in the height of his joy insults the father with menaces, and the daughters with obscenity."

To sum up this Squire: "He is wealthy without followers; he is magnificent without witnesses; he has birth without alliance, and influence without dignity. His neighbours scorn him as a brute; his dependants dread him as an oppressor, and he has only the gloomy comfort of reflecting, that if he is hated, he is likewise feared." [1]

As a country baronet could become the "torment of a province," so a parent could be the torment of a home. Tyrannical fathers were not peculiar to the country, but doubtless in the country, where "the impulses of nature are unrestrained," they permitted themselves a greater licence. Such were the impulses of Squire Western: having discovered that his daughter was in love with Tom Jones, he had her locked up in her room. To Allworthy, who offers his sympathy, he replies: "P—x of your sorrow, it will do me abundance of good, when I have lost my only child, my poor Sophy, that was the joy of my heart, and all the hope and comfort of my age; but I am resolved I will turn her out o'doors; she shall beg and starve, and rot in the streets. Not one hapeny, not a hapeny shall she ever hae o'mine." [2]

This parental tyranny was not inconsistent with a sort of perverted benevolence; sometimes it reached its

<hr>

[1] *Rambler*, No. 142
[2] Fielding, *History of Tom Jones*, Book VI., ch. x.

climax through balked affection. But the essence of the passionate man is his selfishness, and it is his selfishness that makes him contemptible. The type was familiar to Steele: " I have known one of these good-natured passionate men say in a mixed company, even to his own wife or child, such things as the most inveterate enemy of his family would not have spoken, even in imagination. . . . One would think the hectoring, the storming, the sullen, and all the different species and subordinations of the angry should be cured, by knowing they live only as pardoned men ; and how pitiful is the condition of being only suffered ! " [1] So, writes Johnson, " there are indeed many houses which it is impossible to enter familiarly, without discovering that parents are by no means exempt from the intoxications of dominion ; and that he who is in no danger of hearing remonstrances but from his own conscience, will seldom be long without the art of controlling his convictions, and modifying justice by his own will. . . . The regal and parental tyrant differ only in the extent of their dominions, and the number of their slaves. The same passions cause the same miseries ; except that seldom any prince, however despotick, has so far shaken off all awe of the publick eye, as to venture upon those freaks of injustice, which are sometimes indulged under the secrecy of a private dwelling. . . . But the domestick oppressor dooms himself to gaze upon those faces which he clouds with terrour and with sorrow ; and beholds every moment the effects of his own barbarities. He that can bear to give continual pain to those who surround him, and can walk with satisfaction in the gloom of his own presence ; he that can see submissive misery without relenting, and meet without emotion the eye that implores mercy, or demands justice, will scarcely be amended by remonstrance or admonition ; he has found means of stopping the avenues of

[1] *Spectator*, No. 438.

tenderness, and arming his heart against the force of reason." [1]

Tyrants, whether regal, territorial or domestic, are now out of fashion. But those of us who have reached middle age can call Squire Bluster back to memory, and other Blusters eminent in every profession and occupation, and many a parental Bluster who indulged himself in " the intoxication of dominion " and " walked with satisfaction in the gloom of his own presence." Times have changed, and in these days fathers comport themselves towards their sons more like elder brothers — and rather deferential elder brothers. Angry tyrannical squires, if they were ever frequent, are things of the past. They have accommodated themselves to democratic conditions, and sit on County Councils and other bodies with their innumerable committees and sub-committees ; there they find colleagues of all conditions of life, and practise the truly British art of give-and-take. The Local Government Act of 1888 sounded the final knell of Squire Bluster.

Family pride, the custom of entailing estates, and the largeness of families, were in the eighteenth century— and to a lesser degree in the nineteenth—jointly responsible for a serious social problem, How to provide for the Younger Son or Younger Brother. These unfortunate persons had been a mark for Addison's wit. " There is nothing," he wrote, " more easy than to discover a man whose heart is full of his family. Weak minds that have imbibed a strong tincture of the nursery, younger brothers that have been brought up to nothing, superannuated retainers to a great house, have generally their thoughts taken up with little else." [2] He represents a prisoner captured in the rebellion of 1715 as giving this account of his comrades : " One of us had spent his fortune : another was a younger brother : a third had the encumbrance of a

[1] *Rambler*, No. 148.   [2] *Guardian*, No. 137.

father upon his estate." [1] When Peter Plumb, of London, Merchant, was indicted in the Court of Honour for "stealing the wall" of the Honourable Mr Thos. Gules of Gules Hall in the county of Salop, "the prosecutor alleged that he was the cadet of a very ancient family, and that, according to the principles of all the younger brothers of the said family, he had never sullied himself with business, but had chosen rather to starve like a man of honour, than do anything beneath his quality. He produced several witnesses, that he had never employed himself beyond the twisting of a whip, or the making of a pair of nutcrackers, in which he only worked for his diversion, in order to make a present now and then to his friends." [2] Peter Plumb was severely reprimanded for retorting that Mr Gules "was an idle, beggarly fellow, and of no use to the public."

But Mr Will Wimble is the classic example: "Will Wimble is younger brother to a Baronet, and descended from the ancient family of the Wimbles. He is now between forty and fifty; but, being bred to no business, and born to no estate, he generally lives with his elder brother as superintendent of his game. . . . Will Wimble's is the case of many a younger brother of a great family, who had rather see their children starve like gentlemen, than thrive in a trade or profession that is beneath their quality." [3]

Johnson, too, could allow himself a sneer at the younger brother: "He that thinks must think upon something. But tell me, ye that pierce deepest into nature, ye that take the widest surveys of life, inform me, kind shades of *Malbranche* and of *Locke*, what that something can be which excites and continues thought in maiden aunts with small fortunes; in younger brothers that live upon annuities; in traders retired from business; in soldiers

[1] *Freeholder*, No. 3. [2] *Tatler*, No. 256.
[3] *Spectator*, No. 108.

M

absent from their regiments ; or in widows that have no children ? " [1] To such persons he will not even concede the faculty of contemplation, " for they never attend either to the conduct of men, or the works of nature, but rise in the morning, look round them till night in careless stupidity, go to bed and sleep, and rise again in the morning."

This attack strikes me as somewhat ungenerous ; it was fated that Johnson himself should live in comparative idleness for a considerable portion of his own life upon an annuity—granted not by an elder brother, but by the State. But it may be of interest to consider the case of these unprofitable younger brothers, and their preference of a pensioner's existence to an active career. Was the trader really despised by the squire ? If so, at what date did the ostracism begin ?

Lecky says : " It was noticed as a remarkable sign of the democratic spirit that followed the commonwealth, that country gentlemen in England had begun to bind their sons as apprentices to merchants, and also that about the same time the desire to obtain large portions in marriage led to alliances between the aristocracy and the merchants." [2] He quotes the well-known lines of Pope :

" Boastful and rough your first son is a squire,
The next a tradesman meek, and much a liar."

But Sir Walter Besant, in his *London in the Eighteenth Century*,[3] referring to these very lines, remarks : " The tradition of sending the younger sons into trade survived

---

[1] *Idler*, No. 92. Peregrine Langton (uncle of Johnson's friend, Bennet Langton) contrived to live in " plenty and elegance " upon an annuity of £200. He kept two maids and two men in livery. " He had always a post-chaise, and kept three horses " ! Johnson said, " ' he was one of those whom I loved at once by instinct and by reason ' " (Boswell's *Life of Johnson* (Birkbeck Hill), ii. 17, 18).

[2] *England in the Eighteenth Century*, i. 241.   [3] P. 230.

the practice. It is alluded to by Pope (Epistle I.), though in his time the custom had practically ceased." Sir Walter dates the change of custom from about 1700. Dean Inge has written of the Victorian era : " Towards the end of the reign the higher gentry began again to go into trade, *as they had done until the Georges brought in German ideas*, and the way was prepared for the complete destruction of social barriers which the Great War effected." [1]

The Dean's theory will hardly explain the cases of Messrs Will Wimble and Thos. Gules, since they were supposed to flourish—or vegetate—*before* the year 1714 ; but, very possibly, stiff Hanoverian notions of aristocracy and precedence did have the effect of aggravating the armigerous landowner's contempt for the plebeian trader. A more likely cause of the breach was the removal of the London homes of territorial magnates from the City to the new West End squares. [2] Probably the truth is that the smaller or the impoverished gentry, and those who had married City brides, often still found it convenient to educate a son as a merchant, or even as a retail trades-man ; but the richer country gentlemen, and proud personages like Miss Burney's Mr Delvile, grew more and more disdainful of the City and of trade. We remember how Sir Leicester Dedlock, in the earlier part of the Victorian age, condescended to the ironmaster.

Of the many younger sons that figure in Johnson's Essays, only two were engaged in trade. Misocapelus, whose acquaintance we have already made,[3] " was the second son of a country gentleman by the daughter of a wealthy citizen of London. My father, having by his marriage freed the estate from a heavy mortgage, thought himself discharged from all obligations to further

---

[1] *Outspoken Essays*, Second Series, p. 207. (I doubt the completeness of the destruction.)

[2] Sir Walter Besant, *London in the Eighteenth Century*, p. 229.

[3] *Supra*, pp. 152, 167.

thought " (I think Johnson must have composed this sentence hastily), " and entitled to spend the rest of his life in rural pleasures." [1] But his mother was " always recounting the glories of the city," and " by these narratives I was fired with the splendour and dignity of *London*, and of trade." In due course this younger son " was transplanted to town, and, with great satisfaction to myself, bound to a haberdasher." How he was snubbed as a social " outsider " in the vacation and thereby lost his relish for the shop, succeeded to the paternal estate through his elder brother's death, and proved an utter failure as a sportsman, is most amusingly related in *Ramblers* 116 and 123. But the point of the story is that Misocapelus never lost the taint of trade. " A fall, by which my ribs were broken, soon recalled me to domestick pleasures, and I exerted all my art to obtain the favour of the neighbouring ladies ; but wherever I came, there was always some unlucky conversation upon ribands, fillets, pins, or thread, which drove all my stock of compliments out of my head, and overwhelmed me with shame and dejection." And so he had to abandon his " vain endeavours after accomplishments, which, if not early acquired, no endeavours can obtain," and concentrate on " those higher excellencies which are in every man's power, and, though I cannot enchant affection by elegance and ease, hope to secure esteem by honesty and truth."

The second case was different. It is related by Constantius, whose father was the extravagant representative of an impoverished race [2] : " Every man boasted the antiquity of his family, resolved to support the dignity of his birth, and lived in splendour and plenty at the expense of his heir, who, sometimes by a wealthy marriage, and sometimes by lucky legacies, discharged part of the incumbrances, and thought himself entitled to contract new debts, and to leave to his children the same inherit-

[1] *Rambler*, No. 116.   [2] *Ibid.*, No. 192.

ance of embarrassment and distress. Thus the estate
perpetually decayed ; the woods were felled by one, the
park ploughed by another, the fishery let to farmers by a
third ; at last the old hall was pulled down to spare the
cost of reparation, and part of the materials sold to build
a small house with the rest. We were now openly degraded
from our original rank, and my father's brother was
allowed with less reluctance to serve an apprenticeship,
though we never reconciled ourselves heartily to the
sound of haberdasher, but always talked of warehouses
and a merchant, and when the wind happened to blow
loud, affected to pity the hazards of commerce, and to
sympathize with the solicitude of my poor uncle, who
had the true retailer's terrour of adventure, and never
exposed himself or his property to any wider water than
the *Thames*."

These sensitive relations consoled themselves by dis
tinguishing wholesale from retail.[1] The haberdasher
brother, also, was " class-conscious " : " In time, however, by continual profit and small expenses, he grew rich,
and began to turn his thoughts towards rank. He hung
the arms of the family over his parlour-chimney ; pointed
at a chariot decorated only with a cypher ; became of
opinion that money could not make a gentleman ; resented the petulance of upstarts ; told stories of alderman *Puff's* grandfather the porter, wondered that there
was no better method for regulating precedents ; wished
for some dress peculiar to men of fashion ; and when his
servant presented a letter, always enquired whether it
came from his brother the esquire." Finally, he bought

---

[1] Johnson had a proper contempt for this sort of snobbery. In
his *Life of Milton* he ridiculed another form of it—viz. Philips'
plea that Milton was not a schoolmaster, but only took pupils :
" He did not sell literature to all comers at an open shop ; he
was a chamber-milliner, and measured his commodities only to
his friends."

back part of the estate which "his brother the esquire" had sold, and "soon afterwards solicited the office of sheriff, from which all his neighbours were glad to be reprieved, but which he regarded as a resumption of ancestral claims, and a kind of restoration to blood after the attainder of a trade."

Both these stories show that the aristocratic contempt of trade was strong, and that the younger brother, by engaging in it, lost caste. But there were other openings for him:

"My father was the second son of a very ancient and wealthy family. He married a lady of equal birth, whose fortune, joined to his own, might have supported his posterity in honour; but being gay and ambitious, he prevailed on his friends to procure him a post, which gave him an opportunity of displaying his elegance and politeness." [1]

"My father, resolving not to imitate the folly of his ancestors, who had hitherto left the younger sons encumbrances on the eldest, destined me to a lucrative profession; and I, being careful to lose no opportunity of improvement, was, at the usual time in which young men enter into the world, well qualified for the exercise of the business which I had chosen." [2]

"I was the second son of a gentleman, whose estate was barely sufficient to support himself and his heir in the dignity of killing game. He therefore made use of the interest which the alliances of his family afforded him, to procure me a post in the army." [3]

Then there is the tale of "the second son of a gentleman, whose patrimony had been wasted by a long succession of squanderers, till he was unable to support any of his children, except his heir, in the hereditary dignity of idleness." [4]   Being "studious and domestick," this

[1] *Rambler*, No. 149.   [2] *Ibid.*, No. 165.
[3] *Idler*, No. 21.   [4] *Rambler*, No. 153.

younger son won the favour of " an old adventurer, who had been once the intimate friend of my father," and " arrived from the *Indies* with a large fortune." Unhappily this old adventurer died after a short illness, and " I found a will, made at his first arrival, by which my father was appointed the chief inheritor, and nothing was left me but a legacy sufficient to support me in the prosecution of my studies."

But, too often, the younger sons were left " encumbrances on the eldest." [1] As such, certainly their lot was far from enviable ; and yet there was a more desperate plight than that of a younger son. Of George Granville, afterwards Lord Lansdowne, Johnson writes : " He was, as the biographers observe, the younger son of a younger brother : a denomination by which our ancestors proverbially expressed the lowest state of penury and dependance." [2]

The careers (if such a word is suitable) of younger sons in the eighteenth century might make an interesting, but melancholy, study. They were too numerous to be absorbed into the professions ; very many lacked the ability or energy to strike out for themelves, and preferred to quarter themselves on their elder brothers, as did Will Esmond in *The Virginians,* or to live the semi-idle life of " hangers-on " to great houses, or of " led-captains " to wealthy patrons. Probably not a few " took to the

[1] And estates might be encumbered by aunts. " My ancestors, by little and little, wasted their patrimony, till my father had not enough left for the support of his family, without descending to the cultivation of his own grounds, being condemned to pay three sisters the fortunes allotted them by my grandfather, who is suspected to have made his will when he was incapable of adjusting properly the claims of his children, and who, perhaps without design, enriched his daughters by beggaring his son " (*Rambler*, No. 73). These ladies proved to be long-lived, the youngest reaching the age of ninety-three years, five months and six days.

[2] *Lives of the Poets* (Granville).

road " ; of such was William Parsons, the youngest son of a baronet, and nephew of the Duchess of Northumberland, who was hanged for highway robbery in 1751.[1] The nineteenth century gave them a new chance—of making their fortunes in the colonies ; but even in the nineteenth century the tradition endured that trade was no fit occupation for a gentleman. The younger son is found in all the novels, more often in rural surroundings, but sometimes eking out a harmless London existence, like Dickens' Mr Twemlow, first cousin to Lord Snigsworth, " an innocent piece of dinner-furniture that went upon easy castors, and was kept over a livery stable-yard in Duke Street, Saint James's."[2]

The Church, of course, was a refuge for many younger sons. Writing of the year 1685, Macaulay says : " The clergy were regarded as, on the whole, a plebeian class " ; but he adds, in a note : " In the eighteenth century the great increase in the value of benefices produced a change. The younger sons of the nobility were allowed back to the clerical profession."[3] *A fortiori*, we may conclude, the younger sons of the gentry.[4]

But Johnson revered the Church of England, and, in his sketches of rural life, never failed to represent clergymen as scholars and gentlemen. When Melissa was " reduced to a frugal competency, which allowed little beyond neatness and independence," though her " endless train of lovers immediately withdrew," and her friends insulted or neglected her, " there are two persons only whom I cannot charge with having changed their conduct with

[1] *Half-hours with the Highwaymen* (C. G. Harper), ii. 241.
[2] *Our Mutual Friend*, ch. ii.
[3] *History of England*, ch. iii.
[4] *The Connoisseur* (by George Colman and Bonnel Thornton) of 14th January 1756 thus describes the Rev. Jack Quickset, younger brother of Sir Thomas Quickset : " Hunting and shooting are the only busin ess of his life ; foxhounds and pointers lay about in every parlour ; and he is himself, like Pistol, always in boots."

my change of fortune. One is an old curate that has passed his life in the duties of his profession, with great reputation for his knowledge and piety ; the other is a lieutenant of dragoons. The parson made no difficulty in the height of my elevation to check me when I was pert, and instruct me when I blundered ; and if there is any alteration, he is now more timorous lest his freedom should be thought rudeness. The soldier never paid me any particular addresses, but very rigidly observed all the rules of politeness, which he is now so far from relaxing, that whenever he serves the tea, he obstinately carries me the first dish, in defiance of the frowns and whispers of the table." [1] Here were indeed two great gentlemen.

We read of another clergyman being charmed with the society of a learned young lady : " Flavia had read much, and used so often to converse on subjects of learning, that she put all the men in the country to flight, except the old parson, who declared himself much delighted with her company, because she gave him opportunities to recollect the studies of his younger years, and, by some mention of ancient story, had made him rub the dust off his *Homer*, which had lain unregarded in his closet." [2]

Then it was to his parish clergyman that Mercator (the retired London trader who had " commenced lord of a spacious manor ") turned for advice in forming his library : " I then ordered books to be procured, and by the direction of the vicar had in a few weeks a closet elegantly furnished." [3]

But the most amiable and tactful parson in the Essays was he who came to the rescue of the conceited young scholar Verecundulus. Verecundulus was seized with shyness at a dinner-party, where he had intended to dazzle the guests with his wit and learning : " To the questions of curiosity, or the appeals of complaisance, I could seldom

[1] *Rambler*, No. 75.   [2] *Ibid.*, No. 84.

[3] *Adventurer*, No. 102.

answer but with negative monosyllables, or professions
of ignorance ; for the subjects on which they conversed,
were such as are seldom discussed in books, and were
therefore out of my range of knowledge. At length an
old clergyman, who rightly conjectured the reason of
my conciseness, relieved me by some questions about the
present state of natural knowledge, and engaged me, by
an appearance of doubt and opposition, in the explication
and defence of the *Newtonian* philosophy. The consciousness of my own abilities rescued me from depression, and
long familiarity with my subject enabled me to discourse
with ease and volubility ; but, however I might please
myself, I found very little added by my demonstrations
to the satisfaction of the company ; and my antagonist,
who knew the laws of conversation too well to detain their
attention long upon an unpleasing topick, after he had
commended my acuteness and comprehension, dismissed
the controversy, and resigned me to my former insignifi-
cance and perplexity." But this clergyman had done for
Verecundulus all that a man could do.

5. THE CITY LIFE

" After that they get on in trade, and the more they think of
making a fortune the less they think of virtue." *Plato's Republic*
(Jowett's translation), Book VIII.

JOHNSON was a Londoner, but he held in lordly contempt
the habits and standards of the City. This contempt is
evident in many of his Essays,[1] besides appearing in his
other works and in his conversation.

" Commerce," he wrote in the *Preface* to the *Dictionary*,
" however necessary, however lucrative, as it depraves
the manners, corrupts the language." Boswell once asked

[1] It is principally in the *Idlers* that he writes of City life and
character.

him if a merchant might not be a man of enlarged mind,
" such as Addison in *The Spectator* describes Sir Andrew
Freeport to have been. JOHNSON. ' Why, Sir, we may
suppose any fictitious character. We may suppose a
philosophical day-labourer, who is happy in reflecting
that, by his labour, he contributes to the fertility of the
earth, and to the support of his fellow-creatures ; but
we find no such philosophical day-labourer. A merchant
may, perhaps, be a man of enlarged mind, but there is
nothing in trade connected with an enlarged mind.' " [1]
Both the man of birth and the man of letters despised
the citizen. " The West End on one side and Grub Street
on the other, neither of which had the least intercourse
with the City, [2] were completely ignorant of the leaps and
bounds with which the trade and wealth of the London
merchant, and therefore of the London tradesman, advanced in the eighteenth century." [3]   Denizens of Grub
Street, and other authors, were very severe on the trading
classes. The generous-hearted, charitably minded Steele
was an exception. " The courtier, the trader, and the
scholar, should all have an equal pretension to the denomination of a gentleman. That tradesman, who deals
with me in a commodity which I do not understand, with
uprightness, has much more right to that character, than
the courtier that gives me false hopes, or the scholar that
laughs at my ignorance." [4]   But the general view was
expressed by Sir Roger in his discourse on *Punica fides* :
" The Carthaginians were the greatest traders in the
world ; and as gain is the chief end of such a people, they

[1] Boswell's *Life of Johnson* (Birkbeck Hill), v. 328.
[2] If the trader wedded a lady of rank, his life was not supposed
to be enviable. Addison tells the story of a marriage between
Sir John Anvil, a city knight, and Lady Mary Oddly. When Lady
Mary gave a party " she always desires me to be abroad, or to
confine myself to the cock-loft " (*Spectator*, No. 229).
[3] *London in the Eighteenth Century* (Sir Walter Besant), p. 245.
[4] *Tatler*, No. 207.

never pursue any other ; the means to it are never regarded : they will, if it comes easily, get money honestly ;
but if not, they will not scruple to obtain it by fraud, or
cozenage : and indeed, what is the whole business of the
trader's account, but to overreach him who trusts to his
memory ? But were that not so, what can there great and
noble be expected from him whose attention is for ever
fixed upon balancing his books and watching over his
expenses ? And at best, let frugality and parsimony be
the virtues of a merchant, how much is his punctual dealing below a gentleman's charity to the poor, or hospitality
among his neighbours ! " [1]

During the next hundred years the sentiment that
trade was an inferior and almost discreditable pursuit
did not much diminish ; but successful merchants and
bankers and manufacturers were moving from the City to
the suburbs, and from the suburbs to country seats. In
the earlier part of the Georgian era we are struck by the
isolation of the City, by its complete separation from the
" Court End " of the town. Steele writes in Queen Anne's
time of " the ladies within the walls." [2] Johnson, less
politely, refers to " the sons and daughters of lanes and
alleys." [3]

Those walls enclosed scenes of great traditions ; but,
if we may believe Johnson, the greatness had declined
to mere display and the pretentious pomp of office. The
mother of Misocapelus was " always recounting the
glories of the city ; enumerating the succession of mayors ;
celebrating the magnificence of the banquets at *Guildhall*,
and relating the civilities paid her at the companies' feasts
by men, some of whom are now made aldermen, some
have fined for sheriffs, and none are worth less than forty
thousand pounds. She frequently displayed her father's
greatness ; told of the large bills which he had paid at

[1] *Spectator*, No. 174. [2] *Tatler*, No. 109.
[3] *Idler*, No. 12.

sight ; of the sums for which his word would pass on the
Exchange ; the heaps of gold which he used on *Saturday
night* to toss about with a shovel ; the extent of his ware-
house, and the strength of his doors ; and when she relaxed her imagination with lower subjects, described the
furniture of their country-house, or repeated the wit of
the clerks and porters. By these narratives I was fired
with the splendour of *London*, and of trade." [1] Deborah
Ginger, " the unfortunate wife of a city wit," was a lady
of similar ideals : " Thus every day increased our wealth
and our reputation. My husband was often invited to
dinner openly on the *Exchange* by hundred thousand
pounds men [2] ; and whenever I went to any of the halls,
the wives of the aldermen made me low courtesies. We
always took up our notes before the day, and made all
considerable payments by draughts upon our banker.
You will easily believe that I was well enough pleased with
my condition ; for what happiness can be greater than
that of growing every day richer and richer ? I will not
deny that, imagining myself likely to be in a short time
the sheriff's lady, I broke off my acquaintance with some
of my neighbours ; and advised my husband to keep
good company, and not to be seen with men that were
worth nothing." [3]

The tradesman, his shopmen and his apprentices were
finely and even dandiacally dressed, and of ceremonious
behaviour. " In the afternoon," writes Sir Walter Besant,
" when the ladies came along in their coaches to do their
shopping, he was dressed after the fine fashion of the
time in black velvet and white silk stockings, with silver

---

[1] *Rambler*, No. 116.

[2] I recently heard an esteemed Hebrew friend use this very
expression : " My brother was always considered to be a hundred
thousand pounds man." This sum was commonly known as a
" plum."

[3] *Idler*, No. 47.

buttons and buckles, with silver lace in his hat, his wig carefully dressed, and fine lace ruffles at his sleeve. In this array he stood at the door of his shop and invited people to step in, handing the ladies out of their coaches." [1] Goldsmith's Chinese philosopher makes the same report : " Immediately upon entering the mercer's shop, the master and his two men, with wigs plastered with powder, appeared to ask my commands." [2] The apprentice affected a brisk elegance of manner : " I soon caught from my fellow-apprentices the true grace of a counter-bow, the careless air with which a small pair of scales is to be held within the fingers, and the vigour and sprightliness with which the box, after the riband has been cut, is returned to its place." [3] Such were the accomplishments of Misocapelus ; but, finding his occupation despised by his country acquaintances, he writes despondently : " I had now no longer any felicity in contemplating the exact disposition of my powdered curls, the equal plaits of my ruffles, or the gloomy blackness of my shoes."

There was, then, a certain magnificence in the shop ; but the life of the " parlour " behind the shop, the social life of the shopkeeper, was—in Johnson's eyes—a life of meanness, avarice, vulgarity, pretentiousness and emptiness, a life lived with a petty and constricted outlook.

He gibes at the announcements of City weddings: " Many an eye, ranging over the page with eager curiosity in quest of statesmen and heroes, is stopped by a marriage celebrated between Mr *Buckram*, an eminent salesman in *Threadneedle - Street*, and Miss *Dolly Juniper*, the only daughter of an eminent distiller, of the parish of *St Giles's in the Fields*, a young lady adorned with every accomplishment that can give happiness to the married state. Or we are told, amidst our impatience for the event of a battle, that on a certain day Mr *Winker*, a tide-waiter

---

[1] *London in the Eighteenth Century*, p. 237.
[2] *Citizen of the World*, Letter 77.　　　　[3] *Rambler*, No. 116.

at *Yarmouth*, was married to Mrs *Cackle*, a widow lady of great accomplishments, and that as soon as the ceremony was performed they set out in a post-chaise for *Yarmouth*. . . . Whence it arises that on the day of marriage all agree to call thus openly for honours, I am not able to discover. Some, perhaps, think it kind, by a publick declaration, to put an end to the hopes of rivalry and the fears of jealousy, to let parents know that they may set their daughters at liberty whom they have locked up for fear of the bridegroom, or to dismiss to their counters and their offices the amorous youths that had been used to hover round the dwelling of the bride." [1] But Mr Timothy Mushroom gives another solution. Timothy had professed to have been much edified by this *Idler*, and " sent transcripts of it to all the couples that transgressed your principles for the next fortnight. I hoped that they were all vexed, and pleased myself with imagining their misery. But short is the triumph of malignity. I was married last week to Miss *Mohair*, the daughter of a salesman ; and, at my first appearance after the wedding night, was asked by my wife's mother whether I had sent our marriage to *The Advertiser* ? I endeavoured to show how unfit it was to demand the attention of the publick to our domestick affairs ; but she told me, with great vehemence, ' That she would not have it thought to be a stolen match ; that the blood of the *Mohairs* should never be disgraced ; that her husband had served all the parish officers but one ; that she had lived five-and-thirty years at the same house, had paid every body twenty shillings in the pound, and would have me know, though she was not as fine and as flaunting as Mrs *Gingham*, the deputy's wife, she was not ashamed to tell her name, and would show her face with the best of them, and since I had married her daughter——'
At this instant entered my father-in-law, a grave man, from whom I expected succour ; but, upon hearing the

[1] *Idler*, No. 12.

case, he told me, ' That it would be very imprudent to miss such an opportunity of advertising my shop ; and that when notice was given of my marriage, many of my wife's friends would think themselves obliged to be my customers.' I was subdued by clamour on one side, and gravity on the other, and shall be obliged to tell the town, that *three days ago* Timothy Mushroom, *an eminent oilman in* Sea-Coal-Lane, *was married to Miss* Polly Mohair *of* Lothbury, *a beautiful young lady, with a large fortune."* [1] It is to be hoped, for Timothy's sake, that Mrs Mushroom did not inherit all the qualities of Mrs Mohair.

The experiences of Betty Broom, a domestic servant, do not give any more favourable impression of the shop-keeper's home life ; but it must be remembered that her introductions were only to " the families of mean trades-men." It was the practice of her first master " to hire a chaise on *Sunday,* and spend half the wages of the week on *Richmond Hill* ; of *Monday* he commonly lay half in bed, and spent the other half in merriment ; *Tuesday* and *Wednesday* consumed the rest of his money ; and three days every week were passed in extremity of want by us who were left at home, while my master lived on trust at an alehouse. . . . I was then maid to a hatter's wife. There was no want to be dreaded, for they lived in perpetual luxury. My mistress was a diligent woman, and rose early in the morning to set the journeymen to work ; my master was a man much beloved by his neighbours, and sat at one club or other every night. I was obliged to wait on my master at night, and on my mistress in the morning. He seldom came home before two, and she rose at five. I could no more live without sleep than without food, and therefore entreated them to look out for another servant. My next removal was to a linen-draper's, who had six children. My mistress, when I first entered the house, in-formed me that I must never contradict the children, nor

[1] *Idler,* No. 28.

suffer them to cry. I had no desire to offend, and readily promised to do my best. But when I gave them their breakfast I could not help all first ; when I was playing with one in my lap, I was forced to keep the rest in expectation. That which was not gratified always resented the injury with a loud outcry, which put my mistress in a fury at me, and procured sugar-plums to the child. I could not keep six children quiet, who were bribed to be clamorous ; and was therefore dismissed, as a girl honest but not good-natured. I then lived with a couple that kept a petty shop of remnants and cheap linen. I was qualified to make a bill, or keep a book ; and being therefore often called, at a busy time, to serve the customers, expected that I should now be happy in proportion as I was useful. But my mistress appropriated every day part of the profit to some private use, and, as she grew bolder in her thefts, at last deducted such sums that my master began to wonder how he sold so much and gained so little. She pretended to assist his inquiries, and began, very gravely, to hope that *Betty was honest, and yet those sharp girls were apt to be light-fingered.* You will believe that I did not stay there much longer." [1] After this Betty " became under-maid at the house of a mercer in *Cornhill*, whose son was his apprentice. The young gentleman used to sit late at the tavern, without the knowledge of his father ; and I was ordered by my mistress to let him in silently to his bed under the counter, and to be very careful to take away his candle. The hours which I was obliged to watch, whilst the rest of the family was in bed, I considered as supernumerary, and, having no business assigned for them, thought myself at liberty to spend them my own way : I kept myself awake with a book, and for some time liked my state the better for this opportunity of reading. At last, the upper-maid found my book, and showed it to my mistress, who told me that wenches like

[1] *Idler*, No. 26.

N

me might spend their time better ; that she never knew any of the readers that had good designs in their heads ; that she could always find something else to do with her time than to puzzle over books ; and did not like that such a fine lady should sit up for her young master. This was the first time that I found it thought criminal or dangerous to know how to read. I was dismissed decently, lest I should tell tales, and had a small gratuity above my wages." [1] After a much more pleasant period of service " with a gentlewoman of a small fortune, who died of a fever " and " of whom I shall say no more, than that her servant wept upon her grave," Betty took service with the family of an East India director ; but " my behaviour was so different, as they said, from that of a common servant, that they concluded me a gentlewoman in disguise, and turned me out in three weeks, on suspicion of some design which they could not comprehend." [2]

Do we not admire the art with which Johnson indicates the sterling good sense of this charity schoolgirl, and her superiority to her employers ?

Another tradesman to whom we are introduced is Mr Treacle, who makes much complaint of Mrs Treacle [3] : " She walks all the morning sauntering about the shop with her arms through her pocket-holes, or stands gaping at the door-sill, and looking at every person that passes by. She is continually asking me a thousand frivolous questions about every customer that comes in and goes out ; and all the while that I am entering anything in my day-book, she is lolling over the counter, and staring at it, as if I was only scribbling or drawing figures for her amusement. . . . In the afternoons I am sure likewise to have her company, except she is called upon by some of her acquaintance : and then, as we let out all the upper

[1] *Idler*, No. 29.   [2] *Ibid.*
[3] *Ibid.*, No. 15. This paper is said to have been contributed by an unknown correspondent.

part of our house, and have only a little room backwards
for ourselves, they either keep such a chattering, or else
are calling out every moment to me, that I cannot mind
my business for them. . . . But you will pity me much
more when I tell you the manner in which we generally
pass our *Sundays*. In the morning she is commonly too
ill to dress herself to go to church ; she therefore never
gets up till noon ; and, what is still more vexatious, keeps
me in bed with her, when I ought to be busily engaged in
better employment. It is well if she can get her things on
by dinner-time ; and when that is over, I am sure to be
dragged out by her, either to *Georgia*, or *Hornsey Wood*,
or the *White Conduit House*. Yet even these near excursions are so very fatiguing to her, that, besides what it
costs me in tea and hot rolls, and syllabubs, and cakes for
the boy, I am frequently forced to take a hackney-coach,
or drive them out in a one-horse chair. At other times, as
my wife is rather of the fattest, and a very poor walker,
besides bearing her whole weight on my arm, I am obliged
to carry the child myself."

But *audi alteram partem*. " I am the unfortunate wife
of the grocer whose letter you published about ten weeks
ago " (writes Mrs Treacle), " in which he complains, like
a sorry fellow, that I loiter in the shop with my needle-
work in my hand, and that I oblige him to take me out
on *Sundays*, and keep a girl to look after the child. Sweet
Mr *Idler*, if you did but know all, you would give no encouragement to such an unreasonable grumbler. I brought
him three hundred pounds, which set him up in a shop,
and bought in a stock, on which, with good management,
we might live comfortably ; but now I have given him a
shop, I am forced to watch him and the shop too. I will
tell you, Mr *Idler*, how it is. There is an alehouse over the
way with a ninepin alley, to which he is sure to run when
I turn my back, and there loses his money, for he plays
at ninepins as he does everything else. While he is at this

favourite sport, he sets a dirty boy to watch his door, and call him to his customers ; but he is long in coming, and so rude when he comes, that our custom falls off every day. Those who cannot govern themselves, must be governed. I have resolved to keep him for the future behind his counter, and let him bounce at his customers if he dares. . . . On a Sunday, it is true, I make him walk abroad, and sometimes carry the child ; I wonder who should carry it ? But I never take him out till after church-time, nor would do it then, but that, if he is left alone, he will be upon the bed. On a *Sunday*, if he stays at home, he has six meals, and, when he can eat no longer, has twenty stratagems to escape from me to the alehouse ; but I commonly keep the door locked, till *Monday* produces something for him to do." [1]

Gluttony, sloth, purse - pride, frivolity, ostentation, luxury, ignorance, extravagance—such were the failings that Johnson debits to the London citizen and the citizen's wife. But the root of all was their want of an intelligent principle of conduct ; he regards this folk as part of " the innumerable multitudes that, having no motive of desire, or determination of will, lie freezing in perpetual inactivity, till some external impulse puts them in motion." [2] This applies particularly to the women, for the men, at any rate, were obliged to do something —viz. " to mind the shop." The Princess in *Rasselas* thought that " perhaps, what this world can give may be found in the modest habitations of middle fortune ; too low for great designs, and too high for penury and distress." [3] She visited these habitations, and this was her report : " She found their thoughts narrow, their wishes low, and their merriment often artificial. Their pleasures, poor as they were, could not be preserved pure, but were imbittered by petty competitions and worthless emula-

[1] *Idler*, No. 28. [2] *Ibid.*, No. 3.
[3] *Rasselas*, ch. xxiii.

tion. They were always jealous of the beauty of each
other ; of a quality to which solicitude can add nothing,
and from which detraction can take nothing away. Many
were in love with triflers like themselves, and many
fancied they were in love when in truth they were only
idle. Their affection was not fixed on sense or virtue,
and therefore seldom ended but in vexation. Their grief,
however, like their joy, was transient ; every thing floated
in their mind unconnected with the past or future, so that
one desire easily gave way to another, as a second stone
cast into the water effaces and confounds the circles of
the first." [1]

Addison, in an *Essay on the Pleasures of the Imagination*,[2] deplored the fact that " there are, indeed, but very
few who know how to be idle and innocent, or have
a relish of any pleasures that are not criminal ; every
diversion they take is at the expense of some one virtue or
another, and their very first step out of business is into
vice or folly." [3] Johnson's stories of City tradesmen who
try to escape from their environment confirm Addison's
view :

Ned Drugget, who dealt profitably in " remnants,"
pondered long on the pleasures of country life, but the
rural lodging which he at last secured was not very far
from Bow Bells. " I found him at *Islington*, in a room
which overlooked the high road, amusing himself with
looking through the window, which the clouds of dust
would not suffer him to open. . . . After dinner, company
came in, and Mr *Drugget* again repeated the praises of
the country, recommended the pleasures of meditation,
and told them, that he had been all the morning at the

---

[1] *Rasselas*, ch. xxv.   [2] *Spectator*, No. 411.
[3] Dr Blair supposed that Johnson would have said : " Their
very first step out of the regions of business is into the perturba-
tion of vice, or the vacuity of. folly " (Boswell's *Life of Johnson*
(Birkbeck Hill), iii. 172).

window, counting the carriages as they passed before him." [1]

Mr Ginger, the master of a large and splendid shop, and with the shrievalty in sight, became enamoured of the stage and stage-players ; henceforth he neglected his business. He even perpetrated a tragedy, which contained a character called Bombulus. " It is well for me " (wrote Mrs Deborah Ginger), " that I know how to keep a book, for of late he is scarcely ever in the way. Since one of his friends told him that he had a genius for tragick poetry, he has locked himself in an upper room six or seven hours a day ; and, when I carry him any paper to be read or signed, I hear him talking vehemently to himself, some- times of love and beauty, sometimes of friendship and virtue, but more frequently of liberty and his country. I would gladly, Mr *Idler*, be informed what to think of a shopkeeper, who is incessantly talking about liberty ? a word, which, since his acquaintance with polite life, my husband has always in his mouth ; he is, on all occasions, afraid of our liberty, and declares his resolution to hazard all for liberty. What can the man mean ? I am sure he has liberty enough ; it were better for him and me if his liberty was lessened. He has a friend, whom he calls a critick, that comes twice a week to read what he is writing. This critick tells him that his piece is a little irregular, but that some detached scenes will shine prodigiously, and that in the character of *Bombulus* he is wonderfully great. My scribbler then squeezes his hand, calls him the best of friends, thanks him for his sincerity, and tells him that he hates to be flattered. I have reason to believe that he seldom parts with his dear friend without lending him two guineas, and am afraid that he gave bail for him three days ago. . . . When he was behind his counter, he used to be brisk, active, and jocular, like a man that knew what he was doing, and did not fear to look another in

[1] *Idler*, No. 16.

the face; but, among wits and criticks, he is timorous and awkward, and hangs down his head at his own table." [1]

Dick Minim, apprentice to a brewer, inherited a large fortune in the stocks, which enabled him to escape for ever from the City and "commence" critic. Dick's career as a critic was not wholly unsuccessful, but his utterances were not startlingly original. [2]

Sam Softly was bred a sugar-baker, and, like Dick, succeeded to a fortune and retired early from business. Sam spent his life of leisure in driving-excursions, and visiting the stately homes of England, where he made fatuous remarks on the statuary and furniture. "Had *Sam*, as Nature intended, contentedly continued in the calmer and less conspicuous pursuits of sugar-baking, he might have been a respectable and useful character. At present he dissipates his life in a specious idleness, which neither improves himself nor his friends. Those talents which might have benefited society, he exposes to contempt by false pretensions. He affects pleasures which he cannot enjoy, and is acquainted only with those subjects on which he has no right to talk, and which it is no merit to understand." [3]

Tim Wainscot's son was taken early into his father's shop, and "for four years was diligent and sedate, entered the shop before it was opened, and when it was shut, always examined the pins of the window." But, upon an unlucky day (writes Wainscot senior), "a visit was paid him by two of his school-fellows who were placed, I suppose, in the army, because they were fit for nothing better: they came glittering in their military dress, accosted their old acquaintance, and invited him to a tavern, where, as I have been since informed, they ridiculed the meanness of commerce, and wondered how a youth of spirit could spend the prime of life behind a

[1] *Idler*, No. 47.   [2] *Ibid.*, Nos. 60, 61, *supra*, p. 114.
[3] *Ibid.*, No. 93 (by Thomas Warton).

counter." So the shop became odious to Wainscot junior, who also ceased to be competent therein. " He now openly declares his resolution to be a gentleman ; says that his soul is too great for a counting-house ; ridicules the conversation of city taverns ; talks of new plays, and boxes and ladies ; gives duchesses for his toasts ; carries silver, for readiness, in his waistcoat-pocket ; and comes home at night in a chair, with such thunders at the door, as have more than once brought the watchmen from their stands. . . . All this is very provoking ; and yet all this might be borne, if the boy could support his pretensions. But, whatever he may think, he is yet far from the accomplishments which he has endeavoured to purchase at so dear a rate. I have watched him in publick places. He sneaks in like a man that knows he is where he should not be ; he is proud to catch the slightest salutation, and often claims it where it is not intended. Other men receive dignity from dress, but my booby looks always more meanly for his finery. Dear Mr *Idler*, tell him what must at last become of a fop, whom pride will not suffer to be a trader, and whom long habits in a shop forbid to be a gentleman." [1]

" *Dick Serge* was a draper in Cornhill, and passed eight years in prosperous diligence without any care, but to keep his books, or any ambition but to be in time an alderman : but then, by some unaccountable resolution in his understanding, he became enamoured of wit and humour, despised the conversation of pedlars and stock-jobbers, and rambled every night to the regions of gayety, in quest of company suited to his taste. The wits at first flocked about him for sport, and afterwards for interest ; some found their way into his books, and some into his pockets ; the man of adventure was equipped from his shop for the pursuit of a fortune ; and he had sometimes the honour to have his security accepted when his friends

[1] *Idler*, No. 95.

were in distress. Elated with these associations, he soon learned to neglect his shop ; and having drawn his money out of the funds, to avoid the necessity of teasing men of honour for trifling debts, he has been forced to retire hither " (*i.e.* to the Fleet Prison) " till his friends can procure him a post at Court." [1]

We draw the moral " once in the City, always in the City," or, at least, "of" the City. The poor wights who tried to escape (and who shall blame them ?) from this stifling atmosphere of ledgers and counting-houses, and set up as authors or virtuosos or fine gentlemen, incurred the contempt both of those they wished to join and of those they wished to leave.

Their friends in the City—the Deborah Gingers and Tim Wainscots—could not comprehend the desire to migrate, for they had a poor opinion of fashionable folk. Thus spake Mrs Bombasin, " the great silk-mercer's lady," to Zosima, the " daughter of a country gentleman," who applied for her maid's place : " Are you the young woman, says she, that are come to offer yourself ? It is strange when people of substance want a servant, how soon it is the town-talk. But they know they shall have a belly-full that live with me. Not like people at the other end of the town, we dine at one o'clock. But I never take any body without a character ; what friends do you come of ? I then told her that my father was a gentleman, and that we had been unfortunate.—A great misfortune, indeed, to come to me, and have three meals a day !—So your father was a gentleman, and you are a gentlewoman, I suppose— such gentlewomen !—Madam, I did not mean to claim any exemptions, I only answered your inquiry.—Such gentle- women ! people should set their children to good trades, and keep them off the parish. Pray go to the other end of the town, there are gentlewomen, if they would pay their debts. I am sure we have lost enough by gentlewomen.

[1] *Adventurer*, No. 53.

Upon this, her broad face grew broader with triumph, and I was afraid she would have taken me for the pleasure of continuing her insult; but happily the next word was, Pray, Mrs Gentlewoman, troop down stairs.—You may believe I obeyed her." [1]

The " relict of Prune the grocer " would have found in Madam Bombasin a congenial spirit. Mrs Prune's hand and fortune were sought by Leviculus, a needy fortune-hunter: " He soon grew familiar to her dialect, and in a few weeks heard, without any emotion, hints of gay clothes and empty pockets; concurred in many sage remarks on the regard due to people of property; and agreed with her in detestation of the ladies at the other end of the town, who pinched their bellies to buy fine laces, and then pretended to laugh at the city." [2]

Goldsmith made the pawnbroker's widow at Vauxhall express this same brutal contempt for genteel poverty in her retort to Mrs Tibbs. " Mrs Tibbs wondered how people could pretend to know the polite world, who had received all their rudiments of breeding behind a counter; to which the other replied, that though some people sat behind counters, yet they could sit at the head of their own tables too, and carve three good dishes of hot meat whenever they thought proper, which was more than some people could say for themselves, that hardly knew a rabbit and onions from a green goose and gooseberries." [3] It must be admitted that Mrs Tibbs had invited this castigation, but Goldsmith permitted her to vanquish her opponent by showing a superior knowledge of the world, and especially by abusing the Vauxhall viands; thus " the widow was fairly conquered in point of politeness." Probably the City dame would lower her colours when it came to an encounter with one of greater social preten-sions. She was, indeed, apt to boast of her familiarity

[1] *Rambler*, No. 12.   [2] *Ibid.*, No. 182.
[3] *Citizen of the World*, Letter 71.

with the West End, and talk of " her visits at great houses, where she happened to know the cookmaid." [1] If she hated, it was because she was excluded. *Oderint dum metuant* would have been Johnson's sentiment.

It is no accident that these " women in the city "—Mrs Mohair, Mrs Prune, Mrs Bombasin—appear in Johnson's pages as odious creatures. That they *were* odious was his deliberate opinion. " ' High people, Sir (said he), are the best ; take a hundred ladies of quality, you'll find them better wives, better mothers, more willing to sacrifice their own pleasure to their children than a hundred other women. Tradeswomen (I mean the wives of tradesmen) in the city, who are worth from ten to fifteen thousand pounds, are the worst creatures upon the earth, grossly ignorant, and thinking viciousness fashionable.' . . . BOSWELL. ' The notion of the world, Sir, however is, that the morals of women of quality are worse than those in lower stations.' JOHNSON. ' Yes, Sir, the licentiousness of one woman of quality makes more noise than that of a number of women in lower stations ; then, Sir, you are to consider the malignity of women in the city against women of quality, which will make them believe anything of them, such as that they call their coachmen to bed. No, Sir, so far as I have observed, the richer ladies are, they are the better instructed and the more virtuous.' " [2]

" There is nothing in trade," said Johnson, " connected with an enlarged mind." So we may conclude this chapter by inquiring whether this judgment was afterwards modified by his friendship with Henry Thrale the brewer, for so many years Johnson's kind host and generous friend. In the social strata of the eighteenth century Thrale is rather difficult to classify. His father was a self-made man ; " he worked for six shillings a week for twenty years in the great brewery, which afterwards was

[1] *Rambler*, No. 189.
[2] Boswell's *Life of Johnson* (Birkbeck Hill), iii. 353, 354.

his own." [1] But the son was sent to the university, and, by virtue of a relationship to the Cobham family, " was bred up at Stowe, and Stoke, and Oxford, and every genteel place " and was " a very handsome and well-accomplished gentleman." [2] Yet Thrale "stuck to the shop "; he became " unaccountably attached " to his business, and to the house in the Borough adjoining his brewery. In fact, when choosing a bride he made it a *sine qua non* that she should reside there.[3]

Johnson simply regarded his friend as *rara avis in terris*, an exception that proved his rule. Applauding one of Thrale's remarks, he exclaimed : " That was elegantly said of my master, and nobly said, and not in the vulgar way we have been saying it. And where, madam, will you find another man in trade who will make such a speech— who will be capable of making such a speech ? " [4] Here it may be noted how loyally both Johnson and Mrs Thrale (" of good Welsh extraction ") stood by Thrale in his business difficulties. Johnson, in a letter, expounds the true policy of the brewery : " The first consequence of our late trouble ought to be, an endeavour to brew at a cheaper rate ; an endeavour not violent and transient, but steady and continual, prosecuted with total contempt of censure or wonder, and animated by resolution not to stop while more can be done." [5] Mrs Thrale in Thrale's absence exerted herself more practically to regain his wholesale customers : " Careless, of the ' Blue Posts,' has turned refractory, and applied to Hoare's people, who have sent him in their beer. I called on him to-day, however, and by dint of an unwearied solicitation (for I kept him at the

[1] *Autobiography of Mrs Piozzi* (Abraham Hayward), i. 7, 8.
[2] *Ibid.*, 10, 11.
[3] Having myself been born and brought up in a brewery house, I respect Thrale for this fidelity.
[4] *Diary of Madame d'Arblay*, 26th September 1778.
[5] *Autobiography of Mrs Piozzi* (Abraham Hayward), i. 73.

coach side a full half-hour), I got his order for six butts more as the final trial." [1] Hers was indeed

" γυναικὸς ἀνδρόβουλον ἐλπίζον κέαρ."
" A woman's manly-minded, hopeful heart."

On Thrale's death Johnson found the duties of executorship by no means distasteful ; he was loath to give up his occupation of brewer. " All were well pleased to find themselves secured, and the brewhouse *decently*, though not *very* advantageously disposed of, except dear Doctor Johnson, who found some odd delight in signing drafts for hundreds and for thousands, to him a new, and as it appeared delightful occupation. When all was nearly over, however, I cured his honest heart of its incipient passion for trade, by letting him into *some*, and *only* some, of its mysteries." [2]

But when the brewery was finally sold, these were Mrs Thrale's reflections: " ' 'Tis over now, tho', and I'll clear my head of it and all that belongs to it ; I will go to church, give God thanks, receive the Sacrament and forget the frauds, follies, and inconveniences of a commercial life this day.' " [3]

We call to mind that younger son in *The Rambler* [4] whose successful career as a haberdasher enabled him to recover his family estate. " He soon afterwards solicited the office of sheriff, from which all his neighbours were glad to be reprieved, but which he regarded as a resumption of ancestral claims, and a kind of restoration to blood after the attainder of a trade."

So we see that trade was a convenient ladder for gaining, or regaining, the heights of gentility ; it could be kicked away when it had served its purpose. Mrs Thrale sold her brewery and all its " mysteries " to Messrs Barclay & Perkins for £135,000.

[1] *Autobiography of Mrs Piozzi* (Abraham Hayward), i. 70.
[2] *Ibid.*, ii. 48.   [3] *Ibid.*, i. 146.   [4] No. 192, *supra*, p. 182.

6. THE SCHOLAR'S AWKWARDNESS IN SOCIETY

" We see a world of pains taken, and the best years of life spent in collecting a set of thoughts in a college for the conduct of life, and, after all, the man so qualified shall hesitate in a speech to a good suit of clothes, and want common sense before an agreeable woman." STEELE, *Tatler*, No. 30.

THE 33rd *Idler*, written by Thomas Warton of Trinity College, Oxford, purports to be "the *Journal* of a *Senior Fellow*, or *Genuine Idler* just transmitted from *Cambridge*." Four days are accounted for, and the reader receives a general impression of riding, drinking, eating, backgammon, stories in common-room, gout, whist and snuff. We may reasonably discount this story of a Cambridge don written by an Oxford don; but if we turn to an eminent and witty Oxonian's researches about his own university in the eighteenth century,[1] and especially his chapter on "College Life," we may conclude that Thomas Warton's satire is not far from the truth. Mr Godley mentions one other occupation—college business, a matter of perennial interest and a frequent occasion of intrigues and quarrels.[2]

Oxford and Cambridge were isolated from the world. As the City was separated from Westminster, and the country from London, so the Fellows and Scholars of the universities lived lives of their own, apart from the interests of fashion, politics, trade and sport; for even the fury of Oxford's Jacobitism died down after the accession of George III. And there was a peculiar condition of their existence that added to their oddness and eccentricity: "In a College life the society of woemen is wanting,—men grow splenetick."[3] (Now they seem to be

---

[1] *Oxford in the Eighteenth Century* (A. D. Godley).

[2] In this also Cambridge did not differ from Oxford. See Winstanley's *The University of Cambridge in the Eighteenth Century*.

[3] The Rev. Charles Simeon, quoted in Joseph Farington's *Diary*, 13th September 1805.

growing " splenetick " owing to an *excess* of the " society of woemen.")

Lord Chesterfield and Samuel Johnson were very different characters, but both constantly pointed out how poor a figure the scholar made in social life. It was one of Chesterfield's obsessions that Philip Stanhope might develop into a pedant. He was anxious for his son to unite " the knowledge of a Scholar, with the manners of a Courtier ; and to join, what is seldom joined in any of my countrymen, Books and the World. They are commonly twenty years old before they have spoken to any body above their Schoolmaster, and the Fellows of their College. If they happen to have learning, it is only Greek and Latin ; but not one word of Modern History, or Modern Languages. Thus prepared, they go abroad, as they call it ; but, in truth, they stay at home all the while ; for being very awkward, confoundedly ashamed, and not speaking the languages, they go into no foreign company, at least none good." [1] " A man of the best parts, and the greatest learning, if he does not know the World by his own experience and observation, will be very absurd ; and consequently very unwelcome in company. He may say very good things ; but they will probably be so ill-timed, misplaced, or improperly addressed, that he had much better hold his tongue. . . . He puts some people out of countenance ; he shocks others ; and frightens all, who dread what may come out next." [2] " A learned parson, rusting in his cell at Oxford or Cambridge, will reason admirably well upon the nature of man . . . and yet, unfortunately, he knows nothing of man." [3] " At nineteen I left the university of Cambridge, where I was an absolute pedant : when I talked my best, I quoted Horace ; when I aimed at being facetious, I quoted

---

[1] Lord Chesterfield's *Letters to his Son*, No. 118.
[2] *Ibid.*, No. 198.
[3] *Ibid.*, No. 245.

Martial; and when I had a mind to be a fine gentleman,
I talked Ovid." [1]

All these sentiments might have been approved by
Johnson, but what did he think when he read the following
passage?—" There is a man, whose moral character, deep
learning, and superior parts, I acknowledge, admire, and
respect; but whom it is so impossible for me to love, that
I am almost in a fever whenever I am in his company.
His figure (without being deformed) seems made to disgrace or ridicule the common structure of the human
body. His legs and arms are never in the position which,
according to the situation of his body, they ought to be
in; but constantly employed in committing acts of
hostility upon the graces. He throws anywhere, but
down his throat, whatever he means to drink; and only
mangles what he means to carve. Inattentive to all the
regards of social life, he mis-times or mis-places every
thing. He disputes with heat, and indiscriminately;
mindless of the rank, character, and situation of those
with whom he disputes: absolutely ignorant of the
several gradations of familiarity or respect; he is exactly
the same to his superiors, his equals, and his inferiors;
and therefore, by a necessary consequence, absurd to two
of the three. Is it possible to love such a man? No. The
utmost I can do for him is to consider him as a respectable
Hottentot." [2] Did Johnson say to himself, " De te Fabula
narratur "? Dr Birkbeck Hill was sure that this " respectable Hottentot " was not Johnson; Johnson himself
considered that the portrait was of George Lord Lyttelton.
But Boswell writes: " The character of ' a respectable
Hottentot ' in Lord Chesterfield's letters has been generally understood to be meant for Johnson, and I have no
doubt that it was." [3] Boswell's opinion on a contemporary

---

[1] Lord Chesterfield's *Letters to his Son*, No. 229.
[2] *Ibid.*, No. 212.
[3] Boswell's *Life of Johnson* (Birkbeck Hill), i. 266.

matter is not to be lightly rejected. And when we read the passage, do we not instinctively think of Johnson ?

Leaving it to persons of greater erudition to decide who was Chesterfield's "Hottentot," we may observe that Johnson's "Hottentots" display four principal failings or infirmities : (1) Shyness ; (2) Arrogance ; (3) an excessive Sprightliness, or Airiness ; (4) a want of Humanity. Their shyness and arrogance are complementary or reciprocal ; they are the ὑπερβολή and ἔλλειψις by which learned men miss the golden mean of ease and goodbreeding. " A man of letters for the most part spends, in the privacies of study, that season of life in which the manners are to be softened into ease, and polished into elegance ; and, when he has gained knowledge enough to be respected, has neglected the minuter arts by which he might have pleased. When he enters life, if his temper be soft and timorous, he is diffident and bashful, from the knowledge of his defects ; or if he was born with spirit and resolution, he is ferocious and arrogant, from the consciousness of his merit : he is either dissipated by the awe of company, and unable to recollect his reading, and arrange his arguments ; or he is hot and dogmatical, quick in opposition, and tenacious in defence, disabled by his own violence, and confused by his haste to triumph." [1] I think we need not doubt which of these two opposite dispositions (if there must be a choice) would have commended itself to Johnson.

Verecundulus [2] was one of those unfortunate beings who are " dissipated by the awe of company." At the university he had a " shining career, and returned home covered with academical laurels, and fraught with criticism and philosophy. The wit and the scholar excited curiosity, and my acquaintance was solicited by innumerable invitations." But at his first dining-out his sensations were dreadful.

[1] *Rambler*, No. 14. [2] *Ibid.*, No. 157.

"I was blasted with a sudden imbecility, I was quelled by some nameless power which I found impossible to be resisted. My sight was dazzled, my cheeks glowed, my perceptions were confounded ; I was harassed by the multitude of eager salutations, and returned the common civilities with hesitation and impropriety ; the sense of my own blunders increased my confusion, and, before the exchange of ceremonies allowed me to sit down, I was ready to sink under the oppression of surprise ; my voice grew weak, and my knees trembled." A kindly clergyman sought to draw him out, but unfortunately he drew him out too far, and the company was bored by the volubility with which Verecundulus engaged "in the explication and defence of the Newtonian philosophy." [1] But worse things befell the youth when he joined the ladies after dinner. "When I sat down I considered that something pretty was always said to ladies, and resolved to recover my credit by some elegant observation or graceful compliment. I applied myself to the recollection of all that I had read or heard in praise of beauty, and endeavoured to accommodate some classical compliment to the present occasion. I sunk into profound meditation, revolved the characters of the heroines of old, considered whatever the poets have sung in their praise, and, after having borrowed and invented, chosen and rejected a thousand sentiments, which, if I had uttered them, would not have been understood, I was awakened from my dream of learned gallantry by the servant who distributed the tea." The climax of this unhappy scholar's misfortunes was soon to be reached : "I suffered the saucer to drop from my hand. The cup was broken, the lap-dog was scalded, a brocaded petticoat was stained, and the whole assembly was thrown into disorder. I now considered all hopes of reputation was at an end, and while they were consoling and assisting one another, stole away in silence."

[1] *Supra*, p. 186.

As regards the opposite vice of arrogance, Johnson writes : " It is too common for those who have been bred to scholastick professions, and passed much of their time in academies where nothing but learning confers honours, to disregard every other qualification, and to imagine that they shall find mankind ready to pay homage to their knowledge, and to crowd about them for instruction. They therefore step out from their cells into the open world with all the confidence of authority and dignity of importance ; they look round about them at once with ignorance and scorn on a race of beings to whom they are equally unknown and equally contemptible, but whose manners they must imitate, and with whose opinions they must comply, if they desire to pass their time happily among them." [1] Johnson excuses this arrogance of pedantry by pointing out " the natural recurrence of the mind to its common employment. . . . But because we are seldom so far prejudiced in favour of each other, as to search out for palliations, this failure of politeness is imputed always to vanity ; and the harmless collegiate, who, perhaps, intended entertainment and instruction, or at worst only spoke without sufficient reflection upon the character of his hearers, is censured as arrogant or overbearing, and eager to extend his renown, in contempt of the convenience of society, and the laws of conversation." [2]

The illusions fostered by a brilliant university career are illustrated by the fable of Gelaleddin of Bassora,[3] who was " consulted by his fellow-students as an oraculous guide, and admitted as a competent auditor to the conferences of the sages." (We may infer that he was sometimes invited into common-rooms.) Gelaleddin was so puffed up that he refused a professorship, and upon the following considerations :—" ' If I am thus eminent,' said

[1] *Rambler*, No. 137.   [2] *Ibid.*, No. 173.
[3] *Idler*, No. 75.

he, ' in the regions of literature, I shall be yet more conspicuous in any other place ; if I should now devote myself to study and retirement I must pass my life in silence, unacquainted with the delights of wealth, the influence of power, the pomp of greatness, and the charm of elegance, with all that man envies and desires, with all that keeps the world in motion, by the hope of gaining or the fear of losing it. I will therefore depart to *Tauris*, where the Persian monarch resides in all the splendour of absolute dominion.' " To Tauris, accordingly, he proceeded, and " began to display his acquisitions " : but the poorer classes (to whom he belonged) " have no leisure to be pleased with eloquence ; they heard his arguments without reflection, and his pleasantries without a smile. . . . He then frequented places of publick resort, and endeavoured to attract notice by the copiousness of his talk. The sprightly were silenced, and went away to censure, in some other place, his arrogance and his pedantry ; and the dull listened quietly for a while, and then wondered why any man should take pains to obtain so much knowledge which would never do him good." As for the viziers, " he was sometimes admitted to their tables, where he exerted his wit, and diffused his knowledge ; but he observed that where, by endeavour or accident, he had remarkably excelled, he was seldom invited a second time." Disappointed, he returned to his university ; " but he who had been neglected at *Tauris*, was not much regarded at *Bassora* ; he was considered as a fugitive, who returned only because he could live in no other place."

A sad history of failure—but how conditions have improved ! Translate Gelaleddin to modern England, and imagine him a brilliant Balliol graduate of Jowett's day. The Master would have heartily encouraged him to become " more conspicuous in another place." His humble origin would have been no impediment ; and he would probably have risen to be a Cabinet Minister, or at least a *puisne* judge. And, supposing him unsuccessful in politics or law, we may picture him consoled with a fellowship at All Souls—still much regarded at Bassora, and keeping in touch with Tauris. For, whatever be the faults of our age, we find it certainly more feasible than did the men of Johnson's time to " join Books and the World."

But scholars were liable to contract a worse vice than arrogance or conceit ; they were apt to develop a positive inhumanity. There is something almost appalling in Johnson's description of Gelidus : " He has totally divested himself of all human sensations ; he has neither eye for beauty, nor ear for complaint ; he neither rejoices at the good fortune of his nearest friend, nor mourns for any publick or private calamity. Having once received a letter, and given it his servant to read, he was informed, that it was written by his brother, who, being shipwrecked, had swum naked to land, and was destitute of necessaries in a foreign country. Naked and destitute ! says Gelidus, reach down the last volume of meteorological observations, extract an exact account of the wind, and note it carefully in the diary of the weather. The family of Gelidus once broke into his study, to show him that a town at a small distance was on fire, and in a few moments a servant came to tell him that the flame had caught so many houses on both sides, that the inhabitants were confounded, and began to think of rather escaping with their lives than saving their dwellings. What you tell me, says Gelidus, is very probable, for fire naturally acts in a circle." [1] And so Johnson moralises on Gelidus : " Thus lives this great philosopher, insensible to every spectacle of distress, and unmoved by the loudest call of social nature, for want of considering that men are designed for the succour and comfort of each other ; that though there are hours which may be laudably spent upon knowledge not immediately useful, yet the first attention is due to

[1] *Rambler*, No. 24.

practical virtue." Goldsmith's astronomer was of the
same breed as Gelidus : "*Saturday*. The moon is, I find,
at her old pranks. Her appulses, librations and other
irregularities, indeed amaze me. My daughter too is this
morning gone off with a grenadier. No way surprising.
I was never able to give her a relish for wisdom." [1]

Men of learning were sometimes guilty of a greater
offence than becoming shy and breaking tea-cups. Shyness evokes pity, but the manners of one who is " terribly
at ease " are the subject of dislike and ridicule. " Nothing
is more despicable than the airiness and jocularity of a
man bred to severe science, and solitary meditation. To
trifle agreeably is a secret which schools cannot impart ;
that gay negligence and vivacious levity, which charm
down resistance wherever they appear, are never attainable by him who, having spent his first years among
the dust of libraries, enters late into the gay world with
an unpliant attention and established habits. . . . If
he attempts the softer arts of pleasing, and endeavours
to learn the graceful bow and the familiar embrace, the
insinuating accent and the general smile, he will lose the
respect due to the character of learning without arriving
at the envied honour of doing any thing with elegance
and facility." [2]

In his *Lives*, Johnson applies this truth to the case of
Edmund Smith (or Neale): " When he came to London,
his way of life connected him with the licentious and dissolute ; and he affected the airs and gaiety of a man of
pleasure ; but his dress was always deficient ; scholastick
cloudiness still hung about him ; and his merriment was
sure to produce the scorn of his companions." [3]

---

[1] *Citizen of the World*, Letter 92. [2] *Rambler*, No. 173.
[3] *Lives of the Poets* (Smith). We are told of another poet that
he made more successful efforts : " When he had opportunities
of mingling with mankind, he cleared himself . . . from great
part of his scholastick rust " (*ibid.*, Broome).

In *The Rambler* we find two scholars who point the same moral—Euphues and Gelasimus. " Euphues, with great parts and extensive knowledge, has a clouded aspect, and ungracious form ; yet it has been his ambition, from his first entrance into life, to distinguish by particularities in his dress, to outvie beaux in embroidery, to import new trimmings, and to be foremost in the fashion. Euphues has turned on his exterior appearance, that attention which would always have produced esteem, had it been fixed upon his mind ; and though his virtues and abilities have preserved him from the contempt which he has so diligently solicited, he has, at least, raised one impediment to his reputation ; since all can judge of his dress, but few of his understanding ; and many who discern that he is a fop, are unwilling to believe that he can be wise." [1]

The portraiture of Gelasimus is more elaborate : " *Gelasimus* passed the first part of his life in academical privacy and rural retirement, without any other conversation than that of Scholars, grave, studious and abstracted as himself. He cultivated the mathematical science with indefatigable diligence, discovered many useful theorems, discussed with great accuracy the resistance of fluids, and though his priority was not generally acknowledged, was the first who fully explained all the properties of the catenarian curve.

" Learning, when it rises to eminence, will be observed in time, whatever mists may happen to surround it. *Gelasimus*, in his forty-ninth year, was distinguished by those who have the rewards of knowledge in their hands, and called out to display his acquisitions for the honour of his country, and add dignity by his presence to philosophical assemblies. As he did not suspect his unfitness for common affairs, he felt no reluctance to obey the invitation, and what he did not feel he had yet too much honesty to feign. He entered into the world as a larger

[1] *Rambler*, No. 24.

and more populous college, where his performances would be more publick, and his renown further extended ; and imagined that he should find his reputation universally prevalent, and the influence of learning everywhere the same.

" His merit introduced him to splendid tables and elegant acquaintance ; but he did not find himself always qualified to join in the conversation. He was distressed by civilities, which he knew not how to repay, and entangled in many ceremonial perplexities, from which his books and diagrams could not extricate him. He was sometimes unluckily engaged in disputes with ladies, with whom algebraic axioms had no weight, and saw many whose favour and esteem he could not but desire, to whom he was very little recommended by his theories of the tides, or his approximations to the quadrature of the circle.

" *Gelasimus* did not want penetration to discover that no charm was more generally irresistible than that of easy facetiousness and flowing hilarity. He saw that diversion was more frequently welcome than improvement ; that authority and seriousness were rather feared than loved ; and that the grave scholar was a kind of imperious ally, hastily dismissed when his assistance was no longer necessary. He came to a sudden resolution of throwing off those cumbrous ornaments of learning which hindered his reception, and commenced a man of wit and jocularity. Utterly unacquainted with every topick of merriment, ignorant of the modes and follies, the vices and virtues of mankind, and unfurnished with any ideas but such as *Pappus* and *Archimedes* had given him, he began to silence all inquiries with a jest instead of a solution, extended his face with a grin, which he mistook for a smile, and in the place of a scientifick discourse, retailed in a new language, formed between the college and the tavern, the intelligence of the newspaper." [1]

1 *Rambler*, No. 179.

In reading these *Ramblers* we bear in mind Johnson's own good opinion of himself as a " man of the world." " Why, Sir, I am a man of the world. I live in the world, and I take, in some degree, the colour of the world as it moves along. Your father is a judge in a remote part of the island, and all his notions are taken from the old world." [1] He considered himself " a very polite man." He had not " rusted in his cell " at Oxford, but had put his fortune to the test, and at the age of twenty-eight boldly invaded London. He compared himself (1754) with the Reverend Mr Meeke, a Fellow of Pembroke, and was not dissatisfied with the comparison. " On leaving him, Johnson said, ' I used to think Meeke had excellent parts, when we were boys together at the College : but, alas !

' " Lost in a convent's solitary gloom "

I remember, at the classical lecture in the Hall, I could not bear Meeke's superiority, and I tried to sit as far from him as I could, that I might not hear him construe.' [2] . . . I forgot to observe before, that when he left Mr Meeke (as I have told above), he added, ' About the same time of life, Meeke was left behind at Oxford to feed on a Fellowship, and I went to London to get my living : now, Sir, see the difference of our literary characters ! ' " [3]

The difference was great indeed. Meeke was a college don, whose name does not suggest arrogance. When the eighteenth-century don made his rare appearance in London circles, it was probable that he exhibited less arrogance than pedantry. Now Johnson's conversation was certainly guiltless of pedantry ; witness one of Mrs Thrale's anecdotes : " I asked him once concerning the conversation powers of a gentleman with whom I was

---

[1] Boswell's *Life of Johnson* (Birkbeck Hill), i. 427.
[2] *Ibid.*, i. 272.
[3] *Ibid.*, i. 274. (T. Warton's recollections of Johnson.)

myself unacquainted. ' He talked to me at the Club one day ' (replies our Doctor) 'concerning Catiline's conspiracy ; so I withdrew my attention, and thought about Tom Thumb.' " [1] But there are worse conversational offences than pedantry ; there was a failing more peculiar then to the schoolmaster than to the don—an overbearing and domineering behaviour.

Johnson never was a don, but he had been a schoolmaster ; and it must be admitted that in social intercourse his manners were often too pedagogic. Hayward too truly says of a letter to Mrs Thrale (which ought never to have been written) : " Johnson's letter is that of a coarse man who had always been permitted to lecture and dictate with impunity." [2] Horace Walpole writes : " With all the pedantry he had all the gigantic littleness of a country schoolmaster." [3] Walpole was *advocatus diaboli* ; but what says Boswell himself ? When Johnson had described the wife of a " respectable authour " as having " a bottom of good sense," and thereby excited the hilarity of his audience, " His pride could not bear that any expression of his should excite ridicule when he did not intend it ; he therefore resolved to assume and exercise despotick power, glanced sternly around, and called out in a strong tone, ' Where's the merriment ? ' " [4] But this is still more to my point : " No sooner did he, of whom we had been talking thus easily, arrive, than we were all as quiet as a school upon the entrance of the headmaster." [5]

Of Johnson it may be said that if there was a " Beadle within him," there was also a Dominie.

[1] *Autobiography of Mrs Piozzi* (Abraham Hayward), i. 292. Hayward adds : " In the margin is written ' Charles James Fox.' "

[2] *Autobiography of Mrs Piozzi* (Abraham Hayward), i. 247.

[3] *Memoirs of the Reign of George III.*, vol. iv., ch. 7.

[4] Boswell's *Life of Johnson* (Birkbeck Hill), iv. 99.

[5] *Ibid.*, iii. 332.

7. Women and their Education

" The world seems to have formed a universal conspiracy against
our understandings ; our questions are supposed not to expect
answers, our arguments are confuted with a jest, and we are
treated like beings who transgress the limits of our nature whenever we aspire to seriousness or improvement." Generosa's letter
to *Rambler* No. 126.

In a letter to Stella,[1] Swift wrote : " I will not meddle
with the Spectator, let him *fair-sex* it to the world's
end." What did Swift mean when he referred to
Addison as " fair-sexing " it ? I think he implied that
Addison's attitude towards women was one of admiring
but playful condescension. Take a passage in which the
expression occurs—Addison is writing of the rage of party:
" This is, in its nature, a male vice, and made up of many
angry and cruel passions, that are altogether repugnant
to the softness, the modesty, and those endearing qualities
which are natural to the fair sex. Women were formed
to temper mankind and soothe them into tenderness and
compassion ; not to set an edge upon their minds, and
blow up in them those passions which are too apt to rise
of their own accord. When I have seen a pretty mouth
uttering calumnies and invectives, what would I not have
given to have stopt it ! how have I been troubled to see
some of the finest features in the world grow pale, and
tremble with party-rage ! " This emotion makes the
hand of " the fierce and beautiful Penthesilea " to shake,
and a dish of tea is spilt on her petticoat, and so on.[2]
All the essays on Hoops [3] and Patches are written in the
" fair-sexing " vein, as also that exquisite one on *The
Exercise of the Fan*.[4] It is the mood of the indulgent
censor, which Addison could assume to perfection : " I

---

[1] 26th January 1711-1712.   [2] *Spectator*, No. 57.

[3] *E.g. Spectator*, No. 127 : " The fair sex are run into great
extravagancies," etc.

[4] *Spectator*, No. 102.

consider woman as a beautiful romantic animal, that may
be adorned with furs and feathers, pearls and diamonds,
ores and silks. . . . All this I shall indulge them ; but as
for the petticoat I have been speaking of, I neither can
nor will allow it." [1]

Will Honeycomb was a " fair-sexer." He permitted
himself, perhaps, too much the air of a conqueror—the
true " fair-sexer " should always conceal his consciousness
of superiority by a display of chivalrous devotion ; but, in
essentials, Will's view of the sex coincided with that of his
creator. He refers to " those dear confounded creatures,
women." " The women love a gay, lively fellow, and are
never angry at the railleries of one who is their known
admirer. I am always bitter upon them, but well with
them." [2] The " fair-sexer " has flourished ever since, and
is to be found in every rank of life. Miss Burney could
draw him in Sir Clement Willoughby [3] (a " fair-sexer "
with an exceptional sense of humour). The commercial
gentleman at Todgers's who was eloquent about the
Misses Pecksniff at the boarding-house feast was a " fair-
sexer "—" their rugged natures have been softened and
ameliorated that day, by the society of lovely woman " [4] ;
and so was Sir Willoughby Patterne, who " appreciated
Nature's compliment in the fair one's choice of you." [5]

Richardson was a celebrated exponent of this kind of
sentiment. He wrote the 97th *Rambler*, which Johnson
prefaced with the statement that its author " has enlarged
the knowledge of human nature, and taught the passions
to move at the command of virtue " ; but, in an edition
which I possess of Johnson's *Works*, at its conclusion I
find the following note :—" This paper was written by
Richardson, the author of *Clarissa*, *Pamela*, etc., and,
although mean and hacknied in style and sentiment,

[1] *Tatler*, No. 116.   [2] *Spectator*, No. 511.
[3] *Evelina*, Letter No. 13.   [4] *Martin Chuzzlewit*, ch. ix.
[5] *The Egoist*, ch. v.

was the only paper which had a great sale during the publication of *The Rambler*, in its original form. C."

Both as to its style and sentiment this annotator is right, nor can we applaud the public which gave Richardson's *Rambler* a great sale.

"In the time of the SPECTATOR," says Richardson, "modesty and diffidence, gentleness and meekness, were looked upon as the appropriate virtues and characteristick graces of the sex." In those days "the churches were almost the only places where single women were to be seen by strangers." "But some good often resulted, however improper might be their motives. . . . With what ardour have I seen watched for, the rising of a kneeling beauty ; and what additional charms has devotion given to her recommunicated features ! . . . To a man thus put into good humour by a pleasing object, religion itself looked more amiable. The MEN SEEKERS of the SPECTATOR's time loved the holy place for the object's sake, and loved the object for her suitable behaviour in it.[1] Reverence mingled with their love, and they thought that a young lady of such good principles must be addressed only by the man who at least made a show of good principles, whether his heart was yet quite right or not. Nor did the young lady's behaviour, at any time of the service, lessen this reverence. Her eyes were her own, her ears the preacher's."

---

[1] Contrast Steele's more masculine view of these "seekers " : " This jackanapes was fixed at the end of a pew, with the utmost impudence, declaring, by a fixed eye on that seat (where our beauty was placed) the object of his devotion. This obscene sight gave me all the indignation imaginable and I could attend to nothing but the reflection, that the greatest affronts imaginable are such as no one can take notice of " (*Guardian*, No. 65). Miss Jenny Simper frankly avows the motive of her church attendance : " I am a young woman, and have my fortune to make, for which reason I come constantly to church to hear divine service, and make conquests " (*Spectator*, No. 282).

Tennyson has drawn the same picture, but with fewer strokes :

> " She came to the village church
> And sat by a pillar alone,
> An angel watching an urn
> Wept over her, carv'd in stone ;
> And once, but once, she lifted her eyes,
> And suddenly, sweetly, strangely blush'd
> To find they were met by my own."

But Richardson's church-going youth was more fortunate than Tennyson's, and improved into a successful suitor. " She perhaps is not an absolute stranger to the passion of the young gentleman. His eyes, his assiduities, his constant attendance at a church, whither, till of late, he used seldom to come, and a thousand little observances that he paid her, had very probably first forced her to regard, and then inclined her to favour him." And when her hand is sought, " the fair-one is all resignation to her parents. Charming resignation, which inclination opposes not." So all ends well : " He applies to her parents therefore for a near day ; and thinks himself under obligation to them for the cheerful and affectionate manner with which they receive his agreeable application. With this prospect of future happiness, the marriage is celebrated. Gratulations pour in from every quarter. Parents and relations on both sides, brought acquainted in the course of the courtship, can receive the happy couple with countenances illumined, and joyful hearts." (Even the " in-laws " are friendly.) Such is virtuous love ; but as for " the youthful, the gay, the inconsiderate "—" the meteors of a day find themselves " (by a fine confusion of metaphors) " elbowed off the stage of vanity by other flutterers." [1]

What did Johnson really think of this *Rambler* ? We

[1] *Rambler*, No. 97.

know that, as a moralist, he was anti-Fielding [1] and
pro-Richardson, but his opinion of Richardson is also on
record, " that his love of continual superiority was such,
that he took care to be always surrounded by women,
who listened to him implicitly, and did not venture to
controvert his opinions." [2]

Was Johnson a "fair-sexer"? I am afraid he made some
excursions in the art, as will appear later in this chapter,
though (as we shall also see) his common sense appreciated
how much the "fair-sexer" exasperated intelligent women.
But let us first inquire what was his general attitude
towards the female sex. Were they wiser or more foolish,
more or less virtuous, stronger or weaker than men? And
(an important point) how ought they to be educated?

It was an age in which certain persons, who were
highly considered, held lowering views of women; when
elaborate and obsequious courtesy might be the mask of
a bitter contempt. " Women," wrote Lord Chesterfield,
" have, in general, but one object, which is their beauty;
upon which, scarce any flattery is too gross for them to
swallow." [3] " The innocent, but pleasing flattery of their
persons, however gross, is greedily swallowed, and kindly
digested; but a seeming regard for their understandings,
a seeming desire of, and deference for their advice, together with a seeming confidence in their moral virtues,
turns their heads entirely in your favour." [4] " Women
are much more like each other than men; they have,
in truth, but two passions, Vanity and Love; these are
their universal characteristics." [5] Nothing in Philip Stanhope's education was more important than that he should
comprehend woman's inferiority. " I will therefore, upon
this subject, let you into certain *Arcana*, that will be very

[1] *Supra*, p. 75.
[2] Boswell's *Life of Johnson* (Birkbeck Hill), v. 395, 396.
[3] *Letters to his Son*, No. 97.
[4] *Ibid.*, No. 151.   [5] *Ibid.*, No. 177.

useful for you to know, but which you must, with the utmost care, conceal ; and never seem to know. Women, then, are only children of a larger growth ; they have an entertaining tattle, and sometimes wit ; but for solid, reasoning good sense, I never in my life knew one that had it, or who reasoned or acted consequentially for four-and-twenty hours together. Some little passion or humour always breaks in upon their best resolutions. . . . A man of sense only trifles with them, plays with them, humours and flatters them, as he does with a sprightly, forward child ; but he neither consults them about, nor trusts them with serious matters ; though he often makes them believe that he does both ; which is the thing in the world that they are proud of ; for they love mightily to be dabbling in business (which, by the way, they always spoil) ; and being justly distrustful, that men in general look upon them in a trifling light, they almost adore that man who talks more seriously to them, and who seems to consult and trust them : I say, who seems ; for weak men really do, but wise ones only seem to do it. No flattery is too high or too low for them. . . . But these are secrets, which you must keep inviolably, if you would not, like Orpheus, be torn to pieces by the whole sex : on the contrary, a man, who thinks of living in the great world, must be gallant, polite, and attentive to please the women." [1] A strong and skilfully drawn indictment ! But, oddly enough, these inferior creatures and " children of a larger growth " do exercise a sort of sway, which derives from the weakness of men. " They have, from the weakness of men, more or less influence in all Courts : they absolutely stamp every man's character in the *beau monde*, and make it either current, or cry it down, and stop it in payments. It is, therefore, absolutely necessary to manage, please, and flatter them." [2] But whence proceeds this

[1] Lord Chesterfield's *Letters to his Son*, No. 129.
[2] *Ibid.*

strange power of puny woman ? Chesterfield, more
skilled in statecraft than psychology, neither solves, nor
even seems to appreciate, the problem.

Now there are *dicta* of Johnson's that do not show
more " uplift " than these of Chesterfield's—*e.g.* " a lady
seldom listens with attention to any praise but that of her
beauty." [1] Miss Burney chronicles : " Mrs Thrale then
told some other stories of his degrading opinion of us
poor fair sex ; I mean in general, for in particular he does
them noble justice." [2] (This was as to their intelligence.)
" Dr J. The truth is, women, take them in general, have no
idea of grace. Fashion is all they think of. I don't mean
Mrs Thrale and Miss Burney, when I talk of women !—
they are goddesses ! " [3] Johnson could be contemptuous
of women ; but he showed this sign of grace—that he
also pitied them.

Truly, they *ought* to be happy ; but they are not.
" A solitary philosopher would imagine ladies born with
an exemption from care and sorrow, lulled in perpetual
quiet, and feasted with unmingled pleasure ; for, what
can interrupt the content of those, upon whom one age
has laboured after another to confer honours, and accumulate immunities ; those to whom rudeness is infamy,
and insult is cowardice ; whose eye commands the brave,
and whose smile softens the severe ; whom the sailor
travels to adorn, the soldier bleeds to defend, and the poet
wears out life to celebrate ; who claim tribute from every
art and science, and for whom all who approach them
endeavour to multiply delights, without requiring from
them any return but willingness to be pleased. Surely,
among these favourites of nature, thus unacquainted
with toil and danger, felicity must have fixed her residence ; they must know only the changes of more vivid

---

[1] *Rambler*, No. 106.

[2] *Diary of Madame d'Arblay*, 26th August 1778.

[3] *Ibid.*, September 1778.

P

or more gentle joys ; their life must always move either to the slow or sprightly melody of the lyre of gladness ; they can never assemble but to pleasure, or retire but to peace." [1]

It is a fine effort of irony ; and Johnson proceeds to point out, in a less happy vein, some of the minor woes of women's lives that darken the picture : " It is impossible to supply wants as fast as an idle imagination may be able to form them, or to remove all inconveniencies by which elegance refined into impatience may be offended. None are so hard to please, as those who have been always courted with an emulation of civility. There are indeed some strokes which the envy of fate aims immediately at the fair. The mistress of *Catullus* wept for her sparrow many years ago, and lapdogs will be sometimes sick in the present age. The most fashionable brocade is subject to stains ; a pinner, the pride of *Brussels*, may be torn by a careless washer ; a picture may drop from a watch ; or the triumph of a new suit may be interrupted on the first day of its enjoyment, and all distinctions of dress unexpectedly obliterated by a general mourning." [2]

We feel that Addison would have done this better. Let us turn to another *Rambler*,[3] where Johnson is in earnest, expatiating on woman's peculiar share in the general misery of this life :

" The condition of the female sex has been frequently the subject of compassion to medical writers, because their constitution of body is such, that every state of life brings its peculiar diseases : they are placed, according to the proverb, between Scylla and Charybdis, with no other choice than of dangers equally formidable ; and whether they embrace marriage, or determine upon a single life, are exposed, in consequence of their choice, to sickness, misery, and death.

" It were to be wished that so great a degree of natural

[1] *Rambler*, No. 128.   [3] *Ibid.*   [3] No. 39.

infelicity might not be increased by adventitious and artificial miseries; and that beings, whose beauty we cannot behold without admiration, and whose delicacy we cannot contemplate without tenderness, might be suffered to enjoy every alleviation of their sorrows. But, however it has happened, the custom of the world seems to have been formed in a kind of conspiracy against them, though it does not appear but they had themselves an equal share in its establishment; and prescriptions which, by whomsoever they were begun, are now of long continuance, and by consequence of great authority, seem to have almost excluded them from content, in whatsoever condition they shall pass their lives.

"If they refuse the society of men, and continue in that state which is reasonably supposed to place happiness most in their own power, they seldom give those that frequent their conversation, any exalted notions of the blessing of liberty; for whether it be that they are angry to see with what inconsiderate eagerness other heedless females rush into slavery, or with what absurd vanity the married ladies boast the change of their condition, and condemn the heroines who endeavour to assert the natural dignity of their sex; whether they are conscious that like barren countries they are free, only because they were never thought to deserve the trouble of a conquest, or imagine that their sincerity is not always unsuspected, when they declare their contempt of men; it is certain, that they generally appear to have some great and incessant cause of uneasiness, and that many of them have at last been persuaded, by powerful rhetoricians, to try the life which they had so long contemned, and put on the bridal ornaments at a time when they least became them.

"What are the real causes of the impatience which the ladies discover in a virgin state, I shall perhaps take some other occasion to examine. That it is not to be envied for its happiness, appears from the solicitude with which it is avoided ; from the opinion universally prevalent among the sex, that no woman continues long in it, but because she is not invited to forsake it ; from the disposition always shown to treat old maids as the refuse of the world ; and from the willingness with which it is often quitted at last, by those whose experience has enabled them to judge at leisure, and decide with authority.

" Yet such is life, that whatever is proposed, it is much easier to find reasons for rejecting than embracing. Marriage, though a certain security from the reproach and solitude of antiquated virginity, has yet, as it is usually conducted, many disadvantages, that take away much from the pleasure which society promises, and might afford, if pleasures and pains were honestly shared, and mutual confidence inviolably preserved.

" The miseries, indeed, which many ladies suffer under conjugal vexations, are to be considered with great pity, because their husbands are often not taken by them as objects of affection, but forced upon them by authority and violence, or by persuasion and importunity, equally resistless when urged by those whom they have been always accustomed to reverence and obey ; and it very seldom appears that those who are thus despotick in the disposal of their children, pay any regard to their domestick and personal felicity, or think it so much to be inquired whether they will be happy, as whether they will be rich.

" It may be urged, in extenuation of this crime, which parents, not in any other respect to be numbered with robbers and assassins, frequently commit, that, in their estimation, riches and happiness are equivalent terms. They have passed their lives with no other wish than of adding acre to acre, and filling one bag after another, and imagine the advantage of a daughter sufficiently considered, when they have secured her a large jointure, and given her reasonable expectations of living in the midst of those pleasures with which she has seen her father and mother solacing their age.

" There is an economical oracle received among the prudential past of the world, which advises fathers *to marry their daughters, lest they should marry themselves* ; by which I suppose it is implied, that women left to their own conduct generally unite themselves with such partners as can contribute very little to their felicity. Who was the author of this maxim, or with what intention it was originally uttered, I have not yet discovered ; but imagine that however solemnly it may be transmitted, or however implicitly received, it can confer no authority which nature has denied ; it cannot license Titius to be unjust, lest Caia should be imprudent ; nor give right to imprison for life, lest liberty should be ill employed.

" That the ladies have sometimes incurred imputations which might naturally produce edicts not much in their favour, must be confessed by their warmest advocates ; and I have indeed seldom observed that when the tenderness or virtue of their parents has preserved them from forced marriage, and left them at large to chuse their own path in the labyrinth of life, they have made any great advantage of their liberty. They commonly take the opportunity of independence to trifle away youth and lose their bloom in a hurry of diversions, recurring in a succession too great to leave room for any settled reflection ; they see the world without gaining experience, and at last regulate their choice by motives trifling as those of a girl, or mercenary as those of a miser." [1]

So the " custom of the world " was against women, whether they married or remained single. And the " custom of the world," to which in this *Rambler* Johnson

[1] *Rambler*, No. 39.

conformed, was to make cheap fun of spinsters, to whom the world then gave neither career nor employment ; it was even the fashion " to treat old maids as the refuse of the world." A loveless marriage enforced by a mercenary parent held out poor prospects ; but if women were left to their own choice the result was scarcely any better. " They see the world without gaining experience, and at last regulate their choice by motives trifling as those of a girl, or mercenary as those of a miser." [1] One chooses a " Philotryphus, a man vain, glittering, and thoughtless as herself, who has spent a small fortune in equipage and dress, and was shining in the last suit for which his tailor would give him credit." Another succumbs to " Cotylus, the younger brother of a duke, a man without elegance of mien, beauty of person, or force of understanding ; who, while he courted her, could not always forbear allusions to her birth, and hints how cheaply she would purchase an alliance to so illustrious a family." [2]

Nor did Johnson, though he married for love himself, believe in love-matches, the unions of " twin-souls," or the junction of " affinities." " BOSWELL. ' Pray, Sir, do you not suppose that there are fifty women in the world, with any one of whom a man may be as happy, as with any woman in particular ? ' JOHNSON. ' Ay, Sir, fifty thousand.' BOSWELL. ' Then, Sir, you are not of opinion that certain men and certain women are made for each other ; and that they cannot be happy if they miss their counterparts.' [3] JOHNSON. ' To be sure not, Sir. I believe marriages would in general be as happy, and often more so, if they were all made by the Lord Chancellor, upon a due

---

[1] *Rambler*, No. 39.   [2] *Ibid.*

[3] It was said of Sir Thomas Browne's wife that she was " a lady of such symmetrical proportion to her worthy husband, both in the graces of her body and mind, that they seemed to come together by a kind of natural magnetism " (*Religio Medici*, edited by W. Nevison, M.A. (Preface)).

consideration of characters and circumstances, without the parties having any choice in the matter.' " [1]

In spite of all its dangers and disadvantages, and whatever trouble it might bring to woman, " Marriage," said Johnson, " is the best state for a man in general ; and every man is a worse man, in proportion as he is unfit for the married state." [2] Francis Quarles wrote :

> " The sacred academy of a man's life
> Is holy wedlock in a happy wife."

But if the wife is *not* happy the academy will lose its sacred character. It cannot be said that marriage, as presented by Johnson the Essayist, was a happy business, though it might still have its uses as a period of probation, or a school of virtue. " I am not so much inclined to wonder," wrote the *Rambler*, " that marriage is sometimes unhappy, as that it appears so little loaded with calamity." [3]

As for woman's virtue, Johnson held it to be weak and her conduct over-susceptible to influence : " It may be particularly observed of women, that they are for the most part good or bad, as they fall amongst those who practise vice or virtue ; and that neither education nor reason gives them much security against the influence of example. Whether it be that they have less courage to stand against opposition, or that their desire of admiration makes them sacrifice their principles to the poor pleasure of worthless praise, it is certain, whatever be the cause, that female goodness seldom keeps its ground

---

[1] Boswell's *Life of Johnson* (Birkbeck Hill), ii. 461. Like the Lord Chancellor in *Iolanthe* :
> " And in my Court I sit all day,
> Giving agreeable girls away."

[2] *Ibid.*, 457.

[3] *Rambler*, No. 45. The Princess Nekayah could give only a negative testimonial to marriage : " Marriage has many pains, but celibacy no pleasures " (*Rasselas*, ch. xxvi.).

against laughter, flattery, or fashion." [1] But if they are thus weak and easily beguiled, at whose door lies the fault ? Johnson confesses that man is responsible for the vanity of woman : " We see women universally jealous of the reputation of their beauty, and frequently look with contempt on the care with which they study their complexions, endeavour to preserve or to supply the bloom of youth, regulate every ornament, twist their hair into curls, and shade their faces from the weather. We recommend the care of their nobler part, and tell them how little addition is made by all their arts to the graces of the mind. But when was it known that female goodness or knowledge was able to attract that officiousness, or inspire that ardour, which beauty produces whenever it appears ? And with what hope can we endeavour to persuade the ladies, that the time spent on the toilet is vanity, when they have every moment some new conviction, that their interest is more effectually promoted by a riband well disposed, than by the brightest act of heroick virtue." [2]

Next we notice that though woman is weak and vain, and though this weakness and vanity is due to man's preference of beauty to intellect, Johnson demands a higher standard of chastity from the wife than from the husband. If the husband goes astray, it is almost always because the wife has been lacking in complaisance : " Confusion of progeny constitutes the essence of the crime ; and therefore a woman who breaks her marriage vows is much more criminal than a man who does it. A man, to be sure, is criminal in the sight of GOD : but he does not

[1] *Ibid.*, No. 70.

[2] *Rambler*, No. 66. " A fine face," says Pride in Goldsmith's allegory, " is already at the point of perfection ; and a fine lady should endeavour to keep it so : the impression it would receive from thought, would but disturb its whole economy " (*Citizen of the World*, Letter 76).

do his wife a very material injury, if he does not insult
her ; if, for instance, from mere wantonness of appetite, he
steals privately to her chambermaid. Sir, a wife ought not
greatly to resent this. I would not receive home a daughter
who had run away from her husband on that account.
A wife should study to retain her husband by more attention to please him. Sir, a man will not, once in a hundred
instances, leave his wife and go to a harlot, if his wife has
not been negligent of pleasing." [1] And here is another
reason why women should be the more virtuous sex : " If
we require more perfection from women than from ourselves, it is doing them honour. And women have not
the same temptations that we have : they may always
live in virtuous company ; men must mix in the world indiscriminately." [2] " ' Still, Doctor,' pleaded Mrs Knowles,
a Quaker lady, ' I cannot help thinking it a hardship
that more indulgence is allowed to men than to women.
It gives a superiority to men, to which I do not see how
they are entitled.' JOHNSON. ' It is plain, Madam, one or
other must have the superiority. As Shakespeare says,
" If two men ride on a horse, one must ride behind." ' " [3]
We seem here to reach *Realpolitik* in this discussion.

Johnson said of Milton : " There appears in his books
something like a Turkish contempt of females, as sub-
ordinate and inferior beings. . . . He thought women
made only for obedience, and man only for rebellion." [4]
As to man's right to rebel, Johnson and Milton were poles
asunder ; but, as to woman's duty to obey, the foregoing

---

[1] Boswell's *Life of Johnson* (Birkbeck Hill), ii. 56. Johnson reiter-
ates this argument, that the chastity of women is all-important
" as all property depends upon it " (*ibid.*, 457) ; but is it not
equally applicable to the man who commits adultery with a
married woman, and thereby occasions " confusion of progeny " ?

[2] Boswell's *Life of Johnson* (Birkbeck Hill), iii. 287.

[3] *Ibid.* Boswell then developed an argument that even in heaven
the inferiority of women must continue, to which Johnson assented.

[4] *Lives of the Poets* (Milton).

extracts from Johnson's writings and sayings are not out
of harmony with the chorus in *Samson Agonistes* :

> " Therefore God's universal law
> Gave to the man despotic power
> Over his female in due awe,
> Nor from that right to part an hour,
> Smile she or lour."

What did Johnson think of the mind of woman, and
its capability of being trained ? " I have often thought,"
wrote Addison, " there has not been sufficient pains taken
in finding out proper employments and diversions for the
fair ones. Their amusements seem contrived for them,
rather as they are women, than as they are reasonable
creatures ; and are more adapted to the sex than the
species." [1] " I have often wondered that learning is not
thought a proper ingredient in the education of a woman
of quality or fortune. Since they have the same improv-
able minds as the male part of the species, why should
they not be cultivated by the same methods ? why
should reason be left to itself in one of the sexes and be
disciplined with so much care in the other." [2] And, as to
their reason requiring discipline, we remember the " young
university disputant " who put his argument to a lady in
a syllogism, " upon which, as he informed us with some
heat, she granted him both the major and the minor, but
denied him the conclusion." [3]

This female logician flourished in 1716. By the middle
of the century there had been a considerable advance
in the education of women ; writing in 1751,[4] Johnson
observes that scholars were not aware of this progress:
" There prevails among men of letters an opinion, that all
appearance of science is particularly hateful to women ;
and that therefore, whoever desires to be well received in

[1] *Spectator*, No. 10.
[3] *Freeholder*, No. 32.
[2] *Guardian*, No. 155.
[4] *Rambler*, No. 173.

female assemblies, must qualify himself by a total rejection of all that is serious, rational, or important ; must consider argument or criticism, as perpetually interdicted ; and devote all his attention to trifles, and all his eloquence to compliment. Students often form their notions of the present generation from the writings of the past, and are not very early informed of those changes which the gradual diffusion of knowledge, or the sudden caprice of fashion, produces in the world. Whatever might be the state of female literature in the last century, there is now no longer any danger lest the scholar should want an adequate audience at the tea-table ; and whoever thinks it necessary to regulate his conversation by antiquated rules, will be rather despised for his futility than caressed for his politeness." Miss Burney, twenty-eight years later, records that, " Dr Johnson was talking to her [Mrs Thrale] and Sir Philip Jennings of the amazing progress made of late years in literature by the women. He said he was himself astonished at it, and told them he well remembered when a woman who could spell a common letter was regarded as all accomplished ; but now they vied with the men in everything." [1]

One reason why education was necessary for women, was that when their minds were unoccupied they turned to mischief—to the detriment of themselves and men. " Perhaps the most powerful fancy might be unable to figure the confusion and slaughter that would be produced by so many piercing eyes and vivid understandings, turned loose at once upon mankind, with no other business than to sparkle and intrigue, to perplex and to destroy." [2] And here it may be mentioned that Johnson did not consider card-playing to be an occupation worthy of a rational creature. Cards were then all-important, and not least important in the estimation of ladies. When Cleora came

[1] *Diary of Madame d'Arblay*, 20th June 1779.
[2] *Rambler*, No. 85.

up from the country to stay with her aunt, after the first civilities she was told " what pity it was to have kept so fine a girl so long in the country ; for the people who did not begin young, seldom dealt their cards handsomely, or played them tolerably." [1] " Papa made me a drudge at whist," writes another lady in this *Rambler*, " till I was tired of it ; and, far from wanting a head, Mr Hoyle, when he had not given me above forty lessons, said I was one of his best scholars." " There is a set of ladies who have outlived most animal pleasures, and, having nothing rational to put in their place, solace with cards the loss of what time has taken away, and the want of what wisdom, having never been courted, has never given." [2] Another *Idler*, discussing the feasibility of women combining against men, suggests that " the gamesters, if they were united, would make a formidable body ; and, since they consider men only as beings that are to lose their money, they might live together without any wish for the officiousness of gallantry or the delights of diversified conversation." [3]

Cards were a poor substitute for the " diversified conversation " in which Johnson delighted.[4] No one more

---

[1] *Rambler*, No. 15.   [2] *Idler*, No. 39.

[3] *Ibid.*, No. 37. Addison frequently satirizes female card-players : " The day lies heavy upon her, until the play-season returns, when, for half-a-dozen hours together, all her faculties are employed in shuffling, cutting, dealing, and sorting out a pack of cards, and no ideas to be discovered, in a soul which calls itself rational, excepting little square figures of painted and spotted paper. Was the understanding, that divine part in our composition, given for such an use ? Is it thus we improve the greatest talent human nature is endowed with ? What would a superior being think, were he shown this intellectual faculty in a female gamester, and, at the same time, told that it was by this she was distinguished from brutes, and allied to angels ? " (*Guardian*, No. 120).

[4] Later in his life (1773) he said : " I am sorry I have not learnt to play at cards. It is very useful in life ; it generates kindness and consolidates society."

enjoyed the society of clever women, and no one more severely censured those who, like Mrs Busy, neglected their daughters' education.[1] As for erudition, " he maintained to me, contrary to the common notion, that a woman would not be the worse wife for being learned." [2] (Boswell, following the " common notion," differed on this point.) But a wife might be too learned for a husband's comfort : " supposing (said he) a wife to be of a studious or argumentative turn, it would be very troublesome ; for instance,—if a woman should continually dwell upon the subject of the Arian heresy." [3] He was jealous of female authors, who took part in the " epidemical conspiracy for the destruction of paper " ; " but as the times past are said to have seen a nation of Amazons, who drew the bow and wielded the battle-axe, formed encampments and wasted nations ; the revolution of years has now produced a generation of Amazons of the pen, who with the spirit of their predecessors have set masculine tyranny at defiance, asserted their claim to the regions of science, and seem resolved to contest the usurpations of virility." [4] And he disliked female pedants, " the deep-read *Misothea*, who declared herself the inexorable enemy of ignorant pertness, and puerile levity ; and scarcely condescended to make tea, but for the linguist, the geometrician, the astronomer, or the poet," [5] or Camilla, who " professed a boundless contempt for the folly, levity, ignorance, and impertinence of her own sex ; and very frequently expressed her wonder that men of learning or experience could submit to trifle away life with beings incapable of solid thought." [6]

It cannot be said that Johnson the Essayist appears as

---

[1] *Supra*, p. 161.

[2] Boswell's *Life of Johnson* (Birkbeck Hill), ii. 76.

[3] *Ibid.*, iv. 32.

[4] *Adventurer*, No. 115.

[5] *Rambler*, No. 113.   [6] *Ibid.*, No. 115.

an enthusiast for female education. He welcomed wit
and intellect in woman, whenever he found them. Mrs
Thrale and Miss Burney were exceptional—they were
" goddesses " ; and of Mrs Elizabeth Carter he wrote :
" I have composed a Greek epigram on Eliza, and think
she ought to be celebrated in as many different languages
as Louis le Grand." [1] But I have an impression that he
would have considered higher education was for the few,
and that for the average woman Mrs Malaprop's standard
was not so very much amiss : " Observe me, Sir Anthony.
I would by no means wish a daughter of mine to be a
progeny of learning ; I don't think so much learning becomes a young woman ; for instance, I would never let her
meddle with Greek, or Hebrew, or Algebra, or Simony,
or Fluxions, or Paradoxes, or such inflammatory branches
of learning ; neither would it be necessary for her to
handle any of your mathematical, astronomical, diabolical
instruments. . . . But, above all, Sir Anthony, she should
be mistress of orthodoxy, that she might not mis-spell,
and mis-pronounce words so shamefully as girls usually
do ; and likewise that she might reprehend the true
meaning of what she is saying."

And probably Mrs Malaprop would have agreed with
the advisers of Perdita, who was annoyed by their insist-
ing that " the great end of female education is to get a
husband." [2] This is rather a hard saying, to which we
need not subscribe ; nevertheless it must be admitted
that the problem of female education is still complicated
and conditioned by the institution of matrimony, and
ever will be. It is possible not to appreciate this, and
yet to be very skilful in organizing hockey for young
ladies.

Clever women, at least, had Johnson's sympathy ; he

[1] *E. Carter : A Woman of Wit and Wisdom* (Alice C. C. Gaussen),
p. 165.

[2] *Adventurer*, No. 74.

could enter into their feelings, and realize (no woman better) how they tired of men's dreary, laboured compliments, and condescending, patronizing airs, and spurned the calm assumption that they must be men's intellectual inferiors. This attitude could be resented. Generosa's castigation of the astronomer, for instance, was well merited ; and, as this lady was mistress of a very caustic wit, I will conclude this chapter by transcribing her letter to the Rambler [1] :

" SIR,

"Your great predecessor, the SPECTATOR, endeavoured to diffuse among his female readers a desire of knowledge ; nor can I charge you, though you do not seem equally attentive to the ladies, with endeavouring to discourage them from any laudable pursuit. But, however either he or you may excite our curiosity, you have not yet informed us how it may be gratified. The world seems to have formed an universal conspiracy against our understandings ; our questions are supposed not to expect answers, our arguments are confuted with a jest, and we are treated like beings who transgress the limits of our nature whenever we aspire to seriousness or improvement.

" I inquired yesterday of a gentleman eminent for astronomical skill, what made the day long in Summer, and short in Winter ; and was told that nature protracted the days in summer, lest ladies should want time to walk in the park ; and the nights in winter, lest they should not have hours sufficient to spend at the card-table.

" I hope you do not doubt but I heard such information with just contempt, and I desire you to discover to this great master of ridicule, that I was far from wanting any intelligence which he could have given me. I asked the question with no other intention than to set him free from

[1] *Rambler*, No. 126.

the necessity of silence, and gave him an opportunity of mingling on equal terms with a polite assembly, from which, however uneasy, he could not then escape, by a kind introduction of the only subject on which I believed him able to speak with propriety.

"I am, etc.,

"GENEROSA."

VI

JOHNSON THE REFORMER

" Scarce can our fields, such crowds at Tyburn die,
With hemp the gallows and the fleet supply."
London. A Poem.

IT remains to record Johnson's condemnation of
certain social evils and cruelties of his day. In all
that he wrote on these matters his humanity is conspicuous. He was a scholar and an author, not a practical
social reformer; but his views were far in advance of
his age, and he has provided many a valuable argument
for the reformers that came after him.

The Frequency of Capital Punishment

The procession to Tyburn was such a common spectacle
that the wretched criminals evoked little pity:

" Have ye not seye som tyme a pale face,
Among a pres, of him that hath be lad
Toward his deth, whereas him gat no grace,
And such a colour in his face hath had,
Men mighte knowe his face that was bystad,
Amonges alle the faces in that route ? "

Chaucer's lines might have been written under Hogarth's
picture of Tom Idle going to execution. Men of education,
like Boswell and George Selwyn, would sit in a grand
stand opposite the gallows watching the victim slowly
choke to death. But Johnson was shocked that such
numbers must suffer the extreme penalty, and that such
multitudes of crimes should be punishable with death.
On this matter he wrote a notable *Rambler* :

Q   241

" On the days when the prisons of this city are emptied
into the grave, let every spectator of the dreadful procession put the same question to his own heart.[1] Few
among those that crowd in thousands to the legal massacre,
and look with carelessness, perhaps with triumph, on the
utmost exacerbations of human misery, would then be
able to return without horrour and dejection. For, who
can congratulate himself upon a life passed without some
act more mischievous to the peace or prosperity of others,
than the theft of a piece of money ?

" It has always been the practice, when any particular
species of robbery becomes prevalent and common, to endeavour its suppression by capital denunciations. Thus,
one generation of malefactors is commonly cut off and
their successors frighted into new expedients ; the art
of thievery is augmented with greater variety of fraud,
and subtilized to higher degrees of dexterity, and more
occult methods of conveyance. The law then renews the
pursuit in the heat of anger, and overtakes the offender
again with death. By this practice capital inflictions are
multiplied, and crimes, very different in their degree of
enormity, are equally subjected to the severest punishment that man has the power of exercising upon man.

" The lawgiver is undoubtedly allowed to estimate the
malignity of an offence, not merely by the loss or pain
which single acts may produce, but by the general alarm
and anxiety arising from the fear of mischief, and in-
security of possession : he therefore exercises the right
which societies are supposed to have over the lives of those
that compose them, not simply to punish a transgression,
but to maintain order, and preserve quiet ; he enforces
those laws with severity that are most in danger of violation, as the commander of a garrison doubles the guard
on that side which is threatened by the enemy.

[1] *I.e.* " who knows whether this man is not less culpable than
me ? "

" This method has been long tried, but tried with so little success, that rapine and violence are hourly increasing, yet few seem willing to despair of its efficacy, and of those who employ their speculations upon the present corruption of the people, some propose the introduction of more horrid, lingering and terrifick punishments ; some are inclined to accelerate the executions ; some to discourage pardons ; and all seem to think that lenity has given confidence to wickedness, and that we can only be rescued from the talons of robbery by inflexible rigour and sanguinary justice.

" Yet since the right of setting an uncertain and arbitrary value upon life has been disputed, and since experience of past times gives us little reason to hope that any reformation will be effected by a periodical havock of our fellow-beings, perhaps it will not be useless to consider what consequences might arise from relaxations of the law, and a more rational and equitable adaptation of penalties to offences.

" Death is, as one of the ancients observes, τὸ τῶν φοβερῶν φοβερώτατον, of dreadful things the most dreadful; an evil, beyond which nothing can be threatened by sublunary power, or feared from human enmity or vengeance. This terrour should, therefore, be reserved as the last resort of authority, as the strongest and most operative of prohibitory sanctions, and placed before the treasure of life, to guard from invasion what cannot be restored. To equal robbery with murder is to reduce murder to robbery, to confound in common minds the gradations of iniquity, and incite the commission of a greater crime to prevent the detection of a less. If only murder were punished with death, very few robbers would stain their hands in blood ; but when, by the last act of cruelty, no new danger is incurred, and greater security may be obtained, upon what principle shall we bid them forbear ? . . .

" From this conviction of the inequality of the punishment to the offence, proceeds the frequent solicitation of pardons. They who would rejoice at the correction of a thief, are yet shocked at the thought of destroying him. His crime shrinks to nothing, compared with his misery; and severity defeats itself by exacting pity.

" The gibbet, indeed, certainly disables those who die upon it from infesting the community; but their death seems not to contribute more to the reformation of their associates, than any other method of separation. A thief seldom passes much of his time in recollection or anticipation, but from robbery hastens to riot, and from riot to robbery; nor, when the grave closes upon his companion, has any other care than to find another.

" The frequency of capital punishments, therefore, rarely hinders the commission of a crime, but naturally and commonly prevents its detection, and is, if we proceed only upon prudential principles, chiefly for that reason to be avoided. Whatever may be urged by casuists or politicians, the greater part of mankind, as they can never think that to pick the pocket and to pierce the heart is equally criminal, will scarcely believe that two malefactors so different in guilt can be justly doomed to the same punishment; nor is the necessity of submitting the conscience to human laws so plainly evinced, so clearly stated, or so generally allowed, but that the pious, the tender, and the just, will always scruple to concur with the community in an act which their private judgment cannot approve.

" He who knows not how often rigorous laws produce total impunity, and how many crimes are concealed and forgotten for fear of hurrying the offender to that state in which there is no repentance, has conversed very little with mankind. And whatever epithets of reproach or contempt this compassion may incur from those who confound cruelty with firmness, I know not whether any wise man would wish it less powerful, or less extensive. . . .

" All laws against wickedness are ineffectual, unless some will inform, and some will prosecute ; but till we mitigate the penalties for mere violations of property, information will always be hated, and prosecution dreaded. The heart of a good man cannot but recoil at the thought of punishing a slight injury with death ; especially when he remembers, that the thief might have procured safety by another crime, from which he was restrained only by his remaining virtue.

" The obligations to assist the exercise of publick justice are indeed strong ; but they will certainly be overpowered by tenderness for life. What is punished with severity contrary to our ideas of adequate retribution, will be seldom discovered ; and multitudes will be suffered to advance from crime to crime, till they deserve death, because, if they had been sooner prosecuted, they would have suffered death before they deserved it." [1]

IMPRISONMENT FOR DEBT

Misargyrus, the heartless rake, may have deserved that his extravagance and dissolute life should consign him to the Fleet. His punishment was embittered by remorse :

" Confinement of any kind is dreadful ; a prison is sometimes able to shock those, who endure it in a good cause : let your imagination, therefore, acquaint you, with what I have not words to express, and conceive, if possible, the horrours of imprisonment attended with reproach and ignominy, of involuntary association with the refuse of mankind, with wretches who were before too abandoned for society, but being now freed from shame

[1] *Rambler*, No. 114.

or fear are hourly improving their vices by consorting with each other." [1]

Misargyrus describes many of his fellow-captives, whose downfall is due to their own folly, " men whom prosperity could not make useful, and whom ruin cannot make wise : but there are among us many who raise different sensations, many that owe their present misery to the seductions of treachery, the strokes of casualty, or the tenderness of pity ; many whose sufferings disgrace society, and whose virtues would adorn it." [2] There was Serenus, " who might have lived in competence and ease," if he could " have looked without emotion on the miseries of another." Serenus offered himself as surety for a friend, but " the debtor, after he had tried every method which art or indigence could prompt, wanted either fidelity or resolution to surrender himself to prison, and left *Serenus* to take his place." [3] There was Candidus, who " gave bonds to a great value " as security for the conduct of a youth to whose father he had been under obligations. The youth stole money and fled, and " the consequence of his flight was the ruin of *Candidus* ; ruin surely undeserved and irreproachable, and such as the laws of a just government ought either to prevent or repair ; nothing is more inequitable than that one man should suffer for the crimes of another, for crimes which he neither prompted nor permitted, which he could neither foresee nor prevent." And there was Lentulus, whom one of his creditors arrested for debt, " but Lentulus instead of endeavouring secretly to pacify him by payment, gave notice to the rest, and offered to divide amongst them the remnant of his fortune : they feasted six hours at his expense, to deliberate on his proposal ; and at last determined, that, as he could not offer more than five

<hr>

[1] *Adventurer*, No. 41. Boswell says the papers signed Mysargyrus were written by Dr Bathurst.

[2] *Adventurer*, No. 53. [3] *Ibid.*, No. 62.

shillings in the pound, it would be more prudent to keep
him in prison, till he could procure from his relations the
payments of his debts." Of merciless creditors Misargyrus
says : " nor can I look with equal hatred upon him, who,
at the hazard of his life, holds out his pistol and demands
my purse, as on him who plunders under shelter of the
law, and by detaining my son or my friend in prison,
extorts from me the price of their liberty." [1]

Two *Idlers* deal with the same subject, wherein Johnson
not only describes the misery of these captives, but argues
how absurd and wasteful was the practice of imprisoning
for debt. " As I was passing lately under one of the gates
of the city, I was struck with horrour by a rueful cry,
which summoned me to remember the poor debtors." [2]
" If these, who thus rigorously exercise the power which
the law has put into their hands, be asked, why they
continue to imprison those whom they know to be unable
to pay them ? one will answer, that his debtor once lived
better than himself ; another, that his wife looked above
her neighbours, and his children went in silk clothes to
the dancing-school ; and another, that he pretended to
be a joker and a wit. Some will reply, that if they were
in debt, they should meet with the same treatment ;
some, that they owe no more than they can pay, and need
therefore give no account of their actions. Some will
confess their resolution, that their debtors shall rot in
jail ; and some will discover, that they hope, by cruelty,
to wring the payment from their friends." Johnson's heart
and reason revolt against these life sentences : " Since
poverty is punished among us as a crime, it ought at least

---

[1] *Adventurer*, No. 62.

[2] *Idler*, No. 22. " More useful still were the ' Box Men.' Eight
of them were appointed from the Charity Men ; their duty was
to stand at the grating over the boxes, imploring the charity of the
passer-by " (Sir W. Besant on the Prison of Ludgate, *London in
the Eighteenth Century*, p. 584).

to be treated with the same lenity as other crimes; the offender ought not to languish at the will of him whom he has offended, but to be allowed some appeal to the justice of his country. There can be no reason why any debtor should be imprisoned, but that he may be compelled to payment; and a term should therefore be fixed, in which the creditor should exhibit his accusation of concealed property. If such property can be discovered, let it be given to the creditor; if the charge is not offered, or cannot be proved, let the prisoner be dismissed." [1] In this *Idler*, also, he exposes the exactions to which prisoners are subjected: "He that once owes more than he can pay, is often obliged to bribe his creditor to patience, by increasing his debt. Worse and worse commodities, at a higher and higher price, are forced upon him; he is impoverished by compulsive traffic, and at last overwhelmed, in the common receptacles of misery, by debts, which, without his own consent, were accumulated on his head."

In the 38th *Idler* Johnson enlarges on the economic folly of the system, and the misery and depravity entailed upon its victims:

"Since the publication of the letter concerning the condition of those who are confined in gaol by their creditors, an inquiry is said to have been made, by which it appears that more than 20,000 are at this time prisoners for debt. . . . It seems to be the opinion of the later computists, that the inhabitants of *England* do not exceed 6,000,000, of which 20,000 is the three-hundredth part. What shall we say of the humanity of a nation that voluntarily sacrifices one in every three hundred to lingering destruction!

"The misfortunes of an individual do not extend their influence to many; yet, if we consider the effects of consanguinity and friendship, and the general reciprocation

[1] *Idler*, No. 22.

of wants and benefits, which make one man dear or necessary to another, it may reasonably be supposed, that every man languishing in prison gives trouble of some kind to two others who love or need him. By this multiplication of misery we see distress extended to the hundredth part of the whole society.

" If we estimate at a shilling a day, what is lost by the inaction and consumed in the support of each man thus chained down to involuntary idleness, the publick loss will rise in one year to £300,000 ; in ten years to more than a sixth part of our circulating coin.

" I am afraid that those who are best acquainted with the state of our prisons will confess that my conjecture is too near the truth, when I suppose that the corrosion of resentment, the heaviness of sorrow, the corruption of confined air, the want of exercise, and sometimes of food, the contagion of diseases, from which there is no retreat, and the severity of tyrants, against whom there can be no resistance, and all the complicated horrours of a prison, put an end every year to the life of one in four of those that are shut up from the common comforts of human life.

" Thus perish yearly 5000 men, overborne with sorrow, consumed by famine, or putrefied by filth. . . . Who would have believed till now, that of every *English* generation, 150,000 perish in our gaols ! that in every century, a nation eminent for science, studious of commerce, ambitious of empire, should willingly lose, in noisome dungeons, 500,000 of its inhabitants ; a number greater than has ever been destroyed in the same time by pestilence and the sword ! "

Then as to the wickedness of prisons,[1] " the misery of

[1] In *The Pickwick Papers*, ch. xlvii., written seventy-seven years after this *Idler*, Mr Perker thus exhorts Mr Pickwick to free Mrs Bardell—and himself—from the Fleet : " It enables you to take the very magnanimous revenge—which I know, my dear

gaols is not half their evil: they are filled with every corruption which poverty and wickedness can generate between them; with all the shameless and profligate enormities that can be produced by the impudence of ignominy, the rage of want, and the malignity of despair. In a prison the awe of the publick eye is lost, and the power of the law is spent; there are few fears, there are no blushes. The lewd inflame the lewd, the audacious harden the audacious. Every one fortifies himself as he can against his own sensibility, endeavours to practise on others the arts which are practised on himself; and gains the kindness of his associates by similitude of manners.

" Thus some sink amidst their misery, and others survive only to propagate villany. It may be hoped, that our lawgivers will at length take away from us this power of starving and depraving one another; but, if there be any reason why this inveterate evil should not be removed in our age, which true policy has enlightened beyond any former time, let those, whose writings form the opinions and the practices of their contemporaries, endeavour to transfer the reproach of such imprisonment from the debtor to the creditor, till universal infamy shall pursue the wretch whose wantonness of power, or revenge of disappointment, condemns another to torture and to ruin; till he shall be hunted through the world as an enemy to man, and find in riches no shelter from contempt."

On this *Idler* Sir Walter Besant makes the remark: " The writer was before his time; there were eighty years more of debtors' prisons before they were finally swept away." [1]

Sir, is one after your own heart—of releasing this woman from a scene of misery and debauchery, to which no man should ever be consigned, if I had my will, but the infliction of which on any woman, is even more frightful and barbarous."

[1] *London in the Eighteenth Century*, p. 565.

SLAVERY

There are two passages in *The Idler* in which Johnson's hatred of slavery makes itself felt. "Of black men," he writes, " the numbers are too great who are now repining under *English* cruelty "[1]; and in *The Indian's Speech to his Countrymen*,[2] " those invaders ranged over the continent, slaughtering in their rage those that resisted, and those that submitted, in their mirth. Of those that remained, some were buried in caverns, and condemned to dig metals for their masters ; some were employed in tilling the ground, of which foreign tyrants devour the produce ; and, when the sword and the mines have destroyed the natives, they supply their place by human beings of another colour, brought from some distant country to perish here under toil and torture."

On the subject of slavery, Johnson's spoken word agrees with his written: "He had always been very zealous against slavery in every form, in which I, with all deference, thought that he discovered ' a zeal without knowledge.' Upon one occasion, when in company with some very grave men at Oxford, his toast was, ' Here's to the next insurrection of the negroes in the West Indies.' His violent prejudice against our West Indian and American settlers appeared whenever there was an opportunity."[3]

The claim of a strong nation to make slaves of a weak nation was to Johnson " the claim of the vulture to the leveret, of the tiger to the fawn."

PROSTITUTION

Johnson, from long residence in the neighbourhood of Fleet Street and the Strand, and from his own acute

[1] *Idler*, No. 87.   [2] *Ibid.*, No. 81.
[3] Boswell's *Life of Johnson* (Birkbeck Hill), iii. 200. Johnson stigmatized Jamaica as " a den of tyrants and a dungeon of slaves " (*ibid.*, ii. 478). Whitefield called it " the suburbs of Hell."

powers of observation, knew all the seamy side of London life. There is a story of his carrying home on his back a poor destitute woman of the streets, and relieving her necessities; of another woman of the town, Bet Flint, he gave an amusing account, but described her as " generally slut and drunkard ; occasionally, whore and thief." [1] But, for all this, " Oh I loved Bet Flint ! "

In *Rambler* No. 107 he addresses himself " to the publick on behalf of those forlorn creatures, the women of the town ; whose misery here might satisfy the most rigorous censor, and whose participation of our common nature might surely induce us to endeavour, at least, their preservation from eternal punishment."

According to this *Rambler*, they all owed their downfall to the solicitations of gentlemen—and none to their own sinful inclinations. " These were all once, if not virtuous, at least innocent ; and might still have continued blameless and easy, but for the arts and insinuations of those whose rank, fortune, or education, furnished them with means to corrupt or to delude them." [2] Thus they had reached a desperate condition : " their sighs, and tears, and groans, are criminal in the eyes of their tyrants, the bully and the bawd, who fatten on their misery, and threaten them with want or a gaol, if they show the least design of escaping from their bondage." He thinks that, in this matter, prevention is better than cure. " To stop the increase of this deplorable multitude, is undoubtedly the first and most pressing consideration. To prevent evil is the great end of government, the end for which vigilance and severity are properly employed." In this essay Johnson does not proceed to explain what particular measures of vigilance and severity are to be employed. But on severity he placed reliance. "BOSWELL. 'So then,

---

[1] Boswell's *Life of Johnson* (Birkbeck Hill), iv. 103.
[2] He did however admit that " bad women multiply the seduction of youth, more rapidly than bad men seduce honest women."

Sir, you would allow of no irregular intercourse whatever between the sexes ? ' JOHNSON. ' To be sure I would not, Sir. I would punish it much more than it is done, and so restrain it. In all countries there has been fornication, as in all countries there has been theft ; but there may be more or less of the one, as well as of the other, in proportion to the force of the law. All men will naturally commit fornication, as all men will naturally steal. And, Sir, it is very absurd to argue, as has been often done, that prostitutes are necessary to prevent the violent effects of appetite from violating the decent order of life ; nay, should be permitted, in order to preserve the chastity of our wives and daughters. Depend upon it, Sir, severe laws, steadily enforced, would be sufficient against those evils, and would promote marriage.' " [1]

Very sad is the tale of Misella.[2] It was told to Johnson (according to Malone) by a poor girl under a tree in King's Bench Walk,[3] and perhaps such tales should be received with caution. Misella's story was that she was a gentleman's daughter and seduced by a wealthy relative, who afterwards abandoned her. Unable to obtain employment, she was driven to the streets for a living. " In this abject state I have now passed four years, the drudge of

[1] Boswell's *Life of Johnson* (Birkbeck Hill), iii. 17. Of such legislation the difficulty lies in the enforcement. " An Act making adultery a capital offence without benefit of clergy, and making other acts of immorality punishable with three months' imprisonment, was passed on the 10th May, 1650. . . . The provisions of the Act were, however, too far advanced for the public sentiment of that age, which, then as now, rebelled against laws making crimes of offences against morality. . . . Trials under the Act where it was impossible to obtain a conviction became yearly more rare, and in 1657 died out altogether in the metropolitan county " (*The Interregnum*, Inderwick, pp. 33-38). Still more hopeless is the task of enforcing legislation against acts that are not even immoral—as is now proved in the United States.

[2] *Rambler*, Nos. 170, 171.

[3] Boswell's *Life of Johnson* (Birkbeck Hill), i. 223*n*.

extortion and the sport of drunkenness; sometimes the property of one man, and sometimes the common prey of accidental lewdness; at one time tricked up for sale by the mistress of a brothel, at another begging in the streets to be relieved from hunger by wickedness; without any hope in the day but of finding some whom folly or excess may expose to my allurements, and without any reflections at night, but such as guilt and terrour impress upon me.

"If those who pass their days in plenty and security, could visit for an hour the dismal receptacles to which the prostitute retires from her nocturnal excursions, and see the wretches that lie crowded together, mad with intemperance, ghastly with famine, nauseous with filth, and noisome with disease; it would not be easy for any degree of abhorrence to harden them against compassion, or to repress the desire which they must immediately feel to rescue such numbers of human beings from a state so dreadful." [1]

Misella (or Johnson ?) does propound a remedy for the evil: "It is said, that in *France* they annually evacuate their streets, and ship their prostitutes and vagabonds to their colonies. If the women that infest this city had the same opportunity of escaping from their miseries, I believe very little force would be necessary; for who among them can dread any change ? Many of us indeed are wholly unqualified for any but the most servile employments, and those perhaps would require the care of a magistrate to hinder them from following the same practices in another country; but others are only precluded by infamy from reformation, and would gladly be delivered on any terms from the necessity of guilt, and the tyranny of chance. For my chance, I should exult at the privilege of banishment, and think myself happy in any region that should restore me once again to honesty and peace." [2]

[1] *Rambler*, No. 171.   [2] *Ibid.*

Misella might " exult at the privilege of banishment " ;
but what colony would have welcomed her and her
unfortunate sisters as immigrants ?

VIVISECTION

The eighteenth century was an age of " sensibility,"
and certain cultivated persons of this period earned the
name of " Feelers " ; but this did not mean that they
felt very much for the sufferings of animals. Bear-baiting
and cock-fighting were favourite sports : Hogarth's brush
has painted horrors of inhumanity in his *Four Stages of
Cruelty*. Nor was there yet much sympathy for the
victims of the vivisector.

Addison often refers to this practice, but only once
with disapproval. On infidels : " another knows how to
write a receipt, or cut up a dog, and forthwith argues
against the immortality of the soul." [1] Here is the passage
in which he makes his protest (as well he might) ; he is
writing on the instinct of animals : " the violence of this
natural love is exemplified by a very barbarous experiment ; which I shall quote at length as I find it in an
excellent author, and hope my readers will pardon the
mentioning such an instance of cruelty, because there
is nothing can so effectually show the strength of that
principle in animals, of which I am speaking. ' A person
who was well skilled in dissections, opened a bitch, and
as she lay in the most exquisite tortures, offered her one
of her young puppies, which she immediately fell a licking ;
and for the time seemed insensible of her own pain : on
the removal, she kept her eyes fixt on it, and began a
wailing sort of cry, which seemed rather to proceed from
the loss of her young one, than the sense of her own
torments.' " [2] In two other cases his commentator, Bishop
Hurd, makes the protest which he thinks Addison himself

[1] *Tatler*, No. 111.   [2] *Spectator*, No. 120.

should have made: " You have often seen a dog opened,
to observe the circulation of the blood, or make any
other useful inquiry." [1]   " There are, besides the above-
mentioned, innumerable retainers to physic, who, for want
of other patients, amuse themselves with the stifling of
cats in an air-pump, cutting up dogs alive, or impaling
of insects upon the point of a needle for microscopical
observations." [2]

Johnson could ridicule " Feelers " ; but his humanity
was real, and extended from man to beast.   This is his
indictment of vivisectors :

" The *Idlers* that sport only with inanimate nature may
claim some indulgence ; if they are useless, they are still
innocent : but there are others, whom I know not how
to mention without more emotion than my love of quiet
willingly admits.   Among the inferiour professors of
medical knowledge, is a race of wretches, whose lives
are only varied by varieties of cruelty ; whose favourite
amusement is to nail dogs to tables and open them alive ;
to try how long life may be continued in various degrees

----

[1] *Tatler*, No. 119.   Hurd's note : " I wonder that a man of
Mr Addison's humanity could speak of *opening a dog*, with so
much unconcern ; or think it justifiable on the pretence of *making
a useful discovery.*"

[2] *Spectator*, No. 21.   Hurd : " There would be no objection to
this raillery, if it were fit that raillery should be at all employed
on a subject of this nature."   Bishop Hurd was described by Sir
Leslie Stephen as " narrow-minded, formal, peevish, cold-blooded
and intolerably conceited " (*English Thought in the Eighteenth
Century*, ii. 348).   But here he appears as a man of humanity.
Some of his notes on Addison's essays *are* " formal " and " peevish "
but one is very amusing—on *Spectator* No. 561 (*Account of the
Widows' Club*) : " After all the severity of this satire, it should be
remembered that the author ventured on a widow, the *Countess
of Warwick* ; who, to speak in the language of this letter, *fairly
laid him out*, within the compass of four years ; an exploit, for
which her ladyship seems to have been well entitled to the chair
of the society."

of mutilation, or with the excision or laceration of the vital parts; to examine whether burning irons are felt more acutely by the bone or tendon; and whether the more lasting agonies are produced by poison forced into the mouth, or injected into the veins.

" It is not without reluctance that I offend the sensibility of the tender mind with images like these. If such cruelties were not practised, it were well that they should not be conceived; but, since they are published every day with ostentation, let me be allowed once to mention them, since I mention them with abhorrence.

" *Mead* has invidiously remarked of *Woodward*, that he gathered shells and stones, and would pass for a philosopher. With pretensions much less reasonable, the anatomical novice tears out the living bowels of an animal, and styles himself physician, prepares himself by familiar cruelty for that profession which he is to exercise upon the tender and the helpless, upon feeble bodies and broken minds, and by which he has opportunities to extend his arts of torture, and continue those experiments upon infancy and age, which he has hitherto tried upon cats and dogs.

" What is alleged in defence of these hateful practices, every one knows; but the truth is, that by knives, fire, and poison, knowledge is not always sought, and is very seldom attained. The experiments that have been tried, are tried again; he that burned an animal with irons yesterday, will be willing to amuse himself by burning another to-morrow. I know not, that by living dissections any discovery has been made by which a single malady is more easily cured. And if the knowledge of physiology has been somewhat increased, he surely buys knowledge dear who learns the use of the lacteals at the expense of his humanity. It is time that universal resentment should arise against these horrid operations, which tend to harden

R

the heart, extinguish those sensations which give man confidence in man, and make the physician more dreadful than the gout or stone." [1]

CHARITY

So we see that everywhere was much oppression and cruelty to kindle Johnson's indignation, and much suffering and distress to move his generous heart to sympathy. And yet there was a brighter side to this dark picture. Johnson could commend the charitable disposition of his fellow-countrymen—in fact he thought that charity was almost the only redeeming feature of an age " which amidst all its vices, and all its follies, has not become infamous for want of charity." [2] He extended his charitable efforts to the relief of French prisoners, and combated an argument that we recognize as familiar : " It has been urged, that charity, like other virtues, may be improperly and unseasonably exerted ; that while we are relieving *Frenchmen*, there remain many *Englishmen* unrelieved ; that while we lavish pity on our enemies, we forget the misery of our friends. Grant this argument all it can prove, and what is the conclusion ?—That to relieve the *French* is a good action, but that a better may be conceived. This is all the result, and this all is very little. To do the best can seldom be the lot of man : it is sufficient if, when opportunities are presented, he is ready to do good. How little virtue could be practised, if beneficence were to wait always for the most proper objects, and the noblest occasions ; occasions that may never happen, and objects that may never be found. It is far from certain, that a single *Englishman* will suffer by the charity to the *French*. New scenes of misery make new impres-

[1] *Idler*, No. 17.

[2] *Postscript to an Essay on Milton's " Paradise Lost."* (The Postscript was written to raise subscriptions for the relief of Mrs Elizabeth Foster, granddaughter of John Milton.)

sions; and much of the charity which produced these donations may be supposed to have been generated by a species of calamity never known among us before." [1]

"Charity, or tenderness for the poor," wrote Johnson,[2] "which is now justly considered, by a great part of mankind, as inseparable from piety, and in which almost all the goodness of the present age consists, is, I think, known only to those who enjoy, either immediately or by transmission, the light of revelation.

"Those ancient nations who have given us the wisest models of government, and the brightest examples of patriotism, whose institutions have been transcribed by all succeeding legislatures, and whose history is studied by every candidate for political or military reputation, have yet left behind them no mention of almshouses or hospitals, of places where age might repose, or sickness be relieved." [3]

Charity, then, was essentially a Christian virtue. Johnson's age, "though not likely to shine hereafter among the most splendid periods of history, has yet given

[1] *Introduction to Proceedings of Committee for Clothing French Prisoners of War.* Goldsmith's Chinese Philosopher praised England for this benefaction to her foe: "I know not whether it proceeds from their superior opulence, that the English are more charitable than the rest of mankind; . . . whatever be the motive, they are not only more charitable than any other nation, but more judicious in distinguishing the properest objects of compassion" (*Citizen of the World*, Letter 23).

[2] *Idler*, No. 4.

[3] "The active, habitual, and detailed charity of private persons, which is so conspicuous a feature in all Christian societies, was scarcely known in antiquity, and there are not more than two or three moralists who have even noticed it. . . . Christianity for the first time made charity a rudimentary virtue, giving it a leading place in the moral type, and in the exhortations of its teachers. . . . When the victory of Christianity was achieved, the enthusiasm for charity displayed itself in the erection of numerous institutions that were altogether unknown to the Pagan World" (Lecky's *History of European Morals*, ch. iv.).

examples of charity, which may be very properly recommended to imitation. The equal distribution of wealth, which long commerce has produced, does not enable any single hand to raise edifices of piety like fortified cities, to appropriate manors to religious uses, or deal out such large and lasting beneficence as was scattered over the land in ancient times, by those who possessed counties or provinces. But no sooner is a new species of misery brought to view, and a design of relieving it professed, than every hand is open to contribute something, every tongue is busied in solicitation, and every art of pleasure is employed for a time in the interest of virtue."

Johnson then pleads for hospitals: " Of some kinds of charity the consequences are dubious ; some evils which beneficence has been busy to remedy, are not certainly known to be very grievous to the sufferer, or detrimental to the community ; but no man can question whether wounds and sickness are not really painful ; whether it be not worthy of a good man's care to restore those to ease and usefulness, from whose labours infants and women expect their bread, and who by a casual hurt, or lingering disease, lie pining in want or anguish, burthensome to others, and weary of themselves."

His next paragraph is eminently practical : " Yet as the hospitals of the present time subsist only by gifts bestowed at pleasure, without any solid fund of support, there is danger lest the blaze of charity, which now burns with so much heat and splendour, should die away for want of lasting fuel ; lest fashion should suddenly withdraw her smile, and inconstancy transfer the publick attention to something which appears more eligible, because it will be new."

Endowments, in fact, are necessary : " Whatever is left in the hands of chance must be subject to vicissitude ; and when any establishment is found to be useful, it ought to be the next care to make it permanent."

But alas ! it seems that, even then, there were rivalries and jealousies in the hospital world : " The most active promoters of the present schemes of charity cannot be cleared from some instances of misconduct, which may awaken contempt or censure, and hasten that neglect which is likely to come too soon of itself. The open competitions between different hospitals, and the animosity with which their patrons oppose one another, may prejudice weak minds against them all. For it will not be easily believed, that any man can, for good reasons, wish to exclude another from doing good. The spirit of charity can only be continued by a reconciliation of these ridiculous feuds ; and therefore, instead of contentions who shall be the only benefactors to the needy, let there be no other struggle than who shall be the first." [1]

[1] *Idler*, No. 4.

VII

CONCLUSION

"Life, in which nothing has been done or suffered to distinguish one day from another, is to him that has passed it, as if it had never been, except that he is conscious how ill he has husbanded the great deposit of his Creator." *Rambler*, No. 41.

WE read in *Cranford* that when Miss Jenkyns was challenged by Captain Brown to give her opinion of *The Pickwick Papers*, she replied: "I must say I don't think they are by any means equal to Dr Johnson. Still, perhaps the author is young. Let him persevere, and who knows what he may become if he will take the great Doctor for his model." "It is quite a different sort of thing, my dear Madam," observed Captain Brown. To the last this lady remained faithful to *The Rambler*,

"Among innumerable false unmoved."

"Did you ever read *The Rambler*? It's a wonderful book — wonderful! . . . better than that strange old book, with the queer name, poor Captain Brown was killed for reading—that book by Mr Boz, you know."

Whether or not Mrs Gaskell meant her readers to recognize it, there is great significance in this antithesis of Johnson to Dickens. *The Pickwick Papers* were indeed "quite a different sort of thing" from *The Rambler*. Between the age of Johnson and the age of Dickens is a great gulf fixed, for amongst other things the French Revolution separated them, which Johnson did not live to see, and which Miss Jenkyns (it is probable) ignored. Dickens, as Mr Chesterton has remarked, was born in " the

262

age under the shadow of the French Revolution." [1] He
was a Radical and an optimist. " He was the voice in
England of this humane intoxication and expansion, this
encouraging of anybody to be anything. His best books
are a carnival of liberty." [2] Johnson was the exact converse : " Dr Johnson takes too sad a view of humanity,
but he is also too satisfied a Conservative." [3]

And Dickens could make fun of all things [4]—even of a
classical education. We can almost conceive him writing
a novel to " expose " it, as he exposed Yorkshire schools,
the Circumlocution Office, and the Court of Chancery.
" Virgil, Horace, Ovid, Terence, Plautus, Cicero," says
the wife of Dr Blimber, " what a world of honey have we
here." [5] Dickens was not educated to enjoy this honey,
but Johnson devoured it with a bear's relish. For him
those hives were never to be surpassed or equalled ; that
of Horace alone supplied him with more than eighty
mottoes for his Essays.[6] He maintained the classical
tradition, and his manner of maintaining it was without
compromise. Greek and Latin, he said, had furnished
the poets with all their materials ; Homer in fact was
the original source, and Latin itself was only the echo of
Greek. " Yet, whatever hope may persuade, or reason
evince, experience can boast of very few additions to
ancient fable. The wars of *Troy*, and the travels of *Ulysses*,
have furnished all succeeding poets with incidents,
characters, and sentiments. The *Romans* are confessed

----

[1] G. K. Chesterton, *Charles Dickens*, p. 5.

[2] *Ibid.*, p. 14.   [3] *Ibid.*, p. 7.

[4] A few years ago *The National Review* published an amusing
article proving that Mr Pickwick was intended to be a humorous
reminder of Johnson, and that the resemblance extended to
their followers—*e.g.* both Boswell and Mr Tupman were fond of
attending fêtes in fancy dress.

[5] *Dombey and Son*, ch. xi.

[6] Juvenal comes next with 35, then Ovid with 25, Martial 22,
Virgil 14.

to have attempted little more than to display in their own tongue the inventions of the *Greeks*. There is, in all their writings, such a perpetual recurrence of allusions to the tales of the fabulous age, that they must be confessed often to want that power of giving pleasure which novelty supplies ; nor can we wonder that they excelled so much in the graces of diction, when we consider how rarely they were employed in search of new thoughts." As for Virgil, " the warmest admirers of the great *Mantuan* poet can extol him for little more than the skill with which he has, by making his hero both a traveller and a warriour, united the beauties of the *Iliad* and the *Odyssey* in one composition : yet his judgment was perhaps sometimes overborne by his avarice of the *Homeric* treasures ; and, for fear of suffering a sparkling ornament to be lost, he has inserted it where it cannot shine with its original splendour. . . . If *Virgil* could be thus seduced by imitation, there will be little hope that common wits should escape." [1] Not only is it true that the classics are the best of literature, but fortunately that which survives is probably the best of the classics : " Of the ancients, enough remains to excite our emulation and direct our endeavours. Many of the works which time has left us, we know to have been those that were most esteemed, and which antiquity itself considered as models ; so that, having the originals, we may without much regret lose the imitations." [2] Although his own *Dictionary* had conferred, as it were, a *status* on the English language, we know Johnson's opinion of modern literature as compared with ancient—that " the most polished of the present *European* tongues are nothing more than barbarous degenerations " [3] from Latin and Greek. If to Burke the constitution of 1688 was the perfection of all political wisdom, to Johnson the classics were the perfection of all language. And who shall gainsay him ?

[1] *Rambler*, No. 121.   [2] *Idler*, No. 66.   [3] *Rambler*, No. 169.

As to the perfection, or imperfection, of his own writings, opinions differ. Some who have not read his Essays, but have bestowed on them only a cursory glance, have pronounced them to be a collection of verbose platitudes ; men who are justly considered well-read have wholly disdained them. But if any reader has persevered through the preceding pages, will he not agree with Sir Walter Raleigh that *The Rambler* is " a splendid repository of wit and wisdom " ? [1] Mr James Bailey, another great Johnsonian critic, will not concede the epithet " splendid." [2] Johnson defines " splendid " as " showy, magnificent, sumptuous, pompous " : the second and third significations can scarcely be denied to Johnson's prose, the fourth—in its depreciatory sense—must sometimes be admitted. Mr Bailey also considers that Sir Walter, in appraising a certain passage from *The Rambler* as " prose which will not suffer much by comparison with the best in the language," is guilty of an " extravagant " utterance.[3] I will give the conclusion of this passage, and ask the reader if Sir Walter's praise is too high. " While we see multitudes passing before us, of whom, perhaps, not one appears to deserve our notice, or excite our sympathy, we should remember, that we likewise are lost in the same throng ; that the eye which happens to glance upon us is turned in a moment on him that follows us, and that the utmost which we can reasonably hope or fear is, to fill a vacant hour with prattle, and be forgotten." [4] Or can we agree with Mr Bailey that Johnson's prose " has no music, no mystery, no gift of suggestion, very little of the higher sort of imagination " ? [5] Or has it " no imagination " ? [6] " The student wastes away in meditation, and the soldier perishes on the ramparts " ; " if they will dress

[1] *Six Essays on Johnson*, p. 12.
[2] *Dr Johnson and his Circle*, p. 195.   [3] *Ibid.*, p. 179.
[4] *Rambler*, No. 159.
[5] *Dr Johnson and his Circle*, p. 165.   [6] *Ibid.*, p. 196.

crippled limbs in embroidery, endeavour at gayety with faltering voices, and darken assemblies of pleasure with the ghastliness of disease "; " those who glitter in dignity and glide away in affluence "; " they fawn among his equipage, and animate his riots "; " those who have burst the shackles of habitual vice "; " the Great, whose followers linger from year to year in expectations, and die at last with petitions in their hands "; " till he shall at last enter into the recesses of voluptuousness, and sloth and despondency close the passage behind him "—have these sentences no imagination? Do not they conjure up vivid or pathetic scenes? Is there not music in the " cadences " of Johnson's prose? Why, many of his sentences stick in the memory (at least they do in mine) like verses of poetry.

But leaving the art of the writer, which (as is inevitable) some will rate higher than others, let us consider what was his " message "; for he did deliver a message to his age. In his " periodical writings " Johnson is pre-eminently a moralist. It is true they contain several essays on literary subjects [1]; but Johnson's chief business is with human beings and their virtues, vices and manners, which he had long and carefully observed and deeply pondered. And what was the sum of his thoughts? Carlyle, who resembled him in his early poverty, his independent spirit and his erudition, preached the gospel of Work. Johnson preached, though he did not vociferate, essentially the same gospel—that man, a rational being, should live a rational life of active virtue, which for Johnson implied a religious life, the life of a Christian.[2] This was his standard, and any aimless, unprofitable occupation was anathema; yet in such occupations most people spent their time. These are the " multitude fluctuating

---

[1] See *supra*, p. 60*n*.

[2] " The Essays professedly serious will be found exactly conformable to the precepts of Christianity " (*Rambler*, No. 208).

in pleasures or immersed in business, without time for intellectual amusements," [1] or " who, not being chained down by their condition to a regular and stated allotment of their hours, are obliged to find themselves business or diversion, and having nothing within that can entertain or employ them, are compelled to try all the arts of destroying time. The numberless expedients practised by this class of mortals to alleviate the burthen of life, are not less shameful, nor, perhaps, much less pitiable, than those to which a trader on the edge of bankruptcy is reduced. I have seen melancholy overspread a whole family at the disappointment of a party for cards ; and when, after the proposal of a thousand schemes, and the despatch of the footman upon a hundred messages, they have submitted, with gloomy resignation, to the misfortune of passing one evening in conversation with each other ; on a sudden, such are the revolutions of the world, an unexpected visiter has brought them relief, acceptable as provision to a starving city, and enabled them to hold out till the next day." [2] These are they " that spin out life in trifles and die without a memorial." [3]

> " Of men the common rout,
> That, wandering loose about,
> Grow up and perish as the summer fly,
> Heads without name, no more remembered."

On their tombstones might be inscribed that epitaph for Colas, which Chesterfield warned his son against deserving [4] :

> " Colas est mort de maladie,
> Tu veux que j'en pleure le sort,
> Que diable veux tu que j'en die ?
> Colas vivoit, Colas est mort."

[1] *Rambler*, No. 2.   [2] *Ibid.*, No. 6.
[3] *Idler*, No. 17.
[4] Lord Chesterfield's *Letters to his Son*, No. 36.

Some of these objectless persons devote themselves to self-adornment, like Euphues, whose ambition it had been "from his first entrance into life, to distinguish himself by particularities in his dress, to outvie beaux in embroidery, to import new trimmings, and to be foremost in the fashion." [1]

Others are dabblers in science: "One passes the day in catching spiders, that he may count their eyes with a microscope; another erects his head, and exhibits the dust of a marigold separated from the flower with a dexterity worthy of *Leewenhoeck* himself. Some turn the wheel of electricity; some suspend rings to a load-stone, and find that what they did yesterday they can do again to-morrow. Some register the changes of the wind, and die fully convinced that the wind is changeable. There are men yet more profound, who have heard that two colourless liquors may produce a colour by union, and that two cold bodies will grow hot if they are mingled; they mingle them, and produce the effect expected, say it is strange, and mingle them again." [2]

Others take to globe-trotting; worse than this, they write books about their travels: "Those who sit idle at home, and are curious to know what is done or suffered in distant countries, may be informed by one of these wanderers, that on a certain day he set out early with the caravan, and in the first hour's march saw, towards the south, a hill covered with trees, then passed over a stream, which ran northward, with a swift course, but which is probably dry in the summer months; that an hour after he saw something to the right which looked at a distance like a castle with towers, but which he discovered afterwards to be a craggy rock; that he then entered a valley, in which he saw several trees tall and flourishing, watered by a rivulet not marked in the maps, of which he was not

[1] *Rambler*, No. 24.
[2] *Idler*, No. 17.

able to learn the name; that the road afterward grew stony, and the country uneven, where he observed among the hills many hollows worn by torrents, and was told that the road was passable only part of the year; that going on they found the remains of a building, once, perhaps, a fortress to secure the pass, or to restrain the robbers, of which the present inhabitants can give no other account than that it is haunted by fairies; that they went to dine at the foot of a rock, and travelled the rest of the day along the banks of a river, from which the road turned aside towards evening, and brought them within sight of a village, which was once a considerable town, but which afforded them neither good victuals nor commodious lodging. . . .

" This is the common style of those sons of enterprise, who visit savage countries, and range through solitude and desolation; who pass a desert, and tell that it is sandy; who cross a valley, and find that it is green. There are others of more delicate sensibility, that visit only the realms of elegance and softness; that wander through *Italian* palaces, and amuse the gentle reader with catalogues of pictures; that hear masses in magnificent churches, and recount the number of pillars or variegations of the pavement." [1] Then Johnson, in one weighty sentence, draws his moral: " He that would travel for the entertainment of others, should remember that the great object of remark is human life." [2] " I came hither," said Rasselas in Egypt, " not to measure fragments of temples, or trace choked aqueducts, but to look upon the various scenes of the present world."

Others there are, who, in order to kill time, have recourse to mere mechanical futilities. Of such was Sober, whose various and half-developed impulses, " though they do not make him sufficiently useful to others, make him at least weary of himself. . . . But there is one time

[1] *Idler*, No. 97.   [2] *Ibid.*

at night when he must go home, that his friends may sleep; and another time in the morning, when all the world agrees to shut out interruption. These are the moments of which poor *Sober* trembles at the thought. But the misery of these tiresome intervals he has many means of alleviating. He has persuaded himself, that the manual arts are undeservedly overlooked; he has observed in many trades the effects of close thought, and just ratiocination. From speculation he proceeded to practice, and supplied himself with the tools of a carpenter, with which he mended his coal-box very successfully, and which he still continues to employ, as he finds occasion." [1]

Then there are the virtuosos—" the numerous and frivolous tribe of insect - mongers, shell - mongers, and pursuers and driers of butterflies," [2] as Chesterfield described them. " Men may be found, who are kept from sleep by the want of a shell particularly variegated ! who are wasting their lives in stratagems to obtain a book in a language which they do not understand ; who pine with envy at the flowers of another man's parterre." [3] " One is a collector of fossils, of which he knows no other use than to show them ; and when he has stocked his own repository, grieves that the stones which he has left behind him should be picked up by another. The florist nurses a tulip, and repines that his rival's beds enjoy the same showers and sunshine with his own." [4] " An irregular contortion of a turbinated shell, which common eyes pass unregarded, will ten times treble its price in the imagination of philosophers. Beauty is far from operating upon collectors as upon low and vulgar minds, even where beauty might be thought the only quality that could

[1] *Idler*, No. 31.
[2] Lord Chesterfield's *Letters to his Son*, No. 138.
[3] *Adventurer*, No. 119.
[4] *Ibid.*, No. 128.

deserve notice. Among the shells that please by their variety of colours, if one can be found accidentally deformed by a cloudy spot, it is boasted as the pride of the collection. China is sometimes purchased for little less than its weight in gold, only because it is old, though neither less brittle, nor better painted than the modern ; and brown china is caught up with ecstasy, though no reason can be imagined for which it should be preferred to common vessels of common clay. The fate of prints and coins is equally inexplicable. Some prints are treasured up as inestimably valuable, because the impression was made before the plate was finished. Of coins the price rises not from the purity of the metal, the excellence of the workmanship, the elegance of the legend, or the chronological use. A piece of which neither the inscription can be read, nor the face distinguished, if there remain of it but enough to show that it is rare, will be sought by contending nations, and dignify the treasury in which it shall be shown." [1]

The virtuoso could be rated as " not wholly unprofitable," [2] and it might be said for the collector's instinct that " by fixing the thoughts upon intellectual pleasures " it " resists the natural encroachments of sensuality, and maintains the mind in her lawful superiority." [3] But a man like Tim Ranger, who could write, " I have health, I have money, and I hope that I have understanding," ought to have considered his life a more responsible matter. Religion and morality must come first, and then (for educated folk) " the care of the nobler part," or, to use

[1] *Idler*, No. 56. Johnson gives us two pictures of collectors. One was the wealthy Tim Ranger (*Idler*, No. 64), who had already been a beau, a rake, and a racing man, and sought a new method of killing time. The other, Quisquilius (*Rambler*, No. 82), ruined himself by collecting : " I have at length bought till I can buy no longer, and the cruelty of my creditors has seized my repository."

[2] *Idler*, No. 56.

[3] *Ibid.*

Addison's words, of " that divine part in our composition." But country squires and squiresses and City tradesmen seemed to Johnson to be " fluctuating in pleasures or immersed in business "—the pleasures of the chase, the business of money-grubbing in order to become " hundred thousand pounds men," or of " adding acre to acre," or of " *con*serving, *re*serving and *pre*serving "— all of them " without time for intellectual amusement " or with any desire therefor. Of some of these, by reason of their education and position in the world, better things might have been expected. The Rev. Dr Taylor, for instance, Johnson's squarson friend, gave offence by his breeding of cattle ; he was, as it were, a virtuoso in live-stock. " Sir, I love him ; but I do not love him more ; my regard for him does not increase. As it is said in the Apocrypha, ' his talk is of bullocks.' " [1]

It is not to be supposed that Johnson thought all men were fit for intellectual occupations. The thresher who " vociferated his heroics in the barn " was not a person to be encouraged, nor the " girl who forsook her samplers to teach kingdoms wisdom." He represented the tradesman as a rather sordid being, but he also observed that men were rarely more innocently employed than when making money. There were certain callings that were deadening to man's intellectual nature, but none the less necessary. From his Fleet Street Olympus Johnson seems to look down on those who lived east of the Fleet river and within the gates of London, on their courtships, homes, shops, and amusements. He often sneers at their civic ambitions. But were not those citizens still less worthy of respect who never aspired to be aldermen or to " fine for sheriff " ? There were dishonest and lazy and incompetent traders

[1] Boswell's *Life of Johnson* (Birkbeck Hill), iii. 181. Taylor had contracted the virtuoso's jealous disposition : " Our bulls and cows are all well ; but we yet hate the man that had seen a bigger bull " (*ibid.*, 150*n*).

then as now; but there were also stout hearts and independent spirits in the City. Lord Mayor Beckford faced and answered an angry King—though probably his famous speech would not have commended him to Johnson. One can envisage the citizen of eighteenth-century London as a petty retailer guzzling at Guildhall feasts, *or* as a public-spirited merchant giving much of his time to the work of local government—according to one's point of view. But men of letters are apt to be satirical upon traders ; they think the trader is richer than his deserts. Boswell once asked: " What is the reason that we are angry at a trader's having opulence ? " Johnson replied : " Why, Sir, the reason is (though I don't undertake to prove that there is a reason), we see no qualities in trade that should entitle a man to superiority. We are not angry at a soldier's getting riches, because we see that he possesses qualities which we have not. If a man returns from a battle, having lost one hand, and with the other full of gold, we feel that he deserves the gold ; but we cannot think that a fellow, by sitting all day at a desk, is entitled to get above us." [1] It is an old and ever-new complaint ; but the soldier's quest is for honour, not for gold. And the man of letters can console himself by reflecting that his vocation is far more interesting than that of the money-grubber ; his call is to serve the Muses, not Mammon—and the Muses give much richer rewards. There *are* writers who have written, and are writing, only for lucre's sake—some journalists, some novelists, some betrayers and exploiters of social and political secrets. These earn the ill-gotten riches which may properly make us indignant.

As there are no amiable traders in Johnson's Essays (except perhaps Ned Drugget), so there are no benevolent squires. His squires are either tyrants or boors. Rural tyrants no doubt existed:

[1] Boswell's *Life of Johnson* (Birkbeck Hill), v. 327, 328.

S

"The man of wealth and pride
Takes up a space that many poor supplied—
Space for his lake, his park's extended bounds,
Space for his horses, equipage, and hounds ;
The robe that wraps his limbs in silken cloth
Has robb'd the neighbouring fields of half their growth ;
His seat, where solitary sports are seen,
Indignant spurns the cottage from the green." [1]

Even the sportsman was reprehensible, and an unprofitable waster of his own time. But I wish Johnson had written some *Ramblers* to show (none could have argued it better) that the community of sport leavened rural life, and that the English country gentleman who resided on his estate—even if he was tempted to do so by the lure of fox-hunting—was playing a more patriotic part than the French Seigneur who dangled at Paris or Versailles. For if sport attracted him to his country seat, he was detained there by duties social, judicial and administrative. Of such duties and their performance we hear little from Johnson.

It was a limitation of Johnson the Moralist that he examined and passed judgment on the pursuits of his fellow-countrymen as good or bad in themselves, without regard to other considerations. Sport may be useless in itself, but useful as a recreation. Or it may stimulate, or be stimulated by, a love of nature : unfortunately Johnson was not

"Breathed on by the rural Pan."

Again, sport may be the expression and safety-valve of a national vigour and energy. After the Boer War, Mr Kipling wrote a scathing verse about "the flannelled fools at the wicket " ; after the Great War these incorrigible "fools," or such survivors of them as were not disabled by their wounds, soon reappeared on our playing-

[1] Goldsmith, *The Deserted Village*, v. 275-282.

fields. Mr Kipling must despair of them : or does he now recognize that certain national instincts are ineradicable ? Again, sport may conduce to " good-neighbourhood," a thing so repellent to the ruralizing man of letters—but so indispensable to the country-side. Habits and manners must be judged by themselves and by their causes. As Mr Bailey says : " Against the discovery that things can neither be rightly judged nor wisely reformed except by examining how they came to be what they are, the whole eighteenth century, and in it Johnson as well as Rousseau and Voltaire, stands naked. . . . Directly it is seen that all life exhibits itself in stages it becomes obvious that the dry light of reason will not provide the materials for true judgment until it has been coloured by a sympathetic insight into the conditions of the particular stage under discussion." [1]

Just as the political economist used to classify labour as " productive " or " non-productive," so Johnson, a man of the eighteenth century, judged men by certain abstract standards. Were their occupations rational ? did they immediately conduce to learning and virtue and religion ? In the same way he applied hard-and-fast rules to the poets—to what extent did they make use of triplets, or hemistichs, or Alexandrines ? And did their Alexandrines break at the sixth syllable ?—" a rule which the modern French poets never violate." In these matters he was a conformer, and he observed some of the literary conventions of the age ; he wrote allegories and Oriental tales. But other rules he attacked as " enacted by despotick antiquity," or " prompted by the desire of extending authority "—e.g. that the acts of a play should be limited to five, or its action to a certain number of hours.[2] He conformed, or rebelled, as he saw fit. In this complete intellectual independence, even more than in

[1] *Dr Johnson and his Circle*, pp. 173, 174.
[2] *Rambler*, No. 156.

his natural powers of mind and argument, lay his strength and prestige. This gave him his lofty position, and made him (like his poet of the garret) one

" ὅς ὑπέρτατα δώματα ναίει."

He dominated all the great men of his century with whom he came in contact ; and yet he was not characteristic of his century, as were Horace Walpole or Chesterfield or Goldsmith. He was *sui generis*. " Johnson is dead," said " Single-speech " Hamilton. " Let us go to the next best : there is nobody ; no man can be said to put you in mind of Johnson." We too feel there was a difference ; but wherein did this difference consist ? The answer is difficult, for it invites the analysis of a great personality ; but his Essays offer a few contributions towards the solution of the problem.

His style of writing was different ; it was nearly always dignified and grand, but sometimes laboured and pompous, and yet the pomp never (or very rarely) obscured the meaning. He is said to have imitated, or been influenced by, Sir Thomas Browne ; but I cannot see the resemblance—except in his Latinizing, in which fell accomplishment Sir Thomas outdid him.[1] Many have tried to write like Johnson, mostly by way of parody ; but the giant's robe hangs loosely on all such imitators.

He never condescended to write obscenities. Pope and Swift and Smollett wrote now and again as if obsessed by an almost morbid filthiness. But Johnson, though he would call a spade a spade, was free from even the comparatively wholesome coarseness of Fielding, nor did he ever exhibit Addison's occasional tendency to be salacious. This fastidiousness is to his honour, and of itself sets him apart from nearly all his contemporaries.

---

[1] *Omniety, transpeciate, ubiquitary, recompensive, amphibology* are some of Sir Thomas's gems. Against the abuse of this Latinization our English language seems to have a self-protective instinct.

In his humanity, which never degenerated into sentimentality, he belongs rather to the nineteenth than the eighteenth century. Herein the true Johnson is Johnson the Essayist, not Johnson the Talker. In argument he could uphold Tyburn, and even the procession to Tyburn: " Sir, executions are intended to draw spectators. If they do not draw spectators they don't answer their purpose. The old method was most satisfactory to all parties ; the publick was gratified by a procession ; the criminal was supported by it. Why is all this to be swept away? "[1] But in *The Rambler*[2] it was a " dreadful procession " to a " legal massacre," and the spectators looked " with carelessness, perhaps with triumph, on the utmost exacerbations of human misery."

In one other respect he differed from his contemporaries. In an age of Deism and of irreligion Johnson was a Christian writer, " almost the only definite Christian among the great writers of the eighteenth century."[3] It is therefore not surprising that some of his essays are scarce distinguishable from sermons. " Sermons are liked in England," wrote M. Taine. He was probably right, for they are still printed on Saturdays in *The Times* newspaper. We have many gifted preachers, who exhort us from the Pulpit and the Press, but none who speaks more sincerely from the depths of his soul than did this strange and wayward, brave and generous man, who lived in the world and dominated it, exulting in his powers

" γηθόμενος σθένεϊ ᾧ,"

but lived also an inner life of religion and meditation, ever asking for forgiveness and ever humbly hoping for grace. This inner life was Johnson's true life, and the true source of his strength. It was not the gladiator of the club

---

[1] Boswell's *Life of Johnson* (Birkbeck Hill), iv. 188.
[2] No. 114.
[3] *Dr Johnson and his Circle* (Mr John Bailey), p. 175.

and tavern, nor the witty Essayist with his deep knowledge of books and men, but the Christian, conscious of his own many sins and imperfections, who wrote [1] :—

"The completion and sum of repentance is a change of life. That sorrow which dictates no caution, that fear which does not quicken our escape, that austerity which fails to rectify our affections, are vain and unavailing. But sorrow and terrour must naturally precede reformation ; for what other cause can produce it ? He, therefore, that feels himself alarmed by his conscience, anxious for the attainment of a better state, and afflicted by the memory of his past faults, may justly conclude, that the great work of repentance is begun, and hope by retirement and prayer, the natural and religious means of strengthening his conviction, to impress upon his mind such a sense of the divine presence, as may overpower the blandishments of secular delights, and enable him to advance from one degree of holiness to another, till death shall set him free from doubt and contest, misery and temptation :

"' What better can we do than prostrate fall
Before him reverent ; and there confess
Humbly our faults, and pardon beg, with tears
Wat'ring the ground, and with our sighs the air
Frequenting, sent from hearts contrite, in sign
Of sorrow unfeign'd, and humiliation meek ? ' "

[1] *Rambler*, No. 110.

INDEX

A

B